UNCIVIL GUARD

NEW **HISPANISMS**

Cultural and Literary Studies

ANNE J. CRUZ, SERIES EDITOR

UNCIVIL GUARD

POLICING, MILITARY CULTURE,
AND THE COMING OF
THE SPANISH CIVIL WAR

FOSTER CHAMBERLIN

LOUISIANA STATE UNIVERSITY PRESS

BATON ROUGE

Published by Louisiana State University Press
lsupress.org

Designer: Kaelin Chappell Broadus
Typefaces: Dolly Pro, text; Sour Mash and Sucrose, display

Cover photo: Members of the Guardia Civil escorting prisoners
in Asturias, 1934. National Digital Archives of Poland.

Maps by Mary Lee Eggart.

Cataloging-in-Publication Data are available from the Library of Congress.

ISBN 978-0-8071-8468-4 (cloth: alk. paper) —
ISBN 978-0-8071-8576-6 (pdf) — ISBN 978-0-8071-8575-9 (epub)

For my parents

CONTENTS

ACKNOWLEDGMENTS

It is said that one never truly ceases to be an advisor, and this is certainly true of Pamela Radcliff, who has been continuously generous in providing me with feedback, advice, and career support even though I have now been her former student for about as long as I was her student. Therefore, my thanks go first to her. I would also like to thank Frank Biess, Judith Hughes, Jeremy Prestholdt, and Richard Biernacki, each of whom provided commentary that aided me in lending this project focus and direction.

Second, I am deeply indebted to David Henderson, who has read more of my chapter drafts than I can count. I asked for his assistance so many times because his eye for the inane remark and the unnecessary word has undoubtably made me a better writer. When I finally received pages back from him that were not covered in red, I knew I had a book.

For their help with related projects that aided me in developing my thinking on military and police culture for this book, I thank Geoffrey Jensen and Sergio Vaquero Martínez. My thanks go likewise to Ángel Alcalde and Francisco J. Leira Castiñeira, the coeditors of the *Crucible of Francoism* volume from which the last chapter in this book is drawn. I offer a special thank you to Matthew Kerry, who provided important suggestions and sources for the chapters on Asturias through a series of lively email exchanges.

Regarding the research in Spain upon which this book is based, funding was provided by the J. William Fulbright Commission, the Harry Frank Guggenheim Foundation, the Ministerio de Educación, Cultura y Deporte de España's HISPANEX Program, and UC San Diego. I want to also thank Eduardo González Calleja for providing guidance and support for my efforts there. My thanks go likewise to the staffs of all the archives I visited, especially the Sección Guardia Civil del Archivo General del Ministerio del Interior. For a return trip to Spain to do additional research, I received funding from Bilkent University. On that trip, the staffs of the Archivo General Militar de Madrid and the Archivo General Militar de Segovia in particular aided me greatly. Finally, I thank the Pérez family, who always made me feel at home in Madrid.

For their suggestions during the publishing process, my thanks go to Clinton Young, Asli Menevse, Alejandro Gómez del Moral, and, above all, the peer reviewers, whose constructive comments resulted in a greatly improved manuscript. My thanks as well to Northern Arizona University's Department of History, which provided funding for mapmaking and indexing. At Louisiana State University Press, I wish to thank Alisa Plant, who took initial interest in the manuscript and guided me into the hands of James Long, whom I heartily thank as well for guiding this book through to publication along with the rest of the staff at LSU Press. I also thank series editor Anne J. Cruz for her comments on the manuscript, Mary Lee Eggart for her beautiful maps, Scot Danforth for his careful copyedits, and Jenny Lillich for the indexing.

Lastly, I thank my family and friends, especially my parents and late grandparents, who have always encouraged me despite my sometimes seemingly quixotic quest to pursue an academic career in European history. Likewise, I thank my wife, Gökçen, who has also always supported me in my efforts as an American studying Spain in Turkey and Arizona.

Portions of the introduction first appeared in "Guardias del orden: La cultura militar de la Guardia Civil," *Ayer* 135, no. 3 (2024): 49–73. Reprinted by permission of the Asociación de Historia Contemporánea.

Portions of chapter 4 first appeared in "The Roots of the July 1936 Coup: The Rebirth of Military Interventionism in the Spanish Infantry Academy, 1893–1927," *War & Society* 40, no. 4 (October 2021): 279–95, copyright © School of the Humanities and Social Science at the University of New South Wales, reprinted by permission of Taylor & Francis Ltd, http://www.tandfonline.com, on behalf of School of the Humanities and Social Science at the University of New South Wales.

Portions of chapter 9 first appeared in "Policing Practices as a Vehicle for Brutalization: The Case of Spain's Civil Guard, 1934–1936," *European History*

Quarterly 50, no. 4 (October 2020): 650–68. Reprinted by permission of SAGE Publications.

A version of chapter 10 appeared in "The Roots of the Repression: The Rebel Civil Guards in the Spanish Civil War," chap. 3 in *The Crucible of Francoism: Combat, Violence, and Ideology in the Spanish Civil War*, ed. Ángel Alcalde, Foster Chamberlin, and Francisco J. Leira-Castiñeira (Brighton: Sussex Academic Press, 2021). Reprinted by permission of Liverpool University Press.

UNCIVIL GUARD

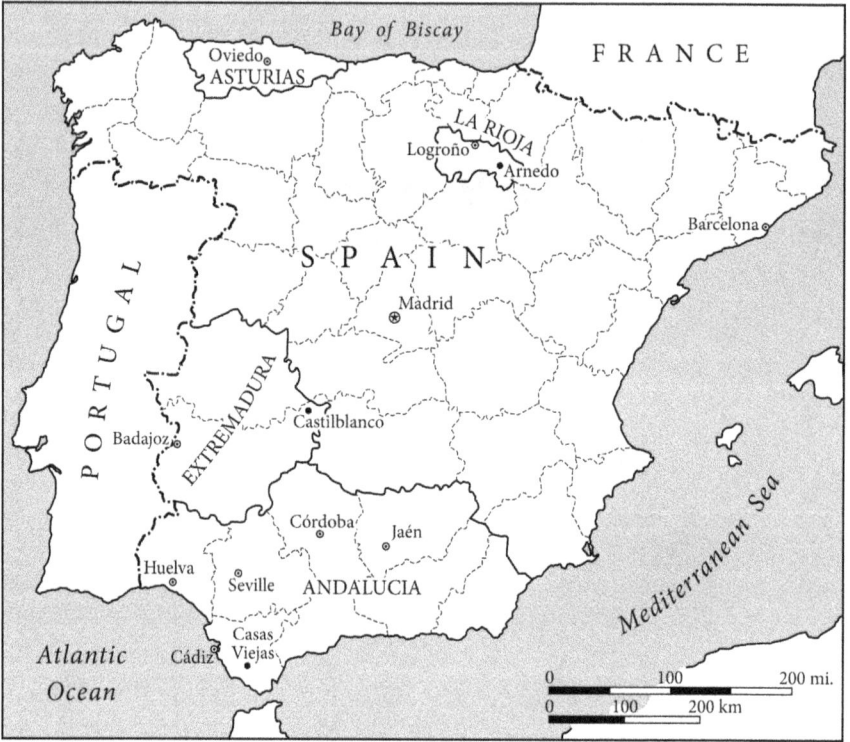

Map of Peninsular Spain indicating the regions, provincial capitals, and towns discussed in the book.

INTRODUCTION

pain's Second Republic period (1931–36) saw more deaths due to political violence in just those five years than did Italy, Germany, or Austria in their respective periods of interwar democratic breakdown.[1] The Second Republic was an experiment in democratic governance that began in April 1931, a time when much of the rest of Europe was already slipping toward authoritarianism and fascism. The republic was declared after the abdication of King Alfonso XIII, at the end of the politically chaotic period that followed the dismissal of General Miguel Primo de Rivera, who had ruled the country as a military dictator from 1923 to 1930. Over the course of the republic's initial five years, its governments passed sweeping reforms that included secularizing education, restructuring the military, granting autonomy to the region of Catalonia, and embarking on a program of land redistribution. Yet this restructuring of Spanish society earned the republic the enmity of traditionalists, fascists, and many within the military. These forces united to launch a coup attempt in July 1936 that only succeeded initially in some areas of the country, thus beginning a civil war between the rebels and those loyal to the republic that would last for almost three years and result in the eventual victory of the rebel forces under General Francisco Franco.[2]

The political violence that plagued the republic even before the outbreak of the war was of enormous significance because it gave those who began the rebellion their main justification for doing so, since it allowed them to argue that they would restore the country to order. However, it was the Civil Guard,

Spain's militarized police force or gendarmerie, that caused more of the deaths in this violence than any other profession.[3] In other words, the public order problem that came to have such grave consequences for the republic was in large part fueled by one of its own police forces—the very force charged with maintaining public order. Given these consequences, the question of why the republic was not more successful at maintaining order and, more importantly, the *perception* of order has been a central facet of the debate over the structural causes of the Civil War. Given how much violence it perpetrated, the Civil Guard is clearly crucial to answering this question, but it is an actor that has usually not been at the center of the study of political violence during the Second Republic.

Apologists for the Civil Guard explain its violence by simply pointing out that guards were often put in confrontational situations in which they were outnumbered and scared, and lethal rifles were the only means they had to defend themselves.[4] Indeed, microsociological research by Randall Collins has highlighted the importance of situational contingencies in determining when violence will occur.[5] This book does not deny the importance of situational factors, but these factors alone would not explain why the number of deaths caused by the Civil Guard was so high compared to police forces in other Western European countries and to other actors in Spain at that time. Critics of the Civil Guard do provide an explanation by arguing that guards were trigger-happy servants of the Right and enemies of the people who were only too willing to open fire on crowds of protesters, often without any provocation.[6] But that explanation makes assumptions about the culture and motivations of the Civil Guard without in-depth study of the force itself. The truth is that both of these explanations are incomplete because they do not take seriously the fact that the Civil Guard was a protagonist in its own right, with a unique culture that shaped its view of events and its actions. This book will study situational factors in detail, but it will also consider how underlying conditions may have tipped the balance in particular situations, turning a confrontation into an episode of violence. In other words, the Civil Guard's actions can best be explained as products of its organizational culture, which was essentially a military culture adapted to civilian policing. Only by examining how a military culture functions in policing situations can the crucial role of the Civil Guard in the Second Republic's efforts to establish order and stability be fully understood.

The core values of the Civil Guard's organizational culture were discipline, sacrifice, loyalty, and political neutrality, all of which were encompassed by the institution's cult of honor. Guards sought to gain this honor by winning the respect of the public. Their organization, therefore, did not explicitly associate itself with either side of the political spectrum, but conservative elites learned to exploit this desire for honor while that same desire only increased mutual animosity with the working classes. Liberals set up the Civil Guard in the nineteenth century to police rural workers just as they were beginning to develop class consciousness and to mobilize politically. When guards did not receive the respect that they felt they deserved from this segment of the population, they turned to violence as a means to create a climate of fear that would serve as a substitute for respect.

This gap between the Civil Guard's culture and the working-class people that the organization policed began early in its history and widened during the Restoration period (1874–1923). By the time of the Second Republic, this organizational culture was unable to adapt to the new challenges presented by the unprecedented mass mobilizations of the time. Instead, guards simply resorted to violence more frequently to defend their honor as they understood it. They were endowed with a culture intended to assist them in maintaining public order, but, by the time of the Second Republic, that culture led them to behaviors that in fact increased the level of violence. Beginning in 1934, many guards also shifted to a more antagonistic conception of their place in society, seeing themselves as confronting the populations they policed instead of protecting them. When the Civil War broke out two years later, most easily transitioned from confrontation to repression.

The literature regarding political violence in Second Republic Spain is especially voluminous because of its importance for the study of the structural origins of the Civil War that followed. Supporters of the Franco dictatorship, past and present, have always played up the political violence of the Second Republic as part of the revolutionary strategy of "the Reds" and as evidence of the republic's instability.[7] They do so as a way to justify the military rebellion of 1936, arguing that it was necessary to restore public order (never mind that the war that the rebellion sparked took some four hundred thousand lives).[8] More academic perspectives, built on social scientist Juan Linz's work that classified the various political parties of the time according to their loyalty to the republic, interpreted the increasing violence through a structural-functionalist approach, thereby seeing it as a consequence of a general polarization in Spanish politics.[9] Some scholars placed blame on a particular political group, while others pointed a finger at the republican regime for failing to incorporate radical groups into a peaceful democratic power system.[10] As in studies of political violence in other European countries, the police (and the Civil Guard in particular) often play an important part in these works but not as an actor with the agency to make its own sociopolitical claims.

There are scholars, however, who have placed the forces of public order at the center of the story. In the 1980s, Manuel Ballbé and Diego López Garrido argued that Spain's militarized approach to public order was the key structural continuity that had consistently blocked the formation of a stable democracy, including during the republic.[11] Today, there is a consensus that their vision of militarization being a continuous obstacle to democratization throughout modern Spanish history needs to be nuanced, given that most other European countries also had roads to democratization that were just as or nearly as rocky and that many stable democracies today have militarized forces that ensure public order. However, agreement on how to achieve that nuance has not been achieved. Eduardo González Calleja argues that it was really the Spanish state's preoccupation with maintaining public order that led its forces of public order to be so violent, while others, like Fernando del Rey and Sergio Vaquero Martínez, find that extremist political discourses were at the root of the violence, preventing a true democratization of the forces of public order.[12] Studying the Civil Guard in particular, Gerald Blaney Jr. argues that Ballbé and López Garrido placed undue emphasis on the corps's military structure and that it should instead be studied as a police force.[13] Blaney draws on the Civil Guard's own internal publications to show that civil guards during the Second Republic thought of themselves as police and saw their mission as maintaining public order in a politically neutral fashion. However, they considered maintaining order to be more important than maintaining loyalty to whatever government was in power.[14] The result was that when the rebellion began in July 1936, somewhere around half betrayed their duty to obey orders from the government and joined the rebels instead.

While scholars from Ballbé to Blaney have focused on the reasons why so many guards proved disloyal to the republic, in studying the institution's vio-

lence, I find the choice between analyzing the Civil Guard as a military institution or a police force to be a false one. Giving a police force a military structure
does not necessarily make it more violent. The question here is what the elements of its military culture are and if those lead the force to employ violence
more frequently. Rather than concentrating solely on the Civil Guard's militarized structure as a causal factor, this book seeks to understand civil guards'
actions in attempting to carry out their policing duties during the Second
Republic by taking into account a multiplicity of factors: continuities in the
organizational culture of their institution; the influence of the discourses of
various political factions at the national level; evolving forms of sociopolitical
claims making; and local dynamics and decisions by individuals at the time
of specific incidents.

To study the nature of the Civil Guard as an institution in its full com-
plexity, this book draws on a concept of organizational culture that begins
with Clifford Geertz's understanding of culture in the semiotic sense as the
patterns of behavior within a society through which humans communicate
symbolic significance.[15] To study the culture of an organization, then, is to
study the patterns of behavior of its members as they are related to and shaped
by that organization and to analyze the symbolic significance of these patterns.
In the 1980s, Edgar Schein applied Geertz's understanding of culture to the
study of business organizations. He defined an organization's culture as a set
of unconscious assumptions about notions as fundamental as "the nature of
reality, truth, time, space, human nature, human activity, and human relationships." He argues that these assumptions emerge as solutions to external
and internal problems that have worked consistently and are therefore taught
to new members to the point where the assumptions are taken for granted.[16]
And so to study an organization's culture means first determining what its
hidden assumptions are and what problems they were meant to solve. Then the
researcher can ask how well the solutions do in solving the problems in question, once these solutions are incorporated into an organization's unconscious
culture, and what unintended consequences they may have.

For a militarized police force like the Civil Guard, two subfields within the
larger field of studies of organizational culture are relevant: military culture
and police culture. Considering military culture first, by the 1990s, military
historians were seizing upon the possibilities of the study of organizational
culture as a way to take a cultural approach to the study of military organiza-

tions.[17] Analyzing organizational culture allows scholars to look beyond official regulations and organizational flowcharts to the unofficial practices and
unconscious assumptions that also influence the behavior of military forces.
What makes military culture a distinct subfield from organizational culture
more broadly is not only that militaries are the object of study but also that
militaries *at war* are the object of study. Hence, one can summarize historian
Isabel Hull's use of the term to define military culture as "a way of understanding why an army acts as it does in war" based on its "habitual practices, de-
fault programs, hidden assumptions, and unreflected cognitive frames."[18] The
thinking here is that even when a military organization is not at war, war is its
purpose, and so the problems that its organizational culture is developed to
solve will concern war.

   Military-culture researchers have observed the problem that the habits that
develop as part of a military organization's culture, usually developed in the
last war or during peacetime, can sometimes diverge from the fulfillment of
that organization's mission—winning the next war.[19] Such was also the case
with the Civil Guard. The habits that emerged from the military culture of the
Civil Guard undermined its policing mission. From the nineteenth century,
the institution developed strong core values of honor, discipline, sacrifice, and
loyalty as its founders sought to shield it from the dangers of corruption and
politicization. But when guards felt their honor and their safety under attack as
their mission required them to confront the new mass political mobilizations
of the Second Republic, they all too easily turned to violence in response. In
other words, the rapid mass political mobilization that accompanied the republic required rapid adaptation on the part of the Civil Guard, but the corps's
strong "institutional inertia," to borrow semanticist S. I. Hayakawa's term,
created a cultural lag that did not allow the force to adapt enough to ensure
order in the republic without deepening the animosity of large segments of
the population toward the forces of public order.[20]

   Military institutions, given their rigid bureaucratic and hierarchical structures, are notoriously slow to adapt to changing circumstances. Studies of military innovation suggest that change only occurs when senior officers are open
to it and are supported by civilian leaders.[21] The organization must be able
to listen to and learn from lower-ranking officers who are gaining practical
lessons from on-the-ground experience in the field.[22] While there were civil
guards advocating practical changes that would reorient the organization to-

ward nonlethal policing methods, neither civilian leaders nor the commanders they appointed listened to these voices. Instead, the change that did occur was a deepening of the civil guards' isolation from the working classes such that many came to believe that active military intervention and political repression were the only ways to ensure they would be properly respected for their sacrifices to the *patria* (fatherland).

What makes this book's analytical approach unique is that it combines the lens of military culture with that of police culture, since the Civil Guard's mission was primarily policing rather than war fighting. In the 1960s, police forces became subject to increased scrutiny and social scientists began to conduct sociological and ethnographical studies of these organizations, seeking to define the "working personality" of the police officer.[23] Many of the defining characteristics of police culture that these researchers identified fit the case of the Civil Guard in the late nineteenth and early twentieth centuries remarkably well. Consistent themes include the high degree of discretion that police officers enjoy and the unpredictability of their work. Usually operating in singles and pairs, police develop their own habits to guide how they will react to the unpredictable and potentially dangerous situations that they will encounter without the immediate presence of a supervisor telling them what to do.[24] The nature of their work, including its potential danger and the need to establish authority, draws policemen together to create a strong sense of solidarity and a conservative mindset, but at the same time this solidarity isolates them from the rest of the community.[25] These values are coupled with strong suspicion of everyone outside of their organization—an "us vs. them" mentality develops.[26] One of the earliest police culture researchers, William A. Westley, argues that concern for their safely leads policemen to demand respect from the hostile public, and they view their own violence as justified if it is used to impose this respect.[27] However, he reaches these conclusions by studying the corrupt police of industrial Gary, Indiana. Can similar dynamics be at work in a much more disciplined force operating in rural areas? I find that the observations made by early efforts to describe a police culture largely do hold true for the Civil Guard and are useful for understanding guards' behaviors and motivations. At the same time, each chapter will consider the political and social context in which guards operated rather than treating them in isolation, thereby addressing criticisms of the police culture concept that it is too deterministic and monolithic and does not take into account external social and cultural influences.[28]

The police culture literature has, with few exceptions, only studied the types of urban police forces present in the United States and England, not the militarized forces that are prevalent in rural areas elsewhere.[29] In this book, I aim to demonstrate the analytical utility of applying these frameworks to such historical examples outside of the English-speaking world. I am not analyzing the militarization of command structures, equipment, and tactics about which there has been much debate in the United States in recent decades but rather forces that are subject directly to military discipline and are considered to be part of the armed forces. To understand these units, one must study them as both policing and military organizations at the same time. While having a military structure does not necessarily make a police force more violent, it can have this effect when it accentuates the disconnect between members' training and values and those of the people that they are policing. It was precisely such a disconnect that led guards to develop patterns of behavior that proved ill-suited to adaptation to the challenges of promoting order and stability in a young democracy with a politically mobilized population.

Among the various factors that composed the Civil Guard's organizational culture (discipline, obedience, political neutrality), this book will highlight honor as that culture's most important component, and the one that most shaped guards' responses to the sociopolitical contestations of the Second Republic period. Historian of the American South Bertram Wyatt-Brown defines honor as "the inner conviction of self-worth . . . the claim of that self-assessment before the public . . . [and] the assessment of the claim by the public, a judgment based on the behavior of the claimant. In other words, honor is reputation."[30] This definition makes clear how crucial public perception is to honor, and this was certainly true in Spain as well, where one definition of the word honor by the Spanish language's governing body, the Royal Spanish Academy, is "glory or good reputation that follows from virtue, from merit or from heroic actions."[31] In these pages, civil guards in particular will be found to be constantly concerned with the image of the institution in the public eye, letting that concern for reputation shape their actions, but also being selective in their interpretation of public opinion so as not to admit that there were any stains on the honor of their institution.

In many societies, conceptions of masculinity are inseparably bound together with those of honor, which is why historian of the American Civil War Lorien Foote alters Wyatt-Brown's definition to read "when a man's self-worth

is based on public reputation and the respect of others."[32] As a masculine domain, the possession of honor, Foote maintains, can help define someone as a
man. Consequently, the civil guards' defense of their honor would also be a defense of their masculinity, and these chapters find that to be the case, especially
during and after the Asturias rebellion, when civil guards perceived attacks
on their families as challenges to the society's whole structure of political and
gender hierarchy.

Both Wyatt-Brown's and Foote's definitions of honor represent it as an
individual trait, but military organizations in particular also have a sense of
collective honor. For the Civil Guard, honor operated both at the individual and
institutional levels: the personal honor an individual civil guard gained or lost
could add to or subtract from the honor of his institution as well. Honor is also
usually thought to exist outside of the state and often in opposition to it. As
social anthropologist Julian Pitt-Rivers explains, the law has never "appealed
to adherents to the code of honor" because a law court "excludes the possibility
of demonstrating personal worth through the display of courage."[33] Yet as a
police force, the Civil Guard was part of the legal system itself. Guards struggled to reconcile the sometimes-conflicting codes of law and honor governing
their behavior, but ultimately their regulations gave them the authority to use
violence when they felt their honor demanded it.

This book is divided into two parts, the first of which outlines the nature and
the development of the Civil Guard's military culture both as an institution
and within the generation of guards that would serve during the Second Republic. It situates these developments in the context of the consolidation of
the liberal state and the beginnings of the political mobilization of the working
classes from the mid-nineteenth through the early twentieth centuries. The
second part then employs case studies to investigate how this culture shaped
the actions of these guards and how it evolved during the republic as they
faced the new mass politics of the period. This interaction between military
culture, democratic politics, and social movements is introduced in chapter
5 and then explored in detail at both the local and national levels in the case
studies of the second part that focus on specific incidents of political violence
involving the Civil Guard.

In part 2, chapters 6 through 9 offer case studies of three of the most prominent incidents of political violence in the Second Republic in order to understand further how the Civil Guard's military culture evolved and shaped its actions during the period. Exploring in-depth examples at the local level is necessary, since this was the sphere in which guards carried out their duties. The thick descriptions presented in theses chapters demonstrate how local contestations for hegemony over public space and even individual decisions could have national consequences, given the tense political atmosphere of the republic. While the examples in these chapters are far from typical (rather, they are three of the republic's most extreme cases of violence), their prominence means that extensive sources are available that permit a closer examination of the nature and evolution of the interactions between the Civil Guard's police culture and political culture at the local level than would be possible with more commonplace examples. In addition, each of these incidents had repercussions on the national stage that contributed to the destabilization of the republic, making the infrequency of such dramatic occurrences less important than the national attention they received.

Each of these chapters examines the origins, unfolding, and aftermath of the incident in question at the local, regional, and national levels. Regarding each of the three incidents, I argue that the cause of the events that transpired was the clash between the Socialists' political culture of mass mobilization, which sought to alter the structures of the republic, and the Civil Guard's organizational culture, which centered on honor. There was a role for individuals too in selecting from the range of possibilities for action within each culture. As the different players vied to shape the narrative of each incident that would be told at the national level, guards had to rely on others to present their version of the story while their own extralegal retribution efforts gave ammunition to their opponents. Offended by even the government's half-hearted efforts to rein them in, many guards came to the conclusion that the military suppression, rather than the policing, of mass politics was the only solution to the perceived lack of respect that mass mobilization engendered.

ONE

FOUNDATION

The Origins of the Civil Guard's
Military Culture

ueen Isabella II is said to have asked why the Civil Guard was called "civil" if it was militarized.[1] It was a fair question, the answer to which lies in the complex rivalries in mid-nineteenth-century Spain between differing ideas of liberalism that were at the heart of the corps's foundation. These frictions would produce an organization with a military structure and civilian policing duties, and the tension between these two would come to define the institution up to the present day. Therefore, if the organizational culture of the Civil Guard in the Second Republic is to be understood, then it is necessary to look back to the origins of that culture, even as far back as the middle of the nineteenth century. This dual identity of the Civil Guard also necessitates understanding both its military and police cultures. The idea of police culture emphasizes the power of the behavioral habits that police officers develop given the large degree of discretion that is inherent in their work.[2] The Civil Guard was certainly no exception to this pattern; however, as a military institution, its written regulations and command structure also exerted an unusually strong influence on guards' behavior. Hence the utility of the military culture frame here, since it examines the tension between formal regulations and unwritten practices. Therefore, because the Civil Guard's foundational documents in particular were so important to its institutional identity, this first chapter will focus on those documents and the creation of the corps's military culture.

The foundation of the Civil Guard was largely the product of the conservative side of Spain's nineteenth-century liberal transformation, which combined a preoccupation with public order and *ancien régime* elitism with a liberal desire for an expansion of private property and state authority. Yet even within the Moderate Party, which represented this more conservative side of Spanish liberalism, there were differing visions of the role of the military in society. The Civil Guard that emerged from these contrasts was a military force tasked with policing civilians. The Duque de Ahumada, the nobleman considered to be the founder of the Civil Guard, is the one who enshrined honor in its regulations as the defining feature of its military culture. In applying the old aristocratic notion of honor to this new, modern police force, he redefined it to mean the approbation of the Civil Guard by the public. He did so to ensure that his civil guards would be firm but just in their enforcement of the law, but he also inadvertently opened the possibility that they would use violence to defend their honor.

A CONTESTED FOUNDATION

The Civil Guard was born of the clash between the *ancien régime* and liberalism that defined the first half of the nineteenth century in Spain and Europe as a whole. After the death of the absolutist king Ferdinand VII in 1833, the country descended into a seven-year war of succession between, in essence, liberals on the one hand and absolutists known as Carlists on the other. The liberals desired a central, parliamentary government subordinated to a constitution and the universal application of the idea of private property, which meant selling Church lands and municipal common lands to private owners. This process, known as *desamortización*, was greatly feared by the peasantry, who stood to lose the critical resource of the common lands, so many joined the Carlists or supported bandits who claimed to be robbing the rich to feed the poor.

The liberals won the war, but they still had to cement their legitimacy after seven years of violence and political instability.[3] Yet the liberals themselves were deeply divided. The Moderate Party was composed of strict centralizers who wanted shared sovereignty between the king and the people and also desired stringent property requirements for voting. They were furthermore against the creation of a national militia, which the more radical Progressive

Party favored, along with looser property requirements for voting and vesting sovereignty entirely in the people. The rivalry between these two liberal factions, as well as tensions with the crown, led to political chaos from 1833 to 1843 and a power vacuum that allowed banditry to surge in the countryside.[4] It also led to frequent interventions in politics in the form limited military uprisings, known as *pronunciamientos*, that pursued specific political objectives.[5]

Such a chaotic environment created a desire among the governing elites for a disciplined police force that could rein in the banditry, prevent a Carlist resurgence, protect the persons and property of those who benefited from the *desamortización*, and generally bring a restoration of order that would be conducive to political stability. In fact, the steady increase in crime in the first decades of the nineteenth century had hatched a plethora of police forces throughout Spain to combat banditry. However, since all of these forces were local in nature, they were too small to have a wide impact and susceptible to bribes from the bandits themselves.[6] For the Progressives, the answer was the National Militia, which was composed of local units in which property owners were the ones keeping order. The problem with the militia was that it was intimately linked to the Progressives and to the popular General Baldomero Espartero in particular, while its local nature made it prone to corruption.[7] As for the Moderates, they envisioned a professional force under direct orders from the national government that could further their centralization and state-building projects. Therefore, when the Moderates, allied with some Progressives, overthrew Espartero's regency government and took power in 1843, they dissolved the militia and moved to replace it with a new, professional force of public order.[8]

The idea of such a force was not entirely new to Spain. In the eighteenth century, there were already a number of militarized regional police forces.[9] However, the core of the Spanish Bourbons' public-order system was the army.[10] Meanwhile, the French Bourbons already possessed a kind of national police force in the form of the Maréchaussée, which could trace its origins at least as far back as the sixteenth century. It had a military structure and a series of small posts around France from which members would conduct patrols.[11] When the French Revolution broke out, the revolutionaries saw the value of this *ancien régime* institution as a force for national unity, and so they simply changed its name to the Gendarmerie Nationale and actually expanded its numbers, which were then further augmented by Napoleon.[12]

Napoleon spread the gendarmerie model across Europe as he conquered the continent. In the case of Spain, Joseph, the brother Napoleon had installed on the Spanish throne, founded a number of police forces, including a Spanish gendarmerie. All of these units disappeared when the French withdrew from Spain in 1814, but King Ferdinand VII did create a customs force, known as the Cuerpo de Carabineros, that had a military structure.[13]

The legacies of both the *ancien régime* and the Napoleonic period meant that all Spanish liberals, whether Moderates or Progressives, desired a militarized public-order system.[14] The Progressives favored the militia, while most Moderates maintained the idea of the gendarmerie. They wanted a strong state to "restore order" and were impressed by the fact that France's gendarmerie had survived the French Revolution.[15] Various attempts were made in the ensuing decades to refound such a force in Spain, but the political turmoil rendered all of them nonstarters.[16] In the early months of 1844, when Moderate Prime Minister Luis González Bravo was considering how to replace the militia, he naturally envisioned a gendarmerie with a military structure and members recruited from the army that would represent the central government throughout the country—centralization being the primary goal of his administration.[17]

Yet from the very beginning, the question of exactly how militarized this new force would be was a central point of debate. Since González Bravo, a former Progressive, was running a civilian government somewhat at odds with a powerful military faction within the Moderates led by General Ramón María Narváez, he wanted to be sure that the new force would be under the control of the civilian Ministry of the Interior and not part of the army. This civilian supervision would ensure that the military's power in the developing centralized state was not further augmented. He proposed naming the force the Corps of Civil Guards (*cuerpo de guardias civiles*) to emphasize its civilian nature.[18] A January 26, 1844, decree declaring the need for a security force contained plenty of criticism about the partiality of the militia model and its failure to protect "respectable interest," but it also suggested that "the service of protection and public security will be exclusively in the charge of the Ministry of the Interior."[19] Another decree, dated March 28 and written by the Ministry of the Interior, created such a corps and gave it the broad mission of providing "order, public security, and the protection of people and properties," noting that "neither the standing army nor the National Militia can attend to this service without harm to their peculiar organization and objectives, without detriment to military discipline, and without unfortunate annoyances and damages of the greatest importance for the wealthy and working classes."[20]

The man chosen to build this new force (which was already being referred to as simply the Civil Guard) would wind up undermining this civilian vision. He was Francisco Javier Girón y Ezpeleta, II Duque de Ahumada, a blue-blooded aristocrat who counted even the Aztec Emperor Moctezuma II among his ancestors. As was common for aristocrats of the period, his family was also a military one, yet it was moderately liberal in its politics. In fact, his father, Pedro Agustín Girón, had been named minister of war when the liberals had seized power in 1820. He had proposed a new force modeled after the French Gendarmerie to be called the Legión de Salvaguardias Nacionales, but the more radical Cortes (as the Spanish parliament was known) rejected the offer. This and other setbacks led Pedro Agustín to resign after just six months in office and Francisco Javier to spend the remainder of the three-year period of liberal rule in exile in Gibraltar.[21]

A decade later and back in Spain, Francisco Javier fought for the liberals as a divisional commander in various actions in the First Carlist War and rose to the rank of field marshal.[22] Politically, he followed in his father's footsteps as a member of the most conservative and militaristic wing of the Moderate Party, which was particularly concerned with public order.[23] He was a natural choice to lead the project of continuing his father's efforts to found a Spanish gendarmerie because he had already worked with the Mossos d'Esquadra police force in Catalonia and had studied other European gendarmeries, and he had had experience with military organization as inspector general of the army.[24] Ahumada would prove the right man for the job, and one whose life as an aristocrat and soldier would profoundly influence the form that the new institution would take. Upon being named to the office on April 12, 1844, he immediately began studying the March 28 decree, and within a week he demonstrated his militarist inclinations by proposing to modify it to give himself almost total control over the organization, placing it entirely under the Ministry of War and giving it a centralized structure that would reduce the provincial governors' control over it.[25]

As it happened, just a couple of weeks later, on May 3, Isabella II replaced González Bravo as prime minister with General Narváez. As the leader of the pro-military faction within the Moderate Party, Narváez was supportive of the Civil Guard project as a whole and of his old friend Ahumada's suggestions to

allow the Ministry of War some control over the new force. Since most ministers of war in the liberal period were generals, these measures would in effect grant the army complete control of public order in Spain.[26] However, the
Ministry of the Interior still wanted a say, and so Narváez compromised. On
May 13, using the excuse that the March 28 decree had been vague, he issued a
new decree placing the Civil Guard partially within the minister of war's portfolio and repealing "all previous orders that oppose this decree."[27] The May 13
decree's article 1 explained the roles of each ministry: "The Civil Guard depends
on the Ministry of War for that which concerns its organization, personnel, discipline, materiel, and payroll, and on the Ministry of the Interior for that which
is related to everyday services and movements." The document also created the
General Inspection, which allows a centralized command structure broad control over the Civil Guard's internal affairs down to the lowest-ranking officer.
The hope was that such an organization would ensure the cohesion of a corps
dispersed all around the country.[28] Despite all this, Narváez, who was not quite
as enthusiastic about militarization as Ahumada, also inserted a clause saying
that the Civil Guard's role was to be distinct from that of the army. In short,
the strength of the military's political power within the ostensibly civilian governments of nineteenth-century Spain had produced a hybrid force with both
military and civilian characteristics, and the tension between these elements
was to become one of the defining features of the Civil Guard's history.[29]

   This tension between the military and civilian competencies over the Civil
Guard was apparent in the first task its organizers faced—creating the regulations for the new force. Ahumada himself drafted a set of regulations that
resembled the French model, in which the gendarmerie could receive orders
from Interior Ministry officials, but the force was considered to be part of the
army (and thus under the auspices of the Ministry of War).[30] However, Spain's
Ministry of the Interior also drafted its own regulations for the Civil Guard,
which, naturally, gave it more direct control over the institution than Ahumada's version did. Narváez favored the Ministry of Interior in this case, and it
published the Civil Guard's *Reglamento para el servicio* (Service Regulations) on
October 9, 1844. These regulations reject the French Gendarmerie model and
echo the March 28 decree in declaring the mission of the Civil Guard to be "the
protection of people and property," envisioning it as primarily a policing rather
than a military force.[31] But they also state that the Civil Guard's goal is "public
order" rather than "order [and] public security," a slight change in wording

that shifts the emphasis from the security of the citizenry to an abstract idea of "order" that could presumably be defended at the expense of an individual's safety.[32] Furthermore, the document concludes by stating that part of the Civil Guard's mission is ensuring the tranquility of "the persons and property of honorable and peaceful men," not the tranquility of all citizens.[33]

This idea of the Civil Guard as a force to ensure public order is reinforced by the *Reglamento*'s chapter 3, which enumerates the corps's duties. The first few articles of the chapter are all about maintaining public order. Article 26 instructs civil guards to "stamp out and repress any riot or disorder that occurs in their presence," even if they have not received specific orders to do so. If such action is necessary, article 27 contains instructions on how the commander should proceed:

1° He will evaluate the means that prudence dictates for persuading the members of the crowd to disperse and not continue altering public order.

2° When these means are ineffective, he will threaten them with the use of force.

3° If despite this intimidation the rioters persist with the same disobedience, he will reestablish tranquility and the rule of law with the vigorous use of force.

The key articles of the *Reglamento para el servicio* remained little altered up through the Second Republic.[34] Therefore, given that civil guards received almost no training in crowd control, article 27 constituted some of the only instruction that they had on how to proceed in confrontational situations. The vagueness of these directives left plenty of room for improvisation and for unwritten patterns of behavior to develop.[35] Article 27's third step allowed guards to initiate violence if their orders were not respected. Naturally, article 28 also stipulates that "if the rioters or agitators make use of any violent means during the first warnings, the Civil Guard will also employ force from that point on without preceding with other notifications or warnings."

In one final illustration of the ambiguities about the military character of the Civil Guard that lie in the very foundations of the institution, the Ministry of War issued its own *Reglamento militar* (Military Regulations) just six days after the Interior Ministry's *Reglamento para el servicio*. Ahumada's suggestions

influenced the drafting of the *Reglamento militar*, but it was ultimately composed by a Ministry of War commission. The document never even mentions
the minister of the interior's roles and confers on the inspector general (for-
merly the director general) broad powers to shape the centralized organization
and discipline of the corps, envisioning it as a branch of the army.[36]

The idea that the Civil Guard would be under two different ministries and
governed by two different sets of regulations, known as dual dependency,
would come to define the institution. Questions of organization and promotion would be controlled by the Ministry of War and channeled through the
Civil Guard's command structure, while instructions about duties to perform
would be given by the Ministry of the Interior and civil governors at the provincial level. Town mayors could also give civil guards instructions as long as
they did not interfere with orders from these higher authorities. This complex
system, born of the political contradictions of mid-nineteenth-century Spain,
gave the Civil Guard military discipline and some civilian control, but it also
created tensions with local communities and ambiguities regarding what the
Civil Guard's mission was.

Developed amidst the political chaos of mid-nineteenth-century Spain, the
Civil Guard's militarized structure was a manifestation of the desires of Moderate liberalism for centralized state control and, above all, for order. At the same
time, the character of the new force reflected the debates within the Moderate
Party between military and civilian influences, as well as between *ancien régime*
and liberal influences. The outcome was the perpetually ambiguous position
of the Civil Guard as a militarized force carrying out a civilian policing mission
under the orders of both civilian and military officials.

AHUMADA AND HONOR

Studies of organizational culture have identified the founders of an organization as the most important influences on the formation of its culture.[37] Since he
did not entirely get his way with the drafting of the regulations, the Duque de
Ahumada was not the sole founder of the Civil Guard, but his outsized impact
as its first inspector general and his status as a legendary father figure did give
the corps a firm foundation upon which to construct a strong organizational
culture.[38] In other words, for a strongly hierarchical organization like the Civil

Guard, it makes sense to find the origins of its culture in Ahumada's early leadership, especially because the focus of this book will be on how low-ranking
civil guards interpreted the values he instilled in their institution.

The duke's most important legacy was the *Cartilla del Guardia Civil*, a hand-
book he wrote that was originally meant simply to complement and clarify
the two different sets of regulations—from the Ministries of the Interior and
of War—but that took on a life of its own as the fundamental text defining
the Civil Guard's values.[39] The *Cartilla* was largely memorized and kept in the
breast pocket of a guard's uniform at all times—it is sometimes referred to
as the "Bible of the Civil Guard."[40] First issued in 1845, it became so revered
that it was never substantially altered after one revision in 1852. As José Díaz
Valderrama, one of the first Civil Guard historians, wrote in 1858, "The guards
not only know the articles from memory but also record them in their hearts,
on the doors of their rooms, and even on the walls of their homes."[41]

With the initial work of creating the regulations over, Ahumada had more
time to think beyond the model of the French Gendarmerie as he was writing
the *Cartilla*.[42] He wound up defining what the moral code of the Civil Guard
would be in the document's famous first article: "Honor must be the principal
watchword of the civil guard; he must, therefore, preserve it without stain.
Once lost it can never be recovered."[43] In other words, Ahumada took the idea
of honor from his own aristocratic background and applied it to this quint-
essentially liberal institution. The match appears an odd one because it asked
an institution tasked with the liberal project of enforcing the written law to be
governed in part by an extralegal system arbitrated, as emphasized in Wyatt-
Brown's definition of honor, by approbation from the public rather than the
courts' readings of the law.

Ahumada's efforts can also be seen as part of a broader trend of extending
the ability to have honor to the non-noble classes. In the Middle Ages, honor
was thought to be virtually synonymous with the military role of the nobility;
in this sense, honor and violence have gone hand-in-hand for centuries.[44] By at
least the early modern period, commoners also had their own sense of honor
that they defended in duels and in the courts, even if the aristocratic notion
of honor was still the one exclusively discussed in morality texts and drama-
tized in honor plays.[45] By the eighteenth century, Enlightenment thinkers were
advocating for an official extension of honor from the nobility to members of
various professions such as artisans as well, thereby disconnecting honor and

violence.[46] In Spain, this extension was made official in the Royal Dispatch of 1783, but at first the effect of the measure was limited.[47] After the French Revolution and the Napoleonic Era, the idea of honor as the exclusive domain of the nobility was certainly on the wane, but the bourgeoisie came to embrace honor more strongly than ever to assert the superiority of their rising class.[48] This shift led army officers also to increase their emphasis on honor as a way to maintain their image of themselves as part of this new gentlemanly milieu, just as the number of nobles in the army steadily declined during the nineteenth century.[49]

For Ahumada, honor was particularly important for civil guards as model representatives of the liberals' idea of the Spanish nation around the country. As honor had once been a factor helping aristocrats to maintain their elite social status, so he hoped that it would now aid guards in gaining an elite status in the towns they policed, granting them the respect they needed to be obeyed and shielding them from corruption. As article 2 of the *Cartilla* states, "The greatest prestige and moral strength are the corps's first elements, and assuring the morality of its members is the fundamental basis for the existence of this institution."[50] Whereas previous police forces in Spain had disappeared as soon as the governments that founded them fell from power, Ahumada hoped that by making the Civil Guard loyal to the abstract idea of honor, it would come to represent more than just the Moderate Party and thereby be acceptable to whoever succeeded the Moderates in power.[51] He was transforming the old aristocratic value of honor from a hallmark of the *ancien régime* to a method for creating the kind of professional, bureaucratic force that liberals so desired.[52]

As Ahumada saw it, honor would have another benefit in guiding civil guards in their policing duties. It would automatically temper their behavior by having them always keep in mind what the public would think of their actions. Article 4 of the *Cartilla* prohibits physical or verbal maltreatment of the citizenry because, as the next article explains, "Always faithful to his duty, calm when in danger and carrying out his functions with dignity, prudence, and firmness, the civil guard will be more respected than one who with threats alone manages to alienate everyone." In other words, the *Cartilla* attempts to make honor a guard's guide in judging how to apply force as stipulated in articles 27 and 28 of the *Reglamento para el servicio*. Therefore, Ahumada goes on to state in the famous article 7 of the *Cartilla* that a guard's "first weapons should be persuasion and moral strength, resorting to those [weapons] that he carries with him only when he sees himself offended by others or [when] his words have not been enough. In this case, he will always leave in good stead the honor of his arms."[53] While this article advocates a nonviolent approach to policing, it also suggests that violence is acceptable if a guard's honor is offended, even if only verbally. Given that the *Cartilla* states that his honor could never be regained if lost, he was under tremendous pressure to defend it. Therefore, as defined in the *Cartilla*, honor could be a force working to restrain or encourage a guard to use violence, depending on the situation. Ahumada seems to have hoped that honor would ensure that guards employed the broad powers given to them in articles 27 and 28 of the *Reglamento para el servicio* with prudence, but he did not foresee that it could drive them to use violence with abandon as well.

Ahumada's concern that his men's behavior be respectable went so far that he ordered them to be subject to on-duty discipline at all times.[54] Indeed, the *Cartilla* regulates every aspect of a guard's life, not just his official duties. Ahumada understood that appearances matter to public perception; therefore, the *Cartilla* demands of a civil guard that he have a courteous but serious and sober attitude while on patrol and that he pay meticulous attention to his uniform and personal appearance; in addition, it stipulates such details as how often he should shave, that he should not greet friends he may see with shouts or nicknames, and that he should be polite when asking to enter a domicile or view documentation. The *Reglamento militar* regulates his private life as well: it contains prohibitions on patronizing gambling houses, having a bad reputation, causing a public scandal, or associating with suspicious persons.[55]

In addition to honor, Ahumada saw a military structure as key to enabling the Civil Guard to be immune to corruption and ultimately loyal only to the central government. Militarization meant isolation from local influences. Housing in barracks and strict discipline would serve to distinguish civil guards from the people they policed while enhancing unit solidarity. Ahumada also insisted that his organization be composed entirely of volunteers from the army. An all-volunteer force meant that these men would be committed to the institution, and the fact that they had been in the army would also make them accustomed to a job that entailed what he called sacrifice—the willingness to endure harsh physical conditions (Ahumada's physical requirements were even stricter than the army's) and danger for one's country. Since most enlisted men came from a peasant class excluded from the political system, he (and Narváez) hoped that they would not enter the force with political predispositions. As a consequence, Ahumada had to find a way to elevate these men to a social level in which they would value the idea of property, the protection of which would be one of their primary duties.[56] Therefore, he insisted that all recruits know how to read and write (also essential skills for checking documentation and writing tickets and reports) and that their pay be higher than that of members of the army (which would also help prevent corruption). Unfortunately, the low literacy rate in Spain, along with the fact that the pay was still barely enough to survive on, meant that the Civil Guard was to have persistent problems finding enough volunteers who met its qualifications.[57]

The role of the charismatic founding figure played by Ahumada was key to ensuring that the Civil Guard outlived its predecessors and developed a strong organizational culture that would give it continuity and a sense of identity. Drawing on his aristocratic background, he hoped that making honor and military discipline the centerpieces of that culture would elevate guards of humble origins to a privileged position in society that would confer authority upon them. At the same time, honor served as an extralegal limit on that authority, with concern for their reputations in the public eye functioning as a self-regulating mechanism. However, when guards confronted new challenges to the sociopolitical order as the nineteenth century drew to a close, their continued adherence to the unique military culture that Ahumada had endowed to them would have consequences that he could not have foreseen.

The tensions within the organizational culture that shaped the Civil Guard's actions during the Second Republic dated back to the very foundations of the institution. Regarding its official structure, the dual dependency compromise worked out between the more and less militaristic factions of the Moderate Party began the identity crisis of the Civil Guard that has lasted up to the present day. The question of whether the institution should be under the Ministry of War or the Ministry of the Interior might seem an academic one, but it spoke to the larger issue of how much control the civilian government would have over the corps.

Another factor that contributed to the ambiguities of the Civil Guard's culture was the code of honor that the institution's principal founder, the Duque de Ahumada, inscribed in the *Cartilla*. By establishing honor as the basis for that culture, he could encapsulate all the military values that he thought were most important for his men to have: discipline, obedience, a capacity for sacrifice, and political neutrality. By synthesizing the liberal idea of progress and an aristocrat's understanding of tradition, he believed that giving his men a sense of honor would make them immune to corruption and political partisanship as well as restraining them in the use of force because they would have a sense of accountability to the public. The result was the paradoxical situation of a military culture being applied to the context of civilian policing. The tensions built into this culture could produce violence instead of limiting it. Much depended on the social and political context in which the Civil Guard would be deployed. When this professional military unit enforced the dictates of the central government on a rural Spain accustomed to the informal structures of town life, respect from all classes of society was not the result.

TWO

ON PATROL

The Police Culture of the Civil Guard

n September 1, 1844, the Civil Guard went on patrol for the first time, parading through Madrid with the Duque de Ahumada at its head and General Narváez looking on. The corps expanded gradually outward from Madrid across all of Spain over the next two years, its deployment a symbol of the expanding power of the central government.[1] The organization's numbers grew quickly to match the expansion—from an initial 1,870 men to 5,015 just two years later.[2] Regional organization was based on the provincial system that was established in 1833, thereby linking the Civil Guard to yet another liberal project meant to standardize the relations of the central government with all areas of the country. Each town of any size was given a Civil Guard post of usually six men but sometimes as few as four.

This chapter considers how these small detachments of guards went about policing Spain's rural communities. It examines how the Civil Guard's military culture influenced the corps's day-to-day policing of civilians, and it will need to take up the lens of police culture as well in order to do so. Police culture permits the study of the practices and habits that guards developed over the course of their day-to-day policing activities as they sought to balance the mandates of their regulations with on-the-ground realities. Whereas most studies of police culture have concentrated on urban police forces, this chapter will examine the patterns of behavior that emerge in a force living in and policing rural communities. It begins by taking up the military elements of a guard's life, such as living in a barracks and being subject to strict discipline, which were intended to isolate him from the corrupting influences of small-town life while elevating his class status so that he would be respected and obeyed. However, this isolation from the everyday townsperson also brought guards closer to other town elites, such as landowners and clergy.

First, the chapter concentrates on these structures of a civil guard's life, many of which were designed by Ahumada himself. Then it considers how this distancing process from most of the population was exacerbated by guards' daily policing duties. The chapter stands outside of the chronological order of the book, taking examples from the mid-nineteenth century up through the Second Republic, because my contention is that the Civil Guard's police culture changed remarkably little throughout this period. The strong values bequeathed to the institution by the foundational documents resulted in significant cultural continuity over the first ninety years of its existence. This stability proved an asset that ensured its survival in the turbulent years of the mid-nineteenth century but wound up being a hinderance to its ability to adapt to the rapidly changing social and political circumstances of the early-twentieth-century Spain. The Civil Guard's policing practices were intended to win respect from the pueblo[3] through fighting crime and maintaining order, but they instead bred resentment because the Civil Guard attempted to impose the dictates of the central government upon local communities that largely operated under their own informal methods of social regulation. Unwilling to admit they were not receiving the respect they felt they deserved, yet still bound to maintain political neutrality, guards deemed the town elites who praised them to be the "good" citizens—and the only ones whose opinions mattered.

INTERNAL STRUCTURES

Housing and Family

Perhaps Ahumada's most important strategy for ensuring his men were honorable was to combine their police stations and quarters into one building, called the *casa-cuartel* (house-quarters).[4] These *casas-cuarteles* were intentionally isolated—often placed at the edge of town at a crossroads or other strategic point—to ensure that guards formed tight bonds with one another.[5] The buildings allowed them to both live and work together in close proximity, rather than with townspeople who might seek to corrupt them.[6] Developing rela-tionships with locals was dangerous because, in rural Spain, friendship could imply an expectation that quid pro quo favors would be exchanged.[7]

The design of the *casas-cuarteles* was meant to provide a military lifestyle even in a remote town. They were rather spartan structures, bearing a closer resemblance to a barracks than a police station.[8] A typical layout included a dormitory for unmarried guards and small units for the families of married ones, a slightly larger unit and a small office for the station commandant, a kitchen area, a stable, and a central patio and armaments room where a daily meeting would take place. An unmarried guard's personal possessions were expected to fit into a single chest.

In Ahumada's rush to deploy the Civil Guard around the country, he be-gan the practice of having municipalities pay for guards' lodging as a way to facilitate the process, but in so doing he undermined his efforts to keep the force neutral by making it dependent on local politicians' good will.[9] Given the limited funds available to most municipalities, the state of a guard's *casa-cuartel* was often quite decrepit, and guards were frequently housed in whatever building the local authorities had available. Ahumada commonly arranged for former monasteries and convents seized in the *desamortización* to be converted to this new purpose. By 1850, 30 percent of his men were housed in such structures, even though the Ministry of Health had declared many of them uninhabitable.[10]

Civil guards also frequently found themselves fairly isolated from the out-side world because of poor roads and a lack of telegraph and telephone lines. While the *casas-cuarteles* may have been barracks, they were certainly not forts, as the walls were often quite flimsy. This combination of poor communication (even if there was a telegraph or telephone line, it was easily cut) and poor-quality housing made the *casa-cuartel* potentially vulnerable to assault by the pueblo itself. However, at least according to Civil Guard historian Fernando Rivas, no such assault had ever been successfully carried out prior to the Sec-ond Republic, no doubt because the pueblo lacked military arms.[11] Another result of the lack of government money for housing was that without funding for expansions of the *casas-cuarteles*, guards sometimes had to be off-site in rented apartments. Here one sees how the government's budgetary restraints helped prevent the full isolation of the civil guards from civilian society. Those men and their wives who lived outside of the *casas-cuarteles* could and did form relationships with their landlords and neighbors.

In 1860, Ahumada took another measure to ensure that his men were not influenced by local ties by ordering that a guard could not be posted in his hometown or that of his wife, thereby removing them from the proximity of any friends and relatives they might have.[12] However, there were limits on this approach to isolating guards as well. They could still be stationed *near* their hometowns, and many obtained transfers to their native provinces.[13] In addition, they often remained at the same post for years (especially if it was near their hometowns), which makes it highly unlikely that they resisted forming any bonds with the local communities where they were stationed.

As Ahumada saw it, in addition to keeping guards isolated, the *casa-cuartel* had the added benefit of allowing them to live with their families, placing their military professional lives and civilian family lives in the same building.[14] Even as guards abided by their own military code of honor, they would also have to take into consideration townspeople's criteria for honor, which was less of a strict code than a rhetoric that included the reputation of a man's family and his financial creditability.[15] Therefore, Ahumada encouraged guards to get married and have children because he believed the public would have greater respect for civil guards who were middle-class family men.[16] One reason why he pushed for high pay for his civil guards was so that they could afford to raise families, especially since he prohibited them from contracting debts (an inability to pay such debts might dishonor them). Given that being a guard was a career position, it is safe to say that most were married and had children. Nevertheless, Ahumada also placed restrictions on marriages to ensure that guards were augmenting rather than diminishing the honor of the corps. He required that the groom be at least twenty-eight years of age, that he be economically solvent, and that his bride obtain a letter of good conduct from her town mayor or priest.[17]

Marriage was another limit on a civil guard's isolation because, although wives and children lived within the confines of the *casa-cuartel*, they had to venture out into the community for shopping and schooling at the very least. Guards also sometimes married women from the towns where they were stationed. To counteract the potential for undue influence, if a guard did marry a local woman, he was always transferred. Moving out of her hometown must have been difficult for many guards' wives, but such a marriage also had benefits. It offered poor women from rural areas housing, a steady family income, and upward social mobility. While they may have previously held some form of employment, they were now to be housewives.

With wives' greater status came greater responsibility. Their presence meant that the Civil Guard had to interest itself in the private lives not only of its members but also of their wives and families in order to safeguard its cherished reputation. Therefore, when an officer inspected a post, he evaluated the personal conduct of both the guards and their families.[18] Although the Civil Guard's sense of honor was not exactly the same as that of the pueblo, it did recognize the important role that women had in rural Spanish society's conception of honor in its efforts to win the respect of that society.

To take an extreme example of how important civil guards considered the reputation of their wives, in 1935, when some items were stolen from a civil guard's chest at a post in the province of Huelva, an investigative judge determined that the wife of the post commandant (a corporal) was the thief. The *Revista Técnica de la Guardia Civil* (*Civil Guard Technical Review, RTGC*), the corps's professional journal from 1910 to 1936, describes what happened next:

> When the corporal got the news, he did not get upset and said, "I will look into it." And after a few seconds two detonations disturbed the peace of the station.
>
> What happened? We don't know. What's certain is that the corporal killed his spouse with his pistol and committed suicide immediately.

The author of the article, Lieutenant Colonel Lara, is not sure what to make of this case, for he is unable to decide whether the corporal's duty to obey the laws against murder and suicide or his duty to uphold his honor was more important. Lara begins by condemning what he calls a crime against divine and social law but then spends most of the rest of the article praising the corporal's sense of honor. Even if Lara cannot condone the corporal's actions, he can empathize with his decision to use violence to defend his honor: "Surely in an act of limitless affection toward the mother of his children, [he] took her life so that she would not have to endure the shame."[19] In this example, the corporal chose safeguarding his family's shame (and thereby his honor and that of his institution) over obeying the written law. In an institution where honor could never be regained once lost, the only solution seemed to him to be death.

Discipline

As Ahumada saw it, civil guards would be members of both their biological families and the institutional family of the Civil Guard itself. Not only did he bring this family together in the *casas-cuarteles* but also he saw enforcing strict discipline and hierarchy as part of inoculating his guards from corruption and winning them the respect of the public.[20] As the head of his biological family and one of the leading figures of the town where he was stationed, a guard's authority reigned almost supreme, but within the institution he submitted to the stern parental authority of his officers. Because of this need to distinguish guards from civilians, guards had more restrictions placed on their lives than the civilians who lived around them did. The *Reglamento militar* provided the key distinction in decreeing that civil guards accused of crimes would be tried in military courts.[21] But beyond the regulations, the guards' code of honor also demanded conformity and obedience to superiors. Discipline was harsh because, it was thought, it had to be in order to maintain that moral standard believed necessary for winning the respect of the people. In the words of the *Reglamento militar*, "Discipline, an essential element in all military bodies, is of more and greater importance in the Civil Guard, since the dispersion of its individuals makes even more necessary in this corps the rigorous completion of their duties, constant emulation [of superiors], blind obedience, love of service, unity of sentiments and honor, and the good name of the institution. Given these considerations, no offense, not even the lightest, is concealable in the civil guards."[22]

The Civil Guard's concern for discipline required that commanding officers, who were corporals or sergeants in small posts, have tremendous power over their men. Much of the commanders' power stemmed from the fact that they could take many disciplinary actions against their men without the approval of any higher authority or jury.[23] A commander who took a dislike to one of his men could make life very difficult for him. He even had control of his subordinates' movements—permission was needed to travel outside the province where one was stationed—and leave was rarely granted.

One reason why officers were given such power was that since their men would be spread out in small posts around the country, it was impossible for a commissioned officer to be stationed at every post, and there was a danger that each post would develop its own culture, replicating the disunity that had previously so hindered policing in Spain. Therefore, the periodic inspections that the *Reglamento militar* required officers to perform took on special importance, and officers were encouraged to take a paternalistic attitude toward their men by being themselves models of good conduct and by policing everything from the enlisted man's dress and equipment to his recordkeeping and even his moral and personal conduct.[24] The inspections were a serious business. Officers who found that regulations had been violated had the power to impose disciplinary measures.[25]

Service records indicate that officers did punish civil guards and lower-ranking officers for even the slightest offenses. Not only disobedience but also simple inexactitude in the completion of duty could result in a note on one's record. The range of violations was quite wide, but many had to do with laziness or sloppiness—dodging inspections, not reporting for duty, making mistakes in filling out reports, or not reporting or failing to investigate an incident. Of course, these reprimands or short periods of house arrest were just slaps on the wrist; the real punishment was the unfavorable note in one's service record—a stain on one's honor that officers went to every effort to have expunged.

In keeping with the Civil Guard's concern about regulating the private lives of its members, violations of its moral regulations seem to have been the most common cause for disciplinary action after punishments for sloppiness in the completion of duty. Bringing what was seen as the moral turpitude of the masses into the supposedly isolated *casa-cuartel* was especially frowned upon. There are enough examples in the service records to conclude that violating a moral regulation was another way in which guards blurred the strict division that they were supposed to maintain between the military *casa-cuartel* and the civilian pueblo.

Even though the officers who judged these cases were concerned about the public's opinion of the civil guards, ultimately they were only legally responsible to their superior officers, not the public. The Code of Military Justice was strict in its enforcement of discipline inside the Civil Guard, but it also served as a shield from civilian interference. According to article 28 of the *Reglamento militar*, "The civil guard, as a solider, is free from all responsibility when he has executed well and faithfully the orders of his superiors."[26] In effect, this regulation, plus the fact that military jurisdiction meant that guards would be tried by other military men, ensured that guards simply did not receive convictions for crimes related to the use of violence. One is led to agree with Eduardo González Calleja, who goes so far as to say that the system gave guards a measure of impunity.[27] Of course, they were subject to some restrictions; for example, they were barred from arbitrarily detaining people, mistreating prisoners, or entering a domicile without authorization.[28] However, guards suspected of violating such regulations were always judged by other members of the military, never by civilians. Guards were much more likely to be disciplined for violations of the regulations than for abuses committed against the public.

The theme of isolation, highlighted by early scholars of police culture, emerges from this description of the structures of a civil guard's daily life.[29] In fact, in the case of the Civil Guard the isolation was even more pronounced than it would be in a civilian force because of the housing in barracks, the frequent transfers, the restrictions on marriage, and the military discipline. Yet, as later scholars of police culture pointed out, this isolation was never complete.[30] Policing duties, funding necessities, family, social events, and their desire for honor itself all put guards in contact with the communities they policed; however, most of that contact was with a town's elite. Perhaps most importantly, the institution's placement under military jurisdiction meant that guards answered for their actions only to the military. While guards could hope to win favor in the court of public opinion, the pueblo had no formal mechanism for truly holding them to account.

RELATIONSHIPS WITH THE PUEBLO

The civil guards' housing arrangements and strict discipline may have had some success in isolating them from corrupting local influences, but that isolation did not encourage warm relations with the public. The Civil Guard and the pueblo were also separated by their starkly contrasting understandings of law and justice. Guards were often a town's only direct representatives of the central government and its laws. Yet in a society where things were accomplished at least as much through personal relationships and favors as through official channels, these institutions must have had only vague meaning for many local residents.[31] The pueblo and the guards' conceptions of law and justice were so different that occasionally guards would even protect criminals if a town tried to lynch them, making clear that the pueblo's self-policing would not be permitted to extend to criminal justice—that was the exclusive domain of the governmental authorities.[32]

Nevertheless, given that their duties, as well as their very survival, required interaction with the public, civil guards had to find a way to coexist with, and at least be tolerated by, the pueblo.[33] Although a strict commitment to enforcing the law without favoritism was a component of the guards' honor code, so was having the support of the public; at times, the former commitment had to be relaxed in order to maintain the latter. Since in rural Spain business was often conducted through friendship networks, a guard who truly had no friends in the pueblo would be rather ineffectual. Resentment toward the guards was strong enough in many rural areas that they were not going to receive any cooperation from most people, and so they had to identify those who would work with them.[34] Guards labeled such people "good citizens," declared that only the opinions of "good citizens" mattered, and voilà: they had the support of everyone that mattered.[35] Guards justified this thinking by believing that they were allying themselves with other men of honor. While the *Cartilla* advised guards to form their closest friendships with fellow guards, it also acknowledged that "he will do so with those residents of the pueblos who, through their morality and good habits, ought to be respected."[36]

The fact that guards themselves had very limited resources meant that they had to accept some gifts, such as free lodging, *casa-cuartel* improvements, and letters of support. In the clientelist culture of the pueblo, where much was accomplished through the exchange of favors, the idea of the "good citizen" allowed guards to maintain a reciprocal relationship with town elites who exchanged protection for these favors, all without violating their commitment to eschew corrupt practices.[37] The guards' regulations list a multitude of crimes against property for which they could fine or arrest people, and the vast majority of them concern rural forms of property, such as trees and animals.[38] Property owners would often request that a detachment of civil guards be posted on their estates if protesters, strikers, squatters, or thieves threatened their possessions. Frequently, they would offer to provide lodging and pay the Civil Guard's expenses.[39] The practice gave the peasantry the impression that the Civil Guard was in the pay of the landowners. Often, rural estates proved the settings for political violence as peasants, in part angered at the very presence of guards defending large estates, attacked them and were met with their rifles.

The station commandant, in particular, established a special relationship with the town mayor because he had to pay frequent visits to the mayor's house in order to receive information on suspicious persons, news from Madrid of relevant new legislation, and orders from the civil governor.[40] Since mayors could also give orders to civil guards, they often treated them like a town police force or even as their personal servants. Inspectors general frequently complained about guards being asked to perform tasks, such as acting as bodyguards, messengers, or tax collectors, that were not among the duties that they were authorized to carry out.[41]

The commandant's relationship with the mayor was just one component of his position as one of his town's most powerful members. This status was remarkable considering that a commandant in a small town only held the rank of corporal or sergeant, and it marked a dramatic social elevation from his likely origins as a rural laborer. Traditionally, this commandant was part of what opposition groups called the "unholy trinity" of powerful people in the town, the other two being the mayor or cacique, as local clientelist bosses were known, and the local priest.[42] Each member symbolized one of the three main institutions that exhibited external influence on the pueblo: the government, the military, and the Church. The alliance among these forces was real, and it stemmed from the elites' shared goal of maintaining social order, their frequent association with each other, and their distance from the rest of the pueblo because of its resentment of them. However, the collaboration was in no way formalized, and each component's primary loyalty lay with its own institution rather than with the town's other elites.[43]

The Civil Guard's isolation and the solidarity within its ranks resulted in an "us vs. them" mentality typical of a police culture.[44] However, as a result of the Civil Guard's isolation not being complete and of a necessity to adapt to informal local power structures and practical considerations, such as budgetary constraints, the "us" came to include not only civil guards but also other local elites, while the "them" came to mean those without property. Ahumada's measures to give guards an elevated status in town society were intended to earn them a respect that would lend them the authority that they needed to uphold the laws of the centralized liberal state, but the necessities of enforcing the liberal property regime made it impossible to win the favor of everyday townspeople. It was therefore all too easy for guards to enter informal alliances with those who would afford them respect: their fellow town elites. The down-

side of these alliances, of course, was that they only deepened the resentment
felt toward the Civil Guard by everyone else.

DUTIES

A civil guard's primary duty was to maintain public order. On a day-to-day basis, fulfilling this mission meant principally conducting patrols to monitor the
population and prevent crime. At times, it also entailed policing protests and
tracking down suspected criminals. These two duties are considered in this
section. They made total isolation from the pueblo impossible, but the police
culture they created did not necessarily engender a positive relationship with
it either. Instead, the guards' constant monitoring, enforcement of unpopular
laws, and pursuit of criminals, whom local communities may not have viewed
as such, all led to tensions that would sometimes later reach a breaking point
in the politically mobilized atmosphere of the Second Republic.

Patrols

Patrols were the principal task that civil guards performed on a daily basis,
and nowhere did the tensions and contradictions inherent in their job become
more apparent. On the one hand, a guard was to maintain his social distance
from the pueblo, and this distance was reinforced by his military bearing, his
distinctive uniform, his position of authority, and his ability to read and write.
On the other hand, the guard was to involve himself intimately in the life of
the pueblo, monitoring it for criminal activity (ordinary and political) and
protecting private property. His work performing these duties was supposed
to win him the respect of the pueblo, but more often than not it instead bred
resentment as the guard enforced the letter of the law imposed by the central
government over the informal structures of rural life.

   Despite the civil guards' desire for the respect of the pueblo, patrols were
designed more to ensure guards' safety and to shield them from corrupting
influences than to develop warm relations with the community. After morning
inspection, a guard began the task that the station commandant had assigned
to him the night before.[45] While one man was always assigned to be station
orderly for the day, most were sent out on patrol. In 1931, Director General José

Sanjurjo explained the procedure: "When patrols start out they are given a paper bearing their hour of departure, the time at which they must present themselves in the districts they have to patrol, the time they remain at posts, etc.,
and finally the hour and route of their return."[46] By being assigned a different
route every day, civil guards kept criminals guessing as to where they would be
at any given time, and they generally followed circular routes to cover as much
ground as possible.[47] Patrols could be arduous—and frightening if the town
was hostile. One guard recalled his first such experience thus: "The first service
that I did in the Civil Guard was a night patrol through the pueblo and its surroundings . . . That patrol gave us a beating I will remember my whole life: We
looked at all the shadows, dark places, open doors, and riverbanks . . . nothing
escaped our fierce vigilance, such that when six o'clock in the morning arrived
and we finished our service we were covered in mud" and totally exhausted.[48]

Such patrols were usually conducted in pairs known as *parejas*. In fact, this
practice was so common that the *pareja* became one of the characteristic im-
ages associated with the Civil Guard. Within the *pareja*, the more senior guard
acted as commander, leading the way in questioning passersby and handing
out citations (his presumably superior reading and writing skills helped here),
while the junior member stood eight to twelve paces back to serve as a backup
and avoid any surprises.[49] The *pareja* was a manifestation in miniature of the
Civil Guard's militarized approach to policing. A strict hierarchy and division
of roles were maintained even at this most basic level, but the system also
fostered a tradition of mentorship and solidarity. The junior guard could both
learn from and befriend the senior guard, while both were assured that they
would have someone else supporting them no matter what threats they might
face on patrol. In this way, the *pareja* was a metaphor for the relationship that
an individual guard was supposed to have with his institution as a whole; it
would always support him as long as he upheld its honor.

Despite the efforts to have guards maintain their distance from the pueblo
during their patrols, the fact was that they had to interact with it on a daily basis in order both to enforce the state's laws and maintain their honor. To begin
with, they had to get their patrol paper signed and the time noted by the custo-
dians or proprietors of the places they were ordered to visit that day, requiring
at least interaction and cordial relationships with these people.[50] More broadly,
the *Cartilla* states that station commandants "will be sure to get to know the
residents of the pueblos, and very particularly the property owners," and, as

General Sanjurjo put it, "It is part of their duties to ascertain from labourers, passers-by, and shepherds what strangers may have been seen in the district."[51] Therefore, guards were talking with residents all the time; however, far from establishing friendly relations, the goal was to monitor their behavior, including political activity, and to identify any potential miscreants.[52] Guards were the eyes and ears of the state in pueblos that had prized their independence, and guards' observations could travel up the chain of command to the minister of the interior or even the prime minister. Of course, always overwhelmingly outnumbered by the townspeople, guards were also constantly being watched, and they had to be careful not to go beyond what the pueblo would tolerate.[53]

Crime Fighting

Despite the fact that public order was the civil guards' primary mission, most of their time was devoted to fighting crime, if one includes their time spent on patrol.[54] Scholars of police culture emphasize the informal way in which patrolmen usually perform such work. They have a large amount of discretion in terms of when to enforce a law or not, and they often prefer to settle a matter through wit, persuasion, a warning, or even a beating rather than initiate an onerous legal proceeding.[55] Understanding that most crimes can never be solved, most policemen prefer to maintain a general sense of order and only make an arrest for a minor crime if the perpetrator threatens that sense of order.[56] Much of the patrolman's work, from checking on property to resolving disputes to giving directions, involves general order maintenance rather than criminal activity in the first place.[57] Therefore, building knowledge of and relations with local residents is essential so that that knowledge and those relationships can be drawn upon in case a dispute needs to be mediated or other relatively minor problems resolved.[58] Political scientist James Q. Wilson calls this approach the "watchman style" of policing, as opposed to the "legalistic style," which seeks the full enforcement of the law whenever possible.[59] As members of a disciplined military institution with a mandate to enforce the laws of the central state in the countryside, civil guards appear to have tried to practice the legalistic style of policing, but their primary charge of maintaining order, their lack of police training, and their isolated circumstances meant that they, if anything, resorted to informal tactics even more commonly than a civilian, urban police force would.

Since guards received no formal training in investigative work, a scientific approach to which was in any case only beginning to be developed in the late nineteenth and early twentieth centuries, they had to rely on connections with locals and on sometimes-violent methods to bring in criminals, fugitives, and deserters. Of course, enforcing criminal law demanded knowledge of it, and gaining this knowledge must have been a challenge for guards, many of whom had only basic reading and writing skills. The *Cartilla* that they carried with them contained a plethora of different forms and reports that they might need to fill out concerning, for example, checks of passports and hunting and fishing licenses, the pursuit of fugitives and deserters, the breaking up of illegal gambling, and prisoner transport. Hence, the *RTGC* contained extensive discussions of the penal code and other legislation that might aid guards in navigating everyday law enforcement and red tape, leaving little room for articles on managing extraordinary situations.

Certainly, a civil guard's job could be a dangerous one; the crime reports of the *RTGC* reveal frequent shootouts with robbers and murderers. Such violence was particularly prevalent in the nineteenth and early twentieth centuries, when banditry was one of the greatest problems that the Civil Guard faced. Against bandits, its militarization proved effective, as confrontations with them often meant a firefight that required more discipline and armament than a civilian force could offer. In addition, in order to combat the widespread banditry of the chaotic Sexenio Revolucionario period (Revolutionary Sexennium, 1868–74), the government revived an 1821 law nicknamed the *ley de fugas* (fugitive law). It authorized forces of public order to open fire on prisoners attempting to escape. What this meant in reality is that guards were given carte blanche to kill bandits because they could simply claim that anyone shot had been trying to escape. The tactic did reduce the level of banditry, but it also meant that any confrontation could become a fight to the death.[60] Of course, some bandits were in part political criminals, in that they were supported by townspeople as a way of fighting against the expanding power of urban liberalism.[61] The bandits saw themselves as living by their own code of honor, but this folk understanding of the term was not one to which civil guards subscribed.[62] Instead, they saw their violent campaign against banditry as bringing order to the countryside, even if their efforts did not endear them to the working classes.

Given the state's unquestioning support of the Civil Guard's actions, taking to the streets in protest was the only method of redress for members of the working classes who felt more endangered than safe by the presence of the Civil Guard. To take one example, in 1919, civil guards in Gijón (Asturias) shot a boy in the back who was running away from them, claiming he had been hit by a warning shot. A few weeks later, they killed an innocent bystander in the same city during another pursuit. The funerals of both men were attended by thousands. Gijón's workers were far from appreciative of the security that the Civil Guard supposedly brought them; instead, they were asking for protection from the state's own police force.[63] The local republican newspaper, *El Noroeste*, was quite clear that such actions were not winning the Civil Guard the respect of the public: "The Civil Guard has not been instituted to cause terror, but rather trust . . . but when an individual of that corps uses his weapon to kill without reason, indiscriminately, he dishonors the uniform that he wears."[64]

Part of the problem was that guards' almost exclusively military training left them unprepared to conduct criminal investigations. Despite the *RTGC*'s articles on fingerprinting and other new criminological techniques, guards appear to have relied extensively on denunciations, informants, witnesses, and interrogations when investigating crimes. Of course, they were not trained to be detectives. Those were to be found in the Investigation and Vigilance Corps (Cuerpo de Investigación y Vigilancia), but that organization was understaffed even in the cities, and it almost always left rural cases to the Civil Guard.[65] Therefore, lacking much knowledge of investigative techniques, a civil guard had to rely on his knowledge of the people he policed. He laid the groundwork by identifying potential troublemakers while on his patrols from among the less-respected elements of the population.[66] Ahumada himself encouraged guards to acquire knowledge "of those men who because of their bad record or unknown way of life are best monitored by the justice system."[67] Then, when a crime did occur, all a guard had to do was round up the usual suspects and interrogate them to find the perpetrator.[68] Admonishments against brutality in the *RTGC* suggest that some guards used beatings as a way to obtain confessions.[69] Surely, in the view of the guards, a flagrant violation of the law could only come from someone without honor anyway. Guards were encouraged to single out certain groups, such as beggars, vagrants, and Roma people, known in Spain at the time as *gitanos*, for extra vigilance.[70] In fact, station commandants maintained a secret log of those who had criminal records, had acted suspiciously, or held suspicious opinions. It was their duty to make inquiries regarding the conduct of these people and make a yearly note of it. In this way, the commandant tapped into the pueblo's own system of informal social regulation through rumor as a way to aid him in his enforcement of the official laws.

The civil guards' duties of patrolling and fighting crime both put them in contact with townspeople on a daily basis and increased their distance from them. Scholars of police culture identify the perceived (and sometimes real) danger of a policeman's work as one of the key factors shaping police culture's characteristic "us vs. them" mentality, which in turn results in group solidarity within the organization and suspicion of and isolation from those outside of it.[71] The Civil Guard's culture certainly exhibits such characteristics. Guards' patrols in *parejas* were designed for protection and to distinguish them from their surroundings, but the constant monitoring that these practices entailed bred resentment from local populations while strengthening relationships between guards and the town elites with whom they needed to cooperate.

Public order was the civil guards' primary mandate, but in the absence of an effective criminal investigative service in rural areas, they also took on this role. Modern criminal investigative techniques were in their infancy in the late nineteenth and early twentieth centuries, and so roundups of suspicious persons and beatings to obtain confessions became de facto parts of guards' policing practices. Given the risks involved with their fight against banditry, the state also tolerated harsh extrajudicial practices, like the *ley de fugas*. In a rural society that was itself suspicious of outsiders and had an understanding of criminality that differed from that of the central government, none of these practices would win the Civil Guard much respect from the pueblo.

In the late nineteenth and early twentieth centuries, the Civil Guard's organizational culture exhibited all the characteristics most typical of a police culture: isolation, solidarity, an "us vs. them" mentality, informal policing practices, and wide discretion in their activities. As a gendarmerie, these characteristics were accentuated by living in barracks in rural areas but also by a strict adherence to the founding values unique to the Civil Guard. The contradictions built in to the corps's initial structures became both amplified and entrenched by the day-to-day practices that guards developed over time. Isolation, for example, which was maintained through its housing arrangements and strict discipline, was another key to Ahumada's strategy for ensuring that guards were honorable and were enforcing the laws of the state in local communities. Yet policing these communities also inevitably meant becoming a part of them. The distance that guards were supposed to maintain and their efforts to extend governmental authority to local communities meant that they became resented (and even hated), rather than respected, by the lower classes. Relations were much cozier with local elites, who were happy to provide benefits, like procuring housing, as added incentives for protecting their persons and property. However, these relationships only further diminished the reputation of the guards in the eyes of the majority of the pueblo because such associations made them look like the servants of the wealthy.

THREE

BARCELONA

The Civil Guard and the
Emergence of Mass Politics

n the spring of 1897, French newspapers received a stream of letters from
prisoners detained in Barcelona's Montjuïc castle containing horrific accounts of the tortures they had been subjected to there. One letter explained
that "all the torments of the Inquisition were used on me: thirst, sleep
deprivation, exhaustion, the branding iron, the twisting of the testicles, and
the lashes of the bullwhip."[1] Another detailed how as "my arms were bound
together and handcuffed, they whipped me cruelly. The handcuffs abraded all
of the flesh they squeezed, and this torture produced a kind of electrification
in me and sharp burning sensations in all of my body's extremities."[2] Yet another prisoner described being made to wear a helmet that forced the lips to
stretch open while giving the impression that the head was being crushed.[3]
All declared that civil guards were the ones who had administered the torture.

These measures, taken as part of an investigation of an anarchist bombing,
hardly seemed to conform to the Duque de Ahumada's vision of an honorable
Civil Guard. In fact, he had wished that the Civil Guard not be used as a force of
political repression in the first place, but Spanish governments had deployed
it for precisely this purpose from its founding years. It was during the Restoration period that many working-class people came to see the Civil Guard
as a symbol of oppression. Even the civil guards of the period felt that their
reputation had diminished. How had this happened? This chapter is dedicated
to answering that question because the answer explains how tensions between

the working classes and the Civil Guard could reach a violent breaking point during the Second Republic.

While the chapter opens with a look at the origins of the Civil Guard's role as a force of public order, and thereby at the origins of the negative side of its image, I primarily seek the answer to the question posed above in a case study of the events surrounding the "crimes of Montjuïc," the Civil Guard–led investigation and subsequent public outcry that followed a presumably anarchist bombing in Barcelona. By the late nineteenth century, anarchist ideas were spreading around Europe as a reaction to the extreme socioeconomic inequality of the period, as well as the failure of the continent's liberal political systems to offer representation to the working classes.[4] As some anarchists in Spain and other European countries turned to the tactic of terrorist bombings, civil guards were asked to respond to this new form of political contestation even though they were not intended to be police investigators. Their existing police culture, developed over decades of fighting bandits, led them to form a standard response of mass arrests followed by beatings to extract confessions. These methods caused little controversy in the Civil Guard's traditional rural settings, but the effects of their actions were very different when they sought to win glory responding to the sensational terrorist attacks that rocked urban Barcelona in the 1890s. Muckraking journalists and populist politicians used denunciations of the Civil Guard's methods to create an international public outcry that brought anarchists and republican mobilizers together with urban workers to fight for a common cause. The Civil Guard, backed by the military and Restoration governments, responded merely by falling back on their police culture of solidarity and denied any wrongdoing. The Restoration had brought a measure of stability to Spain after decades of political chaos, but it also spawned new forms of mass political contestation that it was unable to control. Likewise, the Civil Guard's strong organizational culture allowed it to weather the storms of the nineteenth century, but, by the end of that century, it lacked the flexibility it needed to counter new challenges that Ahumada could never have imagined.

THE EARLY YEARS

Historians of the Civil Guard who are also members of it (who will be referred to as Civil Guard historians) maintain that their institution was not originally intended to be an instrument for suppressing political protest, but articles 27 and 28 of the *Reglamento para el servicio* suggest otherwise.[5] From the beginning, guards' duties included keeping watch over protests, strikes, and festivals, and they wound up being deployed frequently to urban areas to maintain public order through crowd control, starting as early as 1846.[6] These deployments were known as concentrations. The first major deployment of this kind, called the Great Concentration, saw four thousand guards sent to Madrid to counter the revolutionary disturbances there in 1848, which they did successfully. The seriousness of the threat to General Narváez led him to formalize the mechanisms for concentrating guards in regional capitals, and he authorized the inspector general and regional commanders to do so at their discretion.[7]

Civil Guard historians believe that Ahumada argued against the idea of having the Civil Guard suppress street protests because he thought doing so would undermine his efforts to build a corps that had a reputation for political neutrality.[8] However, it seems more likely that Ahumada also saw the Civil Guard as a force of public order; after all, he coordinated the Great Concentration of 1848. He simply objected to specific deployments that appeared to be defending a particular political faction. For example, just two months after the Civil Guard began operating, the government ordered it to detain certain officers who had been involved in an attempted *pronunciamiento* against the Moderates in power. Ahumada submitted a letter of resignation in protest at such a political use of his corps, but Narváez refused to accept it.[9]

On the other side of the coin, in 1854, when the Progressives launched a major uprising, Ahumada again had no qualms about deploying the Civil Guard to defend the Moderate regime, since the Progressives threatened to dissolve his beloved corps.[10] Crowds battled the Civil Guard in the streets of Madrid (with some street fighters shouting "Death to the Civil Guard") and at other points where civil guards concentrated across the country. According to Civil Guard historian Enrique Martínez Ruiz, the fact that many people saw the institution fighting against the popular uprising in Madrid made the so-called Revolution of 1854 the moment when the Civil Guard's reputation as a force of repression and enemy of the people began.[11] Eventually, the rebellion spread around the country, and the Progressives seized power.

The victory of the Progressives was the greatest threat to the Civil Guard's existence prior to the Civil War of 1936 to 1939. The Progressives were antagonistic toward the force not only because it was associated with the Moderates and had spent the last several years fighting against Progressive conspiracies but also because it was in part formed as an alternative to the National Militia that the Progressives hoped to revive. Fortunately for the Civil Guard, the Progressives shifted to the right once in power as the Democrats became the new party of the populist Left. The Progressives began to see the Civil Guard as a useful instrument for keeping order in the countryside, and so they decided simply to replace Ahumada rather than to dissolve the institution as a whole.[12]

The Civil Guard also survived the 1868 seizure of power by a coalition of left-wing Progressives and Democrats, but the institution's willingness to submit to whichever government was in power was pushed to the limit when Republicans took over in 1873. Republican efforts to restart the National Militia and place the Civil Guard fully under civilian control, along with widespread disorder, proved more than the guards could bear. The next year, many opted to break their commitment to political neutrality by supporting the coup led by General Manuel Pavía that ended the parliamentary republic and paved the way for a restoration of constitutional monarchy.[13] The incident proved that the guards, while serious about upholding their political neutrality as part of their honor, were also willing to make exceptions if they felt a regime endangered their ability to defend their honor by fundamentally altering the nature of their institution or by inhibiting its ability to maintain public order.

A glance at the first decades of the Civil Guard's existence reveals that the force was adept at surviving the changing political winds of the nineteenth century, but these very winds also led it to be frequently deployed to keep public order, a duty that was in fact part of its mission. Its goal was always to maintain its neutrality in such engagements, but favoring one side over another sometimes proved unavoidable. It was in response to these public-order deployments that the first characterizations of guards as enemies of the people were heard.

THE RESTORATION

During the Restoration period, the Civil Guard was truly transformed into the
militarized and often-violent force for suppressing protest that the Second
Republic would inherit. When large numbers of workers took to the streets as
their only means of having a political voice in the Restoration system, governments increasingly drew on the Civil Guard to counter these movements and
maintain the status quo, including in urban areas. Yet without a corresponding
effort to adapt the Civil Guard to its new role, it often responded with violence
to confrontational situations. Guards earned a reputation for brutality, and the
tradition of animosity between the Civil Guard and the working classes become
entrenched. As emerging mass political movements criticized the force, this
animosity was only deepened because guards interpreted the criticism as an
attack on their honor.

The Restoration, at least in its first decades, put an end to the military interventions in politics that had plagued Spain in the mid-nineteenth century.
In a system known as the *turno pacífico*, masterminded by Antonio Cánovas
del Castillo, the country's two main parties, Cánovas's Conservatives and the
Liberals, rotated in and out of power, thereby keeping the government under
civilian control. This rotation depended on a nationwide network of caciques
who could mobilize the votes necessary to ensure that the correct party won
an election. These caciques, some of whom wielded tremendous power at the
local level, presented a new threat to the Civil Guard's goal of political neutrality. They gained influence by bestowing favors upon their clients, and many
supported guards by providing housing for them.[14] Although guards did sometimes return such favors by intimidating people into voting the way the cacique wanted them to, tensions arose when guards refused to do favors because
they could only act upon orders given to them through official channels.[15] In
other words, the Civil Guard did not fit neatly into the local clientelism of the
Restoration, but it was not immune from its influence either. Above all, guards
resented the damage it did to their reputation when the people thought of
them as the servants of the caciques.[16]

Another essential element of Cánovas's strategy was to appease the military through measures like maintaining a bloated officer corps and awarding
ministerial posts to officers. The prominent role of the military in the Restoration system extended to the maintenance of public order as well. Already

rigid in its habit of keeping order with armed force, Restoration governments responded to the perceived sociopolitical threats by further increasing the militarization of the forces of public order, relying heavily on the Civil Guard to put down any kind of disturbance. These forces of order frequently employed violence as a technique for combatting unrest, enabled by states of emergency that gave the military political and judicial powers.[17] Civil guards resented the frequency with which they were called out to quell disturbances and feared the damage such work might do to their reputation with the public. One guard wrote for the Civil Guard's professional journal at the time, *El Heraldo de la Guardia Civil*, that "the most minor alteration of public order, the slightest trace of conflict, is sufficient for the guards to come out to the streets." He criticized these deployments, arguing that "to make the Civil Guard available as a unit for public order or for the municipalities is to misunderstand the mission of the Benemérita [Meritorious, a nickname for the Civil Guard] in quite a sad way."[18]

Suppressing political protest became the most important function of the Civil Guard in this period because the success of the Restoration's *turno* system depended on political demobilization.[19] While Republicans and Carlists continued to threaten insurrection, a new movement also emerged to change the Restoration system: anarchism. There were currents within early anarchist associations that favored abiding by the law in order to operate in the open. But repeated wholesale repressions of these associations by the government weakened the moderate voices within the movement. Many anarchists were drawn to the notion of the "propaganda of the deed," the idea that a spectacular act of violence could inspire workers to join the cause of revolution. Extremists known as "terrorists" believed that any attack upon the bourgeoisie was a form of "propaganda of the deed."[20]

The cycle of anarchist attacks and violent reprisals by Restoration's security forces began in the Andalusian countryside. In 1891, they made indiscriminate arrests of suspected anarchists there in an attempt to suppress the movement. In January of the next year, up to two thousand people attempted to free those prisoners, who were being held in Jerez de la Frontera (Cádiz). The Civil Guard led the investigation following the uprising for a military tribunal and did so by arresting hundreds and torturing them.[21] The outcome of the investigation was four executions that shook Spain's anarchist movement, coming as they did in the wake of the international outcry provoked by the execution of four anarchists in the United States in 1887 after the Haymarket Square bombing in Chicago.[22]

The focal point of anarchist activity, and the Civil Guard's fight against it, then shifted from rural Andalusia to urban Barcelona. The city became the epicenter of political violence as government repression of the anarchist movement there forced some adherents to conclude that terrorism was the only means of resistance.[23] While civil guards had already struggled to suppress anarchism in Andalusia, they would now be working outside of their customary rural setting and their actions would be more visible to writers with international reach. The cycle of violence in the city itself began in earnest in 1893, when anarchists began setting off bombs in public spaces as revenge for the government's harsh repression of the aforementioned uprising in Jerez.[24] The first prominent such incident of that year was the attempted assassination of Captain General Arsenio Martínez Campos. On September 24, the anarchist Paulino Pallás threw two bombs in his direction during a parade but managed to only lightly injure the general while killing a civil guard and a civilian and wounding sixteen others.[25] Pallás was captured immediately by the Civil Guard and police and was executed soon after.[26] One militant anarchist, Juan Montseny, did publish a pamphlet in which he celebrated Pallás as a martyr, but otherwise, given Pallás's clear guilt, the police response to the crime did not illicit public criticism.[27]

Instead, the "anarchists of action" would respond to Pallás's execution in their own way. A friend of his, Santiago Salvador Franch, avenged his death on November 7 of the same year with an explosion in Barcelona's Liceo Theater that killed twenty-two people.[28] This bombing caused widespread indignation and panic among the city's bourgeoisie, prompting the Liberal daily *El Imparcial* to call for special measures against anarchism.[29] The Liberal government responded by deploying civil guards to patrol the streets and theaters of the city, which led them to complain again: "How long is the Civil Guard force going to provide police services that are improper to the Institute?"[30] The government also passed Spain's first piece of antiterrorism legislation, which stipulated harsh penalties, including death, for planning or carrying out attacks using explosives.[31] Finally, the government declared a state of emergency in Barcelona that suspended its citizens' constitutional rights and dispatched a special judge to the city who was charged with investigating the attacks.[32] This judge would be assisted by Civil Guard Lieutenant Narciso Portas Ascanio, who had already had extensive prior experience in restive Cuba and in repressing strikes and protests in Barcelona.[33] The police investigation led by Portas detained two hundred people in the prison of the Montjuïc castle, which had become a symbol of the Spanish state's oppression of Catalonia and was known as "the accursed castle" and "the Catalan Bastille" after it had been used to bombard the city during uprisings in the 1840s.[34] The prisoners were tortured to obtain confessions and denunciations, and two died in custody, including one by suicide.

The fact that the police twice claimed that they had obtained a confession and solved the case but then changed their story did not speak well of their investigative methods. After initially obtaining a confession from one anarchist, Portas then focused his efforts on another. He also confessed and implicated five others.[35] Many prisoners wrote letters to the press explaining that their confessions had been made under forms of torture, like testicle mutilation.[36] Their confessions were indeed proven false when civil guards finally located the true author of the Liceo attack, Santiago Salvador, in Zaragoza, but the six previously accused were still executed as Pallás's accomplices in the September bombing.[37] Despite the suspicious proceedings, the allegations of mistreatment by the prisoners were largely ignored; the press was limited by censorship during the state of emergency.[38] Meanwhile, the government awarded Portas for his efforts with a medal and a pension.[39]

After two-and-a-half years of respite, another major bombing followed on June 7, 1896—this time killing twelve as a Corpus Christi procession made its way down Barcelona's Canvis Nous Street. This newest attack only sharpened the demands of the city's bourgeoisie that the national government do more to combat the anarchist threat, which the Barcelona Police Corps seemed unable to bring under control.[40] The corps's inexperienced and poorly paid inspectors were more accustomed to fighting petty crime than the new phenomenon of terrorism, and their effectiveness was undermined by corruption and an excessive reliance on informants.[41] Therefore, the captain general of Catalonia, Eulogio Despujol, used the fact that one soldier had been injured in the attack to place the case under military jurisdiction. This move allowed him to appoint Lieutenant Colonel Enrique Marzo as investigative judge and Lieutenant Portas as his assistant. Despujol praised these two as having already "made the accomplices of Pallás and Salvador confess."[42] He also convinced Cánovas's government that another state of emergency was necessary for Marzo and Portas to do their work.[43] The government accompanied this with new legislation that tightened the penalties for attacks using explosives and authorized the closure of anarchist newspapers and centers and the deportation of anarchists to penal colonies.[44] Once again, the government had turned to the military to confront the anarchist threat and specifically looked to the Civil Guard as a force for the suppression of anarchism.[45] But in this case, these now-routine decisions would have consequences far beyond what the Cánovas government had anticipated.

Portas's investigative strategy followed a familiar playbook of mass arrests followed by beatings to extract confessions. Yet this time also was different: he was under pressure from Marzo to take severe measures and deliver quick results to satisfy Barcelona's elites.[46] Therefore, the repression in this case exceeded in scale even the one that had followed the Liceo Theater attack. Portas and his men took advantage of their emergency powers to arrest over three hundred people of any and all radical persuasions.[47] This sweeping approach made clear the consequence of the Civil Guard operating in this unfamiliar urban environment: Portas had no idea who had actually set off the bomb. Therefore, he turned to the corrupt local police for help. Police Inspector Daniel Freixa fingered Tomás Ascheri y Fossatti, an unemployed anarchist and foreigner who had acted as an informant for the governor and had accused Freixa of illegal gambling. According to Ascheri, Freixa had already intended to accuse him of planning an attack even before the Canvis Nous bombing.[48] Under torture, Ascheri confessed to Portas and his men and named various accomplices who were really detainees who Portas thought were plausible suspects, since they were socially marginal individuals without support networks.[49] In August, Portas and his men then tortured these "accomplices" to extract confessions from them as well. By the next month, Marzo was ready to release triumphantly his investigative report to the press, announcing that he and his team had solved the case with a neat but dubious explanation of how it all happened.[50]

At first, Portas earned praise for this investigative work. The government was so pleased that it put him in charge of a new Corps of Judicial Police created specifically to combat the anarchist threat.[51] The Civil Guard had previously refused to allow its members to be put in charge of civilian police for fear of bringing dishonor on the institution. But in this instance, the thirst for the prestige to be gained from tackling this new threat of anarchist terrorism was unquenchable. *El Heraldo de la Guardia Civil*, after complaining about civil guards patrolling in Barcelona after the Liceo bombing, now ran an article praising Portas's new appointment.[52] In addition, the journal began a collection to show the support of the Civil Guard for Portas and received over 700 pesetas in donations. Considering that most guards gave only one peseta, this amount indicates that dozens of guards openly demonstrated their support for the lieutenant's efforts.[53]

The December 1896 closed-door trial of the supposed perpetrators of the Canvis Nous bombing took place in a military court because of the anti-anarchist measures that were in place. Despite the fact that twelve people had been killed, the primary charge against the principal accused was not murder but rather insulting the armed forces, since one soldier had also been injured. The prosecutor requested the death penalty for twenty-eight of the accused, with another eighty-seven charged simply for attending meetings of an anarchist-linked center.[54] According to an account of the trial by the accused, the prosecution relied on Marzo's brief and the testimonies of Ascheri and the other principal accused, who, under the close watch of their torturers, had virtually memorized their earlier confessions.[55] However, in their defendant statements and in letters to the press, they all asserted their innocence and renounced their earlier declarations, describing the tortures to which they had been subjected.[56] Meanwhile, most of the military officers who were assigned to defend the accused gave formulaic arguments and were barred from raising issues of maltreatment.[57]

The counter allegations from the accused turned the public's attention from the "attack on Canvis Nous" to the "crimes of Monjuïc" and were also the focus of an appeal to the military's Supreme Court.[58] In April 1897, the court reduced some of the sentences and found sixty-three defendants not guilty, although five were still executed.[59] Throughout these proceedings, from the statements of the prosecutors to the sentences of the two courts, Marzo and Portas's version of events was repeated unquestioningly and almost verbatim as the truth. As for those found not guilty, along with over a hundred other anarchists, the Cánovas government gave them fifteen days to leave the country or face banishment to the Spanish colony of Río de Oro (now known as Western Sahara).[60]

Portas had brought Barcelona's bourgeoisie results, but the court of broader popular opinion would rule that he had taken things too far.[61] His mistake was casting his net too wide, jailing several writers who would make sure to take their own kind of revenge. The first key figure in this effort was Pere Coromines, a young, free-thinking lawyer who was a well-connected member of Barcelona's Catalan-speaking middle class. In letters to his family and in a collection of reflections he wrote about his experience, he describes his outrage at being arrested simply for attending a few anarchist-linked meetings, his fear of being sentenced to death, and his desire to bring the tortures that he had witnessed in Montjuïc to light.[62] Aided by sympathetic members of the castle garrison, he obtained writing materials so that he could draft petitions of complain to the minister of war and so that he could take down the accounts of the prisoners who had been tortured. He then had his family and friends send these accounts to France for publication because the anarchist press was still being censored at this time in Spain.[63]

Another anarchist writer who had been jailed at Montjuïc, Fernando Tarrida de Mármol, lit the fire in France with an outraged article in the literary journal La Revue blanche, which was published soon after he had fled to Paris in October.[64] Most of these early accounts simply complained about the arbitrary detentions. But then Henri Rochefort, a prominent French polemicist editor, picked up the story in L'Intransigeant, where he saw its potential to generate another sensation to complement the controversy he was already stirring in his ongoing coverage of the Dreyfus Affair.[65] He began publishing accounts such as those summarized at the beginning of the chapter that had been dictated by the principal accused and described the horrific tortures to which they had been subjected.[66] Such accounts changed the public's view of the proceedings. One of the writers, José Molas, signed off his letter in a way that sums up how these reports were inverting the narrative that the government was trying to construct through the trial: "I, the victim."[67]

These accounts were similar to the ones that emerged from Portas's investigation of the Liceo bombing, but this time the public outcry was much greater. The reason why seems to have had much to do with a third man, Juan Montseny, whom Portas probably came to regret arresting. Portas apparently detained Montseny out of spite for having penned a tract criticizing his response to the Liceo bombing.[68] Having experienced a bit of it himself, the repression became Montseny's obsession. Forced into exile like the other prisoners found innocent, he began sending his denunciations from London to Madrid for publication under the nom de plume of Federico Urales. His mouthpiece in Spain was *El País*, the paper of the populist Republican firebrand Alejandro Lerroux.[69] *El País*, based in Madrid and thus free from the censorship in effect in Barcelona, was one of the first Spanish papers to break the news about Monjuïc.[70] By taking up this anarchist issue in his Republican paper, Lerroux hoped to convert "the infamies of Montjuïc" into a kind of Spanish Dreyfus Affair that would unify workers around him and the Republican cause.[71] In 1897, he founded a new paper, *El Progreso*, in which he collaborated with Montseny to publish almost daily calls for an investigation into what had taken place at Montjuïc, mixing denunciations of Marzo and Portas with letters of protest, reprints of prisoner accounts, and anticlerical suggestions that the Jesuits were behind it all.[72]

Lerroux and Montseny had some success in getting other anarchist, Republican, and Socialist newspapers to join their chorus demanding a review of the trial by civilian courts and an investigation of the methods used by Portas and his men.[73] The calls for action also spilled out into the streets. One free-thinking activist recalled that the flurry of posters, meetings, songs, and benefit events in support of the Montjuïc prisoners created a new generation of working-class adherents to the anarchist cause in Barcelona.[74] Lerroux used such events for his own purposes as well. At the rallies that the nonpartisan Committee for the Review of the Montjuïc Proceedings held around the country, he stole the show, taking advantage of these occasions to fire up crowds with revolutionary rhetoric as he talked more about himself than the Montjuïc trial.[75] The sensation that he had partially created was uniting anarchists, workers, and even some monarchists around him, all while increasing sales of his newspapers.[76]

Some of the criticisms in the press that came out of Montjuïc were directed at the Civil Guard. Many of the letters from prisoners implicated specific guards on Portas's team by name while also playing on the Civil Guard's sense of honor. For example, in one of their letters to the press, they claimed that one civil guard, who was guarding the prisoners during the trial, ran out of the courtroom exclaiming, "Fuck, what a dishonor for the corps!" when he heard the accused give their statements describing the tortures to which they had been subjected.[77] In the collective memory of Barcelona's working class, the name of Portas became synonymous with the perceived injustice of the Spanish state.[78] Yet another anarchist writer whom Portas had jailed,

Ramón Sempau, went so far as to physically attack the lieutenant on the night of September 4, 1897, wounding him and his second-in-command.[79] While a summary court-martial immediately sentenced Sempau to death, public opinion so favored him over Portas that the would-be assassin was later granted a pardon.[80]

Lerroux was the most vocal of all in his accusations against Portas, publishing choice descriptions of him in *El Progreso* such as "that ferocious beast who opened up his victims just to revel with the voluptuousness of a tiger in their pain and blood."[81] Portas challenged Lerroux to a duel, but, although Lerroux was a notorious duelist, he refused to fight this civil guard over actions that he deemed "unworthy of a gentlemen." Portas took the case to a military honor court, which found not only Portas's honor sufficient but questioned that of Lerroux. The case was one of the few in which a guard attempted to defend his honor through the extralegal means of a duel. Ultimately, the two never did duel each other, but they did get in a brutal fight armed with their canes in 1902 when Portas saw Lerroux walking down a Madrid street.[82]

Civil guards followed the campaign in the press against Portas closely, concerned about the damage to their institution's reputation.[83] Yet while one did write to *El Progreso* to distance his institution from "the stain that Portas has made on our most honorable corps," for the most part, both his corps and the military remained steadfast in their support for the lieutenant.[84] *El Heraldo de la Guardia Civil* continued to laud him, dismissing the accusations against him as having "demonstrated eloquently the uninterrupted energy [he] employed for the discovery and punishment of incessant disturbers of the social order."[85] He also received praise from Capitan General Despujol for "the exceptional aptitudes that he possesses for the elucidation of criminal acts."[86] Meanwhile, hundreds of officers from all branches of the armed forces signed a letter to Marzo congratulating him on his efforts: "They constitute a brilliant page in the annals of Military Justice."[87] Many officials involved in the case, including Portas and his men, were even awarded medals and pensions, but these awards were not announced publicly for fear of backlash from the public.[88]

Those fears were not unwarranted. By 1900, inundated with domestic and foreign demands for review of the Montjuïc proceedings, the Conservative government of Francisco Silvela admitted that the links of the remaining prisoners to the attacks were tenuous, and they were pardoned.[89] It also moved to begin a civilian investigation of the proceedings. Meanwhile, the military's support for Portas was unwavering. Despujol shielded him by insisting that the case remain under military jurisdiction. He added that any allegations against Portas and his civil guards were nothing more than a defamatory campaign led by Coromines, despite the fact that Despujol had previously admitted that "two or three of [the prisoners] had suffered from maltreatment as had also occurred in past anarchist cases."[90] The military prosecutors assigned to the case also concluded that there was nothing to investigate, releasing a scathing report in which they similarly dismissed all allegations as foreign plots to undermine Spain's reputation and political maneuverers masterminded by Coromines and Tarrida de Mármol. All the officers these prosecutors interviewed and who were stationed at Montjuïc at the time of the interrogations, including two doctors who had previously reported treating prisoner injuries, denied witnessing any wrongdoing.[91] The shield that the military had built around Portas held up. In the end, no one was ever prosecuted for the "crimes of Montjuïc," and Portas stayed on as the chief of the Judicial Police until 1901, eventually rising to the rank of brigadier general in the Civil Guard.[92]

In all of the case studies of incidents of political violence in this book, I will examine the relationship between the contingent decisions of individual actors and the influence of structural sociopolitical conditions at the time of the incident. In the case of Barcelona in the 1890s, civil guards were right to be reluctant to enter into the fraught realm of urban policing and to take on the difficult task of combating the new and secretive phenomenon of anarchist terrorism. Yet in the end, their desire to win honor for their institution in this new arena got the better of them. At first, Portas's investigative strategy of using mass arrests and torture to extract confessions yielded little controversy, but after the Corpus Christi bombing he took things too far, arresting writers who would take revenge in their own fashion. Only when these writers' stories were picked up by the yellow press, always on the lookout for a good scandal, did the guards' methods become a sensation that backfired on their search for prestige.

On a more structural level, the Restoration's militarized approach to public order is a key factor in explaining the Civil Guard's involvement in Barcelona in the first place, its ability to violate constitutional rights while conducting its investigations, and the use of military tribunals to try the supposedly guilty parties. But by bringing in the military (including the Civil Guard) to counter the terrorist threat, the government was also asking a notoriously rigid military culture to confront the new phenomenon of an urban anarchist movement that had transnational networks and access to innovative journalistic and mass-mobilizing techniques. In the face of the unprecedented public outcry that followed, the Civil Guard and the military simply fell back on solidarity and denied any wrongdoing. While roundups and forced confessions may have been sufficient for fighting bandits and rural disturbances, a politically mobilized urban working class was more vocal about demanding something more: justice. The tales of the "crimes of Montjuïc" were the first time that the new mass press was used to mobilize public sentiment against military institutions like the Civil Guard. As Spain entered the twentieth century, the sociopolitical values that the Civil Guard represented, such as honor, discipline, authority, and order, would be increasingly difficult to defend in the face of populist mass-mobilizers like Lerroux. In its botched response to the propaganda of the deed, the Civil Guard had created a much more powerful opponent: the propaganda of the word.[93]

THE LATE RESTORATION

The cycle of violence that began with the Jerez uprising and its repression in 1892 ended five years later when an anarchist shot Prime Minister Cánovas in 1897 as revenge for the Montjuïc repression. The assassination prompted the government to extend the law suppressing anarchist centers and newspapers in Barcelona throughout the country.[94] By the first decade of the twentieth century, even as bombings continued in Barcelona, anarchists were turning their strategy away from "propaganda of the deed" to undermining the political demobilization upon which the state depended through strikes and mass protests.[95] Adherents to this new strategy were known as anarcho-syndicalists, and they founded a union called the CNT (Confederación Nacional del Trabajo, or National Confederation of Labor) in 1910. Republicans also turned from plotting insurrections to mass political mobilization around the same time, a trend exemplified by Lerroux's Radical Party, which he founded in 1908.

Having a more militarized Civil Guard confront these mass political mobilizations meant that protesters responded with violence as well. The state was not reluctant to deploy the Civil Guard to urban areas given the inability of urban forces of public order to quell these large-scale mobilizations. Certainly, the Civil Guard had seen plenty of concentrations in the mid-nineteenth century, but most of these had been caused by attempted *pronunciamientos,* rather than mass protests. Urban strikes involved larger, more coordinated efforts, yet the large concentrations of guards sent to counter them were untrained in controlling hostile crowds. The result was an increased likelihood that violence would erupt and a continued decline in the Civil Guard's prestige as it increasingly came to be seen as a repressive force fighting to maintain the power of the rich at the expense of the poor.[96] Guards were aware of this and complained more than ever that the problem was that they were being deployed too frequently to counter social agitations that, in fact, the army was supposed to handle. The reputation of the corps was being undermined by these deployments so much that it was having trouble recruiting new volunteers to join the force.[97] In 1903, the director general even suggested a campaign to inform the public of the precepts of the *Cartilla* and the *reglamentos,* since he feared that people did not realize that even "the most minor aggression against [civil guards] must be quashed with arms that the nation puts in their hands."[98] But the government seemed to feel that it had no choice, apologizing to the director general even as it continued to order deployments of civil guards to Barcelona to counter the continuing unrest there.[99]

Indicative of the emerging new forms of popular mobilization was Barcelona's first general strike in 1902, the harsh suppression of which was avenged by the 1905 bombing of the city's flower market.[100] The violence reached a peak in what is known as the Tragic Week of 1909, when over a hundred people were killed in street fighting as they protested conscription for an unpopular war in Morocco and expressed anticlerical anger by burning convents and churches.[101] Once again, there was international outcry over the repression that followed, this time to the point of precipitating the fall of the Conservative government of Antonio Maura.[102] Between 1917 and 1921, the levels of mass mobilization throughout Spain peaked because of the inspiring example of the Russian Revolution and a huge rise in prices created by demand from the belligerent countries in the First World War. The parliamentary regime's frequent declarations of states of emergency and deployments of the Civil Guard and the army (which often sparked violent confrontations) crippled the CNT but failed to halt the violence.[103] In 1923, General Miguel Primo de Rivera toppled the parliamentary regime in a coup, and the king allowed him to stay on as dictator. Primo de Rivera justified his seizure of power by promising to restore order.

The Civil Guard's mission of maintaining order had always been political in that it meant maintaining a moderate liberal order of private property and enforcing laws promulgated by the national government. From the beginning, the force combatted the Carlists' attempts to restore the *ancien régime* and the more diffuse resistance that banditry represented. The successes that the Civil Guard enjoyed in these areas meant that the *Cartilla* became so revered that it was never substantially updated after 1852, but the contradictions contained within the founding documents only deepened as the Civil Guard sought to maintain order in Spain's evolving sociopolitical landscape. Governments could not resist using the force to restore the peace, as well as to keep it, in both urban and rural areas. Within a few years of its founding, the corps was already assisting Moderate governments in countering the explicitly political mobilizations of the Progressives.

During the expansion of mass politics that began in the 1890s, as Carlism and banditry weakened, keeping order during strikes and other mass protests went from an occasional assignment to the primary mission of the Civil Guard. Spain's growing working classes were developing new methods of political contestation, and guards sought to defend the state and the honor of their institution in the face of these new challenges with the same violence that they had deployed in fighting bandits. The Civil Guard was intended to be strong medicine against the banditry problem, but when its military force was applied to mass protest on a much wider scale, the political impact was greater. Now, the Civil Guard's violence had new political meaning because working-class movements interpreted it as part of a broader class conflict.

Especially damaging to the Civil Guard's reputation and to the stability of the Restoration system as a whole was deployment of the force against the anarchist threat in Barcelona in the 1890s, which pushed the Civil Guard into the realm of directly policing political actions.[104] Now, guards had not only to disperse protests but also to identify and suppress anarchist dissidents, a task for which they were wholly unprepared. In the eyes of the city's working-class population, mobilized by anarchist writers and Republican politicians armed with international propaganda networks, the Civil Guard's old trick of using torture to extract confessions was no longer acceptable. A common feature of police culture is that a sense of solidarity is so strong that a police force will protect even excessively violent members, thereby ironically damaging the reputation that policemen care so much about.[105] Starting here with Portas, this pattern of civil guards supporting members who face even justified criticism will be observed frequently in this book, and a pattern also emerges of civilian governments refusing to hold men like Portas accountable. Instead of seeking a new strategy, they continued to respond to disturbances with military force and martial law.

FOUR

TRAINING

From Soldiers to Civil Guards

abriel Ferreras de Luis was raised in a small town in León Province in the 1910s—a town that he remembered in his memoir primarily for its "ancestral Catholicism" and the festival of its patron saint. At age twelve, he left school and moved south, where he worked up to twelve hours a day on a farm in Seville Province and was subjected to the violent punishments of a cruel overseer. From the beginning, he dreamed of joining the Civil Guard as a way to break the monotony and simply because "the life of the civil guard was not as hard as that of the small farmer." His journey to becoming a civil guard began while he was doing his military service at age twenty. He took classes and memorized the *Reglamento*, finally passing the entrance exam and completing the apprenticeship period. In July 1935, after three years of preparation, Gabriel Ferreras entered the Civil Guard.[1]

Ferreras's story was a typical one: he was a man of a humble and conservative background who sought a better life in the Civil Guard. But how to transform this raw material into a stoic agent of the state able to perform varied policing duties with little supervision? This chapter turns to how new guards were imbued with that culture during their training, what Edgar Schein calls a group's socialization process, focusing on the period from roughly 1893 to 1923, when most of the guards who served during the Second Republic were trained.[2] Most of this preparation consisted of training and service in the army. There, future guards were introduced to a military culture that they would then have to transform into a police culture in the Civil Guard.

The influence of civil guards' prior experiences on their subsequent behavior begins with their social backgrounds. This chapter examines the school for guards' children to develop a sociological profile of the enlisted civil guard. Often, like Ferreras, guards were from a working-class but conservative background; the corps provided an opportunity for upward social mobility through literacy and a privileged place in the local community. At the same time, this elevated position, as well as prior experience in the army, particularly in Morocco, made guards different and therefore isolated from the communities they policed. As for training by the Civil Guard itself, this was conducted solely by station commandants during a six-month apprenticeship period. This one-on-one training allowed recruits to learn through example about the desire for honor and loyalty to the institution characteristic of the Civil Guard, while also experiencing firsthand the way in which guards balanced their duty to follow their regulations and orders with the social structures of the pueblo.

Given the sharp differences in social origins and training between enlisted men and officers, I will treat the two groups separately. Officers had to set an example during their inspections, lead criminal investigations, and carry out administrative functions. Preparation for the job was done almost entirely in the army, where they were trained to lead soldiers rather than policemen. Often the indoctrination process began at a young age since many came from military families, and it continued during their education at the Infantry Academy. Afterward, many officers served in Morocco, where they learned to see their enemies as inferior others, a perception that some would bring back with them to Spain. The only formal training that the Civil Guard itself gave the officers who joined the force was a six-month apprenticeship, during which they had to reorient their sense of honor to be something derived from the respect of the pueblo. However, they did not forget their experiences as members of an isolated military family culturally distant from civilian life.

Taken as a whole, the training of civil guards constituted another contradiction inherent in their institution's culture—they prepared for policing civilians almost exclusively by training for war. While such preparation may have contributed to the Duque de Ahumada's original goal of making them a class apart, it did not engender harmonious and peaceful relations with the populace.

THE MAKING OF AN ENLISTED MAN

The Social Origins of the Civil Guard

As throughout its history, the enlisted men of the Civil Guard during the Second Republic were overwhelmingly working class in origin, and most had been rural day laborers.[3] Enlistment presented advantages to the landless laborer. The corps offered a job with higher pay and less physical exertion. In addition, it held the promise of upward social mobility. Chapter 2 traced how the job could propel a laborer from being at the bottom level of his town's society to being one of its most important and (at least supposedly) respected members.[4] The question was how to transform these rural laborers into local elites who would be respected and obeyed. Ahumada believed that the answer lay in the militarization of the institution and the literacy of its members. The requirement that all volunteers had served in the army was maintained, with the exceptions that sons of civil guards and graduates of the Colegio de Guardias Jóvenes (see below) could also join.[5] Indeed, personnel service records suggest that the vast majority of civil guards came from the army.

For the lower classes, joining the army was very unpopular during the Restoration period. Resistance to the draft was widespread because of the harsh conditions and dangers presented by Spain's colonial wars in Morocco (1909–27). This resistance was strong enough to spark the Tragic Week of 1909.[6] Any male age seventeen to thirty-six who was single and met certain physical requirements could be drafted to serve for three years.[7] The burden of this "blood tax" fell exclusively on the poor because the wealthy could opt out or (after 1912) shorten their service by paying a fee or hiring a substitute.[8] Yet despite the unpopularity of serving at the time, a fair number of future guards actually volunteered to join the army. A large number were also drafted, but the fact that they then joined the Civil Guard indicates that they liked military life enough to volunteer to continue serving in a militarized institution. Therefore, even though guards hailed from the very same social strata as the rural protesters they so often faced, in joining the Civil Guard they had already distinguished themselves by their taste for a military lifestyle.

Another path to joining the Civil Guard was the Colegio de Guardias Jóvenes (School of Young Guards). The institution was founded by Ahumada himself in 1853 as a military school for children of civil guards.[9] Classes were taught by Civil Guard officers and allowed students to earn a *bachiller*, or early

high school diploma.[10] Although only a very small percentage of guards entered the force from the colegio, it is of particular interest because it was one
of the only schools before the Civil War run by the Civil Guard. Therefore, it
provides a unique window on the values, practices, and self-image that guards
thought were important to instill in their successors.

The Colegio de Guardias Jóvenes had great symbolic importance to the
corps. Its affiliated Colegios de Huérfanos del Cuerpo (Schools of Orphans of
the Corps), one for boys and one for girls, cared for orphans of primary-school
age. As part of their institution's paternalistic embrace, these schools ensured
guards that their children would be provided for by the corps itself if any were
killed in the line of duty. Their children would still be raised within the insular
world of the Civil Guard, just as they would have within a *casa-cuartel*. The *guardias jóvenes* became symbols of the respect the corps had for members who had
sacrificed their lives and of its solidarity, for guards routinely gave donations
to help support the colegio.[11]

Aside from instruction in the *Cartilla*, there does not appear to have been
any training in how to perform the civilian policing duties of the Civil Guard at
the Colegio de Guardias Jóvenes.[12] Instead, the emphasis was placed on the core
Civil Guard values of discipline, obedience, and Christian morality. Discipline
reigned supreme and was to be instilled through the monotony of the daily
schedule. As for disobedient students, they were often punished by having to
copy many times a passage by Calderón de la Barca that conveniently summarized the values that they were supposed to learn:

> Here the principal
> duty is to obey,
> and the means of doing it
> is neither to request nor deny anything.
> In sum, here courtesy,
> good behavior, loyalty,
> honor, bravery,
> reputation, repute,
> resolve, obedience,
> fame, honor, and life are
> the measures of good fortune.
> The army is no more than a
> religion of honorable men.[13]

Although Calderón wrote this passage about the army in 1650 (it is from a comic scene in one of his plays in which a veteran gives advice to a new recruit), it summarized the Civil Guard's values remarkably well because of its emphasis on honor through living an obedient and respectable life rather than through the death in battle that a soldier might face.[14] Ironically, these honor plays from Spain's Golden Age presented an idealized and elite version of honor rather than the conception that early modern Spaniards held in their daily lives, but it was precisely to this idealized, imagined version that the Civil Guard sought to link itself as part of a restoration of Spain's supposedly glorious past.[15]

While honor was described as a religion for the Civil Guard, morality at the Colegio de Guardias Jóvenes was also defined by Catholicism—"knowledge of Christian doctrine" was required for entry—and *guardias jóvenes* took classes on the subject.[16] Through the vehicle of the colegio, the Church was able to institutionalize its influence on the Civil Guard as a whole. In 1864, a priest placed an image of the Virgen del Pilar (Virgin of the Pillar) in the school. By the next year, the Virgen del Pilar had become the official patron of the colegio, and, in 1913, her patronage was officially extended to the Civil Guard as a whole.[17] Likewise, a nun wrote the Hymn of the Civil Guard in 1924 for the Colegios de Huérfanos before it was adopted by the corps as a whole.[18] The anthem touches on all of the Civil Guard's most sacred values, including honor, order, loyalty, and nobility. The chorus sums up these values by having guards pledge themselves to the honor of the Civil Guard as an institution and, in addition to the standard king and country, dedicating themselves to their mission of preserving law and order:

> Glory to you, institution.
> For your honor I want to live.
> Long live Spain, Long live the King.
> Long live law and order,
> Long live the honored Civil Guard.[19]

Not all students at the Colegio de Guardias Jóvenes would go on to become guards, but the entire curriculum aimed to produce graduates of a similar social rank. There was training for white-collar professions, such as teacher, telegraph operator, mailman, merchant mariner, accountant, mechanic, metallurgist, electrician, and construction project manager.[20] Indeed, despite the pageantry surrounding the *guardias jóvenes* as symbols of the Civil Guard's in-

TABLE 1. Career Tracks of the 1914 Graduating
Class of the Colegio de Guardias Jóvenes

CAREER	NUMBER OF STUDENTS
Postal	37
Telegraphy	35
Military	10
Undecided	5
Teaching	4
Bachillerato (between a high school diploma and a bachelor's degree)	3
Public Works	2
Civil Engineering	1
Customs	1
Electrician	1
Forestry	1

SOURCE: Ramírez Barreto, *Semblanza histórica*, 85.

stitutional solidarity, most of the students pursued one of these civilian careers rather than becoming civil guards (see table 1), indicating that, even though a large percentage of guards had fathers who had the same profession, a relatively small percentage of guards' sons may have wanted to subject themselves to the hardships and dangers of life in the corps. These alternative career paths offered to *guardias jóvenes* suggest that white-collar workers were understood to be guards' civilian equivalents in terms of socioeconomic status. Certainly, having a son become such a professional would mean that a guard had advanced the social status of his family if he had begun as a farm laborer himself.

Girls at the orphans' school were prepared to have a similar social rank; school regulations described their instruction as "primary education and job training appropriate for their sex."[21] Therefore, the curriculum for girls reveals what the female social equivalent of the male civil guard was thought to be. From age sixteen, the girls were instructed in languages, double-entry bookkeeping, typing, dressmaking, sewing, ironing, hairdressing, and manicuring.[22] In other words, the girls seem to have been also expected to take skilled working-class or white-collar jobs, especially as secretaries or in the clothing industry. At the same time, these classes gave them the skills necessary to make them eligible for marriage to someone of a similar social position.

On-the-Job Training

For the majority who did not attend the colegio, the key element of Ahumada's strategy for ensuring that guards were respectable was at least requiring them to be able to read and write. Therefore, before anyone could join the Civil Guard as an enlisted man, he had to pass an entrance examination to verify that he had a basic level of education. The content of the exam varied greatly over the years, but, by the beginning of the twentieth century, it tested only basic arithmetic, reading, and writing.[23] Even if the exam hardly ensured guards would have all the skills that they needed to do their jobs, it did make membership in the Civil Guard a certification of at least a basic level of education. Since even in the early twentieth century, many Spanish rural laborers still could not read, this certification automatically elevated a new guard to a higher social status than that of the people he worked amongst in the small towns, especially in less-developed southern Spain.[24]

After completing their service in the army and passing the literacy test, aspiring civil guards received six months of apprenticeship-style training, where each aspirant was assigned to a veteran member for individual, experiential, on-the-job training. Those who failed to learn the regulations and prove themselves able to fulfill their duties were let go.[25] Individual training had the advantage of allowing the apprentice to learn by doing and to have the opportunity to practice the tasks he would be performing as a guard in the real world. The method also allowed him to become familiar with the realities of rural policing from someone who was actually on the job. The disadvantage was that, with instruction left up to hundreds of noncommissioned officers, the Civil Guard's administrative apparatus and the government had no control over what trainees were being taught. That the Civil Guard could develop a strong organizational culture without much formal training should not come as a surprise. Schein writes that "it is not necessary for newcomers to attend special training or indoctrination sessions to learn important cultural assumptions. These become quite evident through the daily behavior of the leaders."[26] Police culture researchers agree that these apprentice-style training periods are the primary way in which the informal aspects of police culture are engrained in recruits.[27] Practices both good and bad could be passed down from one generation of guards to another, creating a closed organizational culture in which unofficial habits became more and more entrenched.

Recruits were known as *aspirantes* during their training period. Not yet officially civil guards, they wore civilian clothes and a yellow armband as they shadowed a sergeant. The *aspirantes'* activities as they went about their daily lives were also monitored. They could be called up for service if extra manpower was needed and simply handed a spare firearm and ammunition.[28] When they were ready for formal admission into the Civil Guard, they declared their religion to be Catholicism and performed the ceremony of swearing their loyalty to the flag of Spain by kissing it.[29] They were also read the regulations of the Code of Military Justice "so that claiming ignorance of them would never be an excuse."[30] Thus, from their first day in the corps, guards had already pledged multiple loyalties, not only to the military hierarchy and the government but also to the more abstract idea of the *patria*. Honoring all of these commitments would prove to be a constant balancing act.

After the six-month apprenticeship, station commandants then reinforced the training and indoctrination of enlisted men during educational sessions held at least once a week. Lessons, often developed from sources like the *RTGC*, could be on morality, analysis of new legislation, or developments in criminology, or simply a review of the *Cartilla* and *reglamentos*. These sessions would also reinforce military bearing through drills of maneuvers and marches.[31] The lessons were a time to strengthen morale and the bond between commander and subordinate. In addition, they were an opportunity for the instructor to verify that the loyalty of his men was intact, which would become important when that loyalty was tested at the outset of the Civil War.[32]

In sum, the recruitment and training of enlisted men for the Civil Guard was about elevating working-class recruits to a lower-middle-class social status that would distinguish and distance them from the rural townspeople they were to police. The process began with ensuring recruits had basic writing, reading, and arithmetic skills that many rural laborers did not possess. Then, the policy of voluntary enlistment from the army guaranteed that the Civil Guard was receiving men with a taste for the disciplined military lifestyle to which most Spaniards were resistant. Finally, the apprenticeship period and educational sessions placed responsibility for training a guard entirely within the insular world of his particular *casa-cuartel* and its commandant. By the time an *aspirante* officially entered the Civil Guard, his level of education, his military bearing, and his loyalty to a national institution all separated him from the rest of the rural society that he was to police and that he himself had been a part of just a few years prior.

This recruitment and training process created a pair of problems if the goal was forging an effective force of public order for the twentieth century. The entrance requirements for enlisted personnel produced civil guards who could stand apart from the rural citizens they policed because of their military service and their at least rudimentary education. However, with service in the army being considered their principal training, the Civil Guard offered those who aspired to join its ranks no formal schooling (with the exception of the Colegio de Guardias Jóvenes) and no chance to learn policing techniques from a curriculum developed by the state. Although many guards only possessed the most basic reading, writing, and math skills upon joining the force, their job required knowledge of a large body of civil and military law, as well as the ability to complete official documents and analyze fingerprints.[33] Even at the colegio, discipline and morality were emphasized, but policing was hardly given a thought. The apprenticeship period was the first time that most *aspirantes* would be introduced to the organizational culture of the Civil Guard itself, and this training must have had a profound effect given how fully many guards would embrace its culture. Since they did not learn them anywhere else, it is here that the enlisted men had to become acculturated to all the rhythms and habits of daily life as a civil guard; in other words, its police culture, including how to conduct patrols, check papers, issue fines, make arrests, police festivals and protests, etc. In allowing individual sergeants complete control of this essential period, the state permitted a highly personalized training that could reproduce the Civil Guard's police culture but sacrificed any government control over it, thereby forfeiting this opportunity to influence it from above. The insularity of the enlisted men's training was one reason why the corps's culture had such a high degree of continuity.

THE MAKING OF AN OFFICER

The Social Origins of the Civil Guard Officer

Civil Guard officers constituted a more uniform group than the enlisted men because they came from similar social backgrounds and almost all attended the same school. For about half of the officers who served in the Second Republic, their indoctrination into the insular military community no doubt began in infancy because their fathers had also been in the military.[34] These future officers were born all over the country and in cities and towns both large and small, probably because military families were scattered around the country, following the father wherever he was posted. Almost all of the officers' military fathers were also in the officer corps, and about half of them had been infantry officers. Many also appear to have come from the Cuerpo de Intendencia (Logistics Corps), whereas few were Civil Guard officers. What these numbers suggest is that the Civil Guard's officer corps was a fairly homogeneous body socially, drawn from a military milieu increasingly isolated from civilian society. However, within this milieu, the Civil Guard did provide upward social mobility because it enjoyed a higher prestige within the army than the infantry or especially the Cuerpo de Intendencia.[35]

   That so many Civil Guard officers came from military families was no accident. Ahumada himself had established the requirement that all officers come from the army, and the army favored military sons in its admissions to the Infantry Academy.[36] In addition, the sons of military families often attended preparatory schools specifically designed to ready students for the military academies, giving them a further advantage when taking their entrance examinations.[37] In a time when anything more than a primary school education was thought to be reserved for elites, attending such a military preparatory school identified these boys as members of a class apart.[38]

The Military Academies

My analysis of the training future Civil Guard officers received in the army will concentrate on the second Infantry Academy (1893–1927), because a large majority of the Second Republic's Civil Guard officers attended this school, and, as sociologist of the military Morris Janowitz states, "Education at a service academy is the first and most crucial experience of a professional soldier. The educational experiences of the cadet cannot obliterate his social background, but they leave deep and lasting impressions."[39] Sometimes I will also mention the Infantry Academy's predecessor, the Academia General Militar (General Military Academy), because a few of the highest-ranking Civil Guard officers at the time of the Republic were old enough to have attended that school and because of the continuity between its teachings and those of the Infantry Academy.[40] While most of the courses at the Infantry Academy concerned technical subjects, the entire structure of life there was meant to instill in cadets the importance of blind discipline, sacrifice, and a thirst for glory, all of which were to be channeled toward service to the *patria*. In this way, cadets were trained to become part of a military family that was supposed to be a leader of but also separated from civilian society. This family served the nation, but that did not preclude intervention in politics if the army felt its place within that nation was under threat.

The practice of having centralized schools for the training of officers began in Spain in the early nineteenth century, as the army transitioned to being a force led by professional, middle-class officers rather than aristocrats. These schools took on various forms until 1882, when the creation of the Academia General Militar de Toledo brought the general training programs for all army officers under one roof.[41] While some of the oldest officers had attended the Academia General Militar, most of the prominent officers during the Second Republic and the Civil War had graduated from the second Infantry Academy. The year 1910 alone had a graduating class that included Francisco Franco, Juan Yagüe, Emilio Esteban-Infantes, and Camilo Alonso Vega, who would all go on to become key figures on the Francoist side in the Civil War.[42] And graduating the next year was Lisardo Doval Bravo, a Civil Guard officer who went on to play an infamous role in the Second Republic.[43]

*Moral Training and Nationalist Indoctrination
at the Infantry Academy*

The writings and the recollections of former cadets demonstrate that the Infantry Academy's professors, influenced by the Regenerationist movement of the late nineteenth and early twentieth centuries, further developed the conservative nationalist tone that had already been present in the training at the Academia General Militar.[44] Regenerationism envisioned a revitalization of Spain's education, society, and culture in order to return the country to its former glories.[45] Although the broader movement had begun earlier, Regenerationism's influence on the Infantry Academy began in earnest in 1898 following Spain's defeat in the Spanish-American War. The political bent of instruction began to increase as professors blamed politicians, rather than the military, for the loss.[46] As a nostalgic text on the academy put it, "After periods of military grandeur and its political peak, Spain, like France, had their ordeal of disasters produced by egotism and lack of foresight."[47] Drawing on a selective reading of Clausewitz by Prussian/German officers like Helmuth von Moltke, some instructors advocated reform of the academy's curriculum to prioritize developing cadets' "moral" qualities, which would be necessary if the army was to take a leading role in Spain's regeneration.[48]

The Infantry Academy only had one course specifically dedicated to the moral training that its reformist professors so encouraged. Even this class was in fact about how to give moral instruction to enlisted men, but of course the lessons would be absorbed by the students as well. *La educación moral del soldado* by Enrique Ruiz Fornells was the regulation textbook in this course for decades. The primary military virtues that he urged cadets to instill in their future subordinates were duty, patriotism, discipline, abnegation, valor, and honor, with discipline being the most important of these.[49] Professors believed that such instruction was of special importance for steering the Spanish Army in the right political direction. These virtues remained an accurate summary of the values that Spanish officers consistently emphasized throughout the late nineteenth and early twentieth centuries. The values that civil guards held were much the same, with the exception of honor being elevated to a status equal to or even greater than that of discipline, but guards applied this way of thinking to the very different context of civilian policing.

With only one class on moral education in the curriculum, most moral training took place informally through the examples of professors and the structure of daily life. The academy reformers emphasized the examples of the professors themselves as keys to teaching cadets proper military values. Professors were specially selected to be examples of military virtue, glorified as the most important component of the cadets' education and expected to mold every aspect of course instruction and time spent outside of class alike into a model of how to live a virtuous life.[50] This emphasis on the example of the professors placed responsibly for moral education primarily in the hands of each individual instructor, rather than in the curriculum, thereby giving the instructors the freedom to teach their students largely as they saw fit, even if this instruction went against the wishes of the state.

Beyond what the professors could teach through their examples and classes, the structure of academy life itself was thought to be part of the cadets' moral training, and it was built around instilling the most important of all the virtues cadets were to learn: discipline. The teaching of discipline began with each cadet being assigned a number that was displayed on all his clothing and would stay with him throughout his time at the academy.[51] In this way, the cadet would immediately begin to subsume his individual identity to that of the military collective. Once classes began, cadets followed a strict schedule that spelled out how they would spend every hour of the day, including when they would get up, pray, go to class, study, eat their meals, and go to bed.[52]

Again, German military thinking had a strong influence on the Spanish here, but German ideas came to Spain by way of the French. In fact, France's reaction to its own defeat in the Franco-Prussian War served as a model for how Spanish intellectuals would respond to defeat in the Spanish-American War.[53] The French method of adopting the German model was to extoll the idea of *élan*—a fighting spirit that rejected complicated battlefield maneuver in favor of a blind glorification of the offensive.[54] The rhetoric in the Spanish Army followed a similar line, emphasizing the winning of glory through sacrifice to the *patria*, while still rigidly insisting on blind discipline. For example, a prominent professor at the academy explained that "the military life is not all fun and games; discipline, that harsh law, breaks ambition and limits one to nobler purposes. The soldier does not belong to himself; he is only an atom of the formidable organism that governs him."[55] This glorification of abnegation and discipline was meant to teach blind obedience rather than initiative. While this training had a certain logic for the purpose of building a disciplined army, for the Civil Guard officer who would be even at the junior level managing numerous posts spread over a large area with little supervision, such an emphasis on blind obedience could be of little use.

These arguments about discipline at the academy had an effect on how future officers thought about to whom they owed their loyalty. Instead of being primarily a means of ensuring obedience to the civilian state, discipline now principally referred to loyalty to the army itself, which was represented as a new family that the cadets would join. Cadets learned to earn respect for their obedience from their closed military society rather than from civilian society more broadly. In fact, academy professors hoped to train officers who would be models for civilian society, leaders in enhancing discipline and order. The presence of these ambitions in the thinking of Civil Guard officers was particularly important because they would have the closest contact with that civilian society.

Since the vast majority of Civil Guard officers who served during the Second Republic had attended the Infantry Academy, they had already been imbued with its common set of values even before they entered the corps. The academy had made them accustomed to strict discipline and isolation from civilian society. It had also taught them the importance of sacrifice and honor, even if the army's definition of honor emphasized reputation within the military caste, whereas the Civil Guard's emphasized reputation among the public. In addition, as Regenerationist ideas became prevalent within the officer corps after 1898, the academy increasingly taught cadets that the military had a duty to serve an idealized, abstract *patria* that ranked above even its duty to serve the government in power. During the Second Republic, Civil Guard officers would have to decide whether they were more committed to a conservative notion of the *patria* or their corps's emphasis on serving whatever government was in power.

Prior Experiences in the Army and Morocco

Once future Civil Guard officers graduated from the Infantry Academy, they usually spent a few years as lieutenants in the infantry before joining the Civil Guard. In the infantry, most found themselves far from being the valiant warriors and societal leaders that the academy had taught them to be. They found themselves, rather, as poorly paid and little respected members of the lower end of the middle class.[56] Garrison life meant immense boredom and the lack of any stimulation for motivated young officers. Their days consisted of parades, drills, horseback riding, guard duties, and endless paperwork.[57] Many of them held posts that only existed to give positions to the army's excessive number of officers, and some commanded units that existed only on paper.[58] Lacking any other purpose, such officers looked to the training that they had received at the Infantry Academy and dedicated themselves to following orders and regulations with bureaucratic exactitude.[59] Overall, garrison life must not have been so distasteful to future Civil Guard officers that they opted to give up military life entirely, but it must have also left them wanting a career with more interest and activity.

Life for officers who did tours in Morocco, including many who went on to join the Civil Guard, was the polar opposite of that of the garrison. Although officers faced danger and terrible living conditions in Morocco, life did offer more than boredom, and many future guards saw combat there. With danger

came chances for quick promotion and glory for the bold and ambitious officer. Consequently, officers' attitudes toward Morocco were less clear-cut than
those of enlisted men. Most, like the lower classes, had little taste for the poor
conditions and danger of service there. They preferred the security and pre-
dictability of garrison life and tried to avoid being sent to the protectorate.[60]
There was a select group, however, known as the *africanistas*, who relished the
opportunities in Morocco to live out the code of glory through abnegation and
sacrifice that they had learned at the Infantry Academy.

The *africanistas'* representations of the Moroccans that they were subjugat-
ing were contradictory. On the one hand, their writings and other media of the
time were filled with negative racial stereotypes typical of the colonial period
that sought to justify Spanish intervention in Morocco by presenting the Moroccans as inferior and as needing to be civilized.[61] While Spain's initial incur-
sions into northern Morocco sought "peaceful penetration" with a "civilizing
mission" and a heavy dose of Orientalism, by the time of the Spanish Army's
defeat at Barranco del Lobo in 1909, old stereotypes of the Moroccans as bloodthirsty and cruel were being emphasized once again.[62] Spanish underestima-
tions of the Moroccans as brutal fighters incapable of coordinated operations
contributed to an even more disastrous Spanish defeat at the Battle of Anual in
1921 at the hands of rebels led by Abd el-Krim.[63] Afterward, efforts to mobilize
Spain to take its revenge, crush the rebellion, and "pacify" the protectorate
only accentuated representations of the "Moors" as barbaric and traitorous.[64]

On the other hand, other officers, and sometimes even the same ones, also
argued that there was a commonality between Spaniards and Moroccans, stem-
ming from the former Muslim rule of Spain, that put Spaniards in a unique
position to adopt a parental role toward the Moroccans, especially after el-Krim
was defeated in 1927.[65] These officers even identified with the Moroccans in
certain ways; they appreciated what they perceived to be the Moroccans' toughness and willingness to die.[66] The Legión Española (colloquially referred to as
the Foreign Legion), founded in 1920 by the *africanista* José Millán-Astray, was
particularly known for embracing the harsh life of fighting in Morocco through
slogans like "Long live death!"[67] As these *africanistas* became more accustomed
to this lifestyle, they became more alienated from life in the metropole. As they
came to identify with what they saw as the positive aspects of Morocco and its
people, they projected what they considered to be its negative aspects back
onto peninsular Spaniards.[68]

The Infantry Academy taught officers rigid adherence to the tactical theory and regulations that they had memorized, but these rules had little relevance to counterinsurgency warfare in a colonial context. Given the situation on the ground in Morocco, officers realized that they had to adapt and improvise tactics of their own. They learned to take pride in their reliance on instinct, fancying that it was their *cojones* (balls) that guided them.[69] Especially vexing was the problem of identifying who exactly the rebels were amongst the population.[70] One solution employed for identifying rebels was brutality, for which the Spanish Legion in particular was infamous. It was hoped that the sexual abuse of Moroccan women and the torture and execution of prisoners would make the population too afraid to support the rebellion.[71] Another factor leading to brutality was the army's desire for revenge after the Anual defeat, in which thousands were killed and almost the entire Melilla sector lost to the rebels. As Sebastian Balfour explains, "Like the 1898 Disaster, Anual branded the minds of colonial officers with failure. In the prevailing military ideology, defeat was like losing masculinity. From then on, revenge and reaffirmation became obsessive goals."[72]

Several historians have argued recently that the army officers who led the suppression of the 1934 rebellion in Asturias and led the Francoist side in the Civil War developed their brutality in Morocco.[73] Even though Civil Guard officers were not usually the *africanistas* that played so famous a part in these events, they did sometimes also turn to torture as a means to extract revenge, such as in the suppression of the 1934 Socialist-led revolt. While direct causation is difficult to prove, the fact that large numbers of the guards involved in those events, both officers and enlisted men, had previously served in the Moroccan wars suggests that the brutalizing influence of the conflict may have extended beyond the *africanistas* into Spain's armed forces more generally as well.

Civil Guard Officer Admissions and Training

The Civil Guard was not a particularly popular choice for army officers because advancements were so slow in its closed promotion system.[74] Those who did join the corps were not the *africanistas* who reveled in the hardships and violence of Morocco and hoped for quick promotion there.[75] Instead, the force seems to have been for those for whom the military life did hold enough appeal so that they sought to continue it in a setting that would offer more stimulation and independence than the monotonous existence of the army garrison officer. In addition, the Civil Guard presented the officer who did not foresee himself winning glory as an *africanista* with the opportunity to still hold a position of prestige within the military hierarchy.[76] Suddenly, these advantages made the Civil Guard very attractive when the army, around 1922, altered the rate of its promotions to be about the same as that of the Civil Guard. Admission to the force was by a wait-list based primarily on seniority in the army—there was no exam as there was for enlisted men.[77] Requests for admission to the Civil Guard skyrocketed after 1922 to the point where, two years later, there were five hundred officers on the wait-list to fill around twelve vacancies.

In practice, officers always entered the Civil Guard as either first or second lieutenants. Like the enlisted men, they also had a six-month apprenticeship period, but theirs was known as the *prácticas*, and they shadowed a captain instead of a sergeant.[78] This period was crucial for reorienting the officers' sense of honor from defining it as glory won in battle to respect won from the public. However, there is unfortunately virtually no information available on this key phase in the acculturation process since Civil Guard officers of the time left no memoirs and station records are still not available to the public. One is left to speculate that, as with the enlisted men, this individualized mentorship was a powerful factor in perpetuating the Civil Guard's unique culture, because it was the only training that officers received specific to the corps. By shadowing a captain on the job, the new lieutenant could go beyond the regulations to learn the habits of the institution that governed how Civil Guard officers operated in practice, from their strict emphasis on discipline during inspections to their harsh methods for pursuing criminals to their insistence that their honor be respected by all classes of society.

Given the corps's entrance requirements and its almost total lack of in-house training apart from the apprenticeships, service in the army was clearly considered to be the primary training for the Civil Guard. For the typical officer who would serve under the Second Republic, this training may have begun with coming from a military family. After a military preparatory school and three years at the Infantry Academy, this typical officer knew little else but a military lifestyle with its emphasis on discipline and glory through sacrifice in the name of the *patria*. For both officers and enlisted men, service in the garrisons and for some in Morocco acclimatized them to a military culture that was quite distinct and isolated from civilian society.

The problem with service in the army was that it gave guards no training in a police culture that would allow them to do their jobs as guardians of public order. That task was left to individual sergeants and captains during the apprenticeship period. There, enlisted recruits would gain experience patrolling civilian populations, and officers would learn to inspect and manage a group of Civil Guard posts. A shift in mentality was required as well. Whereas in the army's military culture, honor was to be won through glory in battle, guards had to learn to seek it through respect from the people they policed.

In leaving guards' training entirely in the hands of the army and Civil Guard mentors, civilian authorities gave up an opportunity to steer the Civil Guard's culture in new directions. Therefore—and again recalling the importance of civilian intervention for effecting change in military institutions—this lack of control over training can be added to the list of the ways in which Restoration governments failed to steer the Civil Guard's culture in the direction of the nonviolent maintenance of order. Army service began to distance guards from civilian life even before they joined the force, and professors at the Infantry Academy had free rein to replicate in the next generation the conservative and interventionist shift of the late-Restoration officer corps. Then, the apprenticeships allowed engrained habits within the Civil Guard's police culture to be passed down as well. Despite nineteenth-century liberals' hopes that militarization would make the Civil Guard a professional police force, this apprenticeship system made the occupation resemble a craft as much as a profession. Indeed, James Q. Wilson's description of policing-as-craft fits the Civil Guard perfectly: "Learning is by apprenticeship rather than formal training, procedures and rules are passed along by word of mouth and example rather than by written instructions or published manuals, [and] there is comparatively little specialization of tasks."[79] The system also meant that the guards themselves were the only ones with the power to adapt their training and methods to the increasing need to police the large protests and strikes of the early twentieth century. However, the institution's police culture was too ossified to adapt rapidly to the changing sociopolitical climate of the Second Republic, and when guards were met with challenges to their honor, they fell back on the military culture that they had been introduced to in their army days of seeking glory in battle and of being ultimately responsible to the *patria* rather than the pueblo.

FIVE

THE REPUBLIC

Cultural Continuity and Regime Change

O n May 10, 1931, an angry mob took to the streets in Madrid, demanding, above all, the immediate dissolution of the Civil Guard. The crowd made for the offices of the conservative newspaper *ABC*, and Minister of the Interior Miguel Maura Gamazo ordered a detachment of civil guards to protect the building. He felt that this move was an opportunity "to demonstrate that Republic was not a synonym of anarchy." Because of concerns that the Civil Guard would "remain forever stigmatized as an 'enemy of the Republic,'" Prime Minister Niceto Alcalá Zamora, at the urging of Minister of War Manuel Azaña Díaz and other cabinet members, soon reversed Maura's order and had the guards withdraw, but not before they had killed two in front of the *ABC* offices.[1] Afterward, guards of the urban police force, the Cuerpo de Seguridad (Security Corps), who were armed with swords instead of rifles, were left to deal with the crowds.[2]

The next day, the situation became more serious as the crowds began burning churches and convents around Madrid and other cities. In an indication of its deep skepticism of the Civil Guard's ability to maintain order in a peaceful fashion, the cabinet decided to declare a state of war that would allow it to deploy the army rather than send the Civil Guard into the streets. In the end, the *guardias de seguridad* were able to protect some buildings, and the army dispersed the crowds easily, all without causing a single injury or death.[3] Meanwhile, the Civil Guard killed a total of nine more people in other cities, causing almost all the deaths during these incidents.[4]

The May 1931 burnings of convents brought to the attention of the government the urgency of the question of what the role of the Civil Guard would be
in the nascent Second Republic, with each political faction within the republic
staking out its own position in this regard. This chapter examines how the
contradictions built into the Civil Guard's organizational culture became amplified as it came into contact with the unprecedented political mobilizations
ushered in by the new republic.[5] I establish not only what the positions of the
major players in the republic's sociopolitical struggles were relative to the Civil
Guard but also how these groups expressed their positions. I will concentrate
on the first year of the Second Republic, 1931, in order to do this, but relevant
examples from later years will also be mentioned.

A lack of consensus both among and within the republic's various political
players was a significant hindrance to the regime's consolidation, and what approach each faction would take toward the Civil Guard was a frequent sticking
point. Many republicans were initially skeptical of whether or not this institution, which was accustomed to suppressing mass mobilizations for oligarchic
regimes, could be reconciled with the republic. But they quickly came to see the
Civil Guard as essential for policing the wave of strikes and protests that had
accompanied the republic, and, fearful of losing its loyalty, they turned away
from adapting the force's culture to its new circumstances.

The Socialists, meanwhile, maintained their opposition to the Civil Guard
in principle, but they, too, were divided between more moderate leaders and
more radical rank-and-file members. The latter pushed an oppositional stance
toward the Civil Guard that manifested itself in letters of complaint, newspaper articles, speeches, and protests. Whereas the Civil Guard was accustomed
to policing protests, albeit often with violence, it had to rely on others to defend it in the press and the Cortes. Conservative groups were happy to take
on this role as they sought to adapt to the new political environment with a
mass mobilization of their own. The unfortunate consequence for the Civil
Guard was that it came to appear more in league than ever with landowners
and Catholic conservatives.

This chapter presents the Civil Guard as a political player in its own right.
It did not have a particular political agenda, but rather through its actions it
repeatedly made a specific claim: at whatever cost, its honor should not be
offended. The law permitted the institution to use violence as a response to insult, and its regulations only instructed guards to give a warning and then open

fire with their lethal rifles. However, it was up to the commander at the scene to decide when to apply deadly force, and it is here that the corps's culture of honor sometimes drove the commander to advance to this stage quickly. This pattern of behavior was not new to the Second Republic, but when the number of strikes and protests expanded greatly under the new regime, so, too, did the violence of the Civil Guard. At the same time, republican governments failed to reform the institution's culture and tactics to adapt it to the new normal of policing political contestation in the streets.

GENERAL SANJURJO AND THE
COMING OF THE REPUBLIC

In order to understand the positions of the various political players of the Second Republic vis-à-vis the Civil Guard, one must first understand the Civil Guard's role in the formation of the republic. During the dictatorship of Miguel Primo de Rivera, the general fulfilled his promise to restore public order in Spain by permanently suspending constitutional rights. Having taken over the government, the military now had total control over public order.[6] Some Civil Guard historians see the Primo de Rivera dictatorship as a golden age for the Civil Guard because, by suspending the constitution, the regime gave guards essentially free rein to suppress suspected criminals and political dissidence as they saw fit.[7] The resulting low levels of political violence made their jobs much safer because they could preemptively arrest anyone they thought might cause political conflict.[8] The king and Primo de Rivera also spoke to guards' desires for honor by granting them various medals and forms of recognition. Perhaps the greatest honor they bestowed upon the Civil Guard was making one of Spain's most prestigious army officers, Lieutenant General José Sanjurjo Sacanell, its director general in 1928. Sanjurjo soon developed a unique paternal affection for the guards, who reciprocated by venerating him as a leader who brought honor to their institution.

A look at Sanjurjo's life reveals a man of soaring pride and ambition, but one who was also largely successful in maintaining an image of himself as simply a dutiful soldier, concerned only with service to his country rather than politics. His story reveals much about how guards wanted to see themselves. Perhaps one reason they looked up to him so much was that he won his honor in a way they usually could not as policemen: glory in battle. Morris Janowitz notes that, even as military organizations needed more and more military managers, heroic leaders remained important for maintaining tradition and motivating an organization's members.[9] The jobs of civil guards were by nature largely managerial, but they were drawn to Sanjurjo by his preference for deeds over words, his self-proclaimed political neutrality, and his keen awareness of his public image. In fact, he built around himself much the same fiction as they did around their institution.

Sanjurjo came from a deeply Catholic Carlist family, and, his father having been killed in the Third Carlist War, José began a military life while still a boy in the Colegio de Huérfanos de la Guerra (School of War Orphans) in El Escorial.[10] In 1890, he entered the Academia General Militar in Toledo, where, by his own admission, he was a poor student, preferring adventure novels to textbooks.[11] He explained that "of the military course of study I always liked, more than the texts learned in the loneliness of the study rooms, what it has of adventure, of personal inspiration."[12] A general who won honor by personally leading his men by being first in bravery—that was the kind of officer Sanjurjo wanted to be.

Once he had graduated from the academy, Sanjurjo's primary concern as a young officer was to gain this personal honor, and he aimed to win it on a battlefield. In 1896 Sanjurjo would get his first chance when he was sent to fight in the ongoing conflict in Cuba. There, he gained a reputation for calm in the face of danger and for having particularly warm and friendly relations with the soldiers under his command.[13] When war broke out again in 1909 in Morocco, he was quick to volunteer. In the Rif, where he was to spend much of the next twenty years, he was truly in his element, and he came to prefer life there, with its frequent opportunities for winning further glory, to the comparatively dull life of peninsular Spain.[14] Thus he became a leading *africanista*, in contrast to the civil guards, who had chosen a career in policing rather than staying on in Morocco. His most glorious moment came on February 1, 1914, when, as a major, he was seriously wounded twice but kept fighting for another five hours because he feared if he left the battlefield to go to the hospital, his men would retreat without their leader in front of them.[15] For this action, Sanjurjo received a merit-based promotion and the Cruz Laureada de San Fernando, Spain's highest military award for valor.[16] The first of February 1914 was perhaps his finest moment, when he was most the man he wanted to be, because he was winning honor on the battlefield through his own personal leadership and bravery.

The deed brought him to the rank of lieutenant colonel, a level where leadership was more commonly exercised at an observation post or at an office desk than at the front of a battle where sheer physical tenacity could still be enough to win the day. As he continued to receive merit-based promotions, by 1923, Major General Sanjurjo was in a position of such prominence that he found himself involved in politics as well as office work.[17] Seeing himself as a purely military man, he had previously avoided politics, but he actively supported Primo de Rivera's coup of that year.[18] The two generals grew close as they worked together to achieve victory in Morocco.[19] In 1927, they accomplished this, and Sanjurjo, who received another Cruz de San Fernando for his efforts, became Spain's most prestigious general.[20] But when the war ended, so did his raison d'être in Morocco, and he requested a transfer to the peninsula.[21]

In 1928, Primo de Rivera granted Sanjurjo's wish by having him named director general of the Civil Guard.[22] In so doing, Primo de Rivera put a man who had dedicated his life to gaining honor at the head of an institution where honor reigned as the most important value. The guards quickly grew fond of their new director, and he of them.[23] In addressing them in a warm, paternal tone in his general orders, he won their loyalty just as he had won the loyalty of his troops in Cuba and Morocco. He knew how to flatter guards with remarks like "the benemérito corps is like a well-rehearsed orchestra; its practitioners know its mission perfectly, and the one who leads hardly has to do anything except keep the baton in his hand."[24] Of course, his task was made easy by the fact that the guards were glad to have the general add his personal prestige to that of their institution.

Around the same time that Sanjurjo was made director general, Primo de Rivera's popularity was on the wane, and republicans began to launch a series of revolts aiming to overthrow both the dictatorship and the monarchy. As usual, guards led the way in suppressing these uprisings, but they realized that putting down these increasingly popular movements was beginning to damage their reputation. Both republicans and monarchists understood that having the support of the Civil Guard was essential, and so they each courted it in their own way. The republicans distributed a manifesto to Civil Guard posts and promised to restore order. As for the king, he offered a pay raise, gave the Civil Guard a medal, and made its nickname Benemérita official, while the military press spread rumors that the republicans wanted to dissolve the corps.[25] Guards, caught between their commitment to serve the government in power and a public that was turning against that government, took a wait-and-see attitude.[26]

By 1931, Primo de Rivera had resigned, and it had become clear that the elections that had been called for April 12 would be a de facto plebiscite on whether or not the monarchy should go as well. As usual, the guards professed their "profound political neutrality" regarding these developments.[27] When republican parties won the elections by a large majority in urban areas, the will of the people was clear, but the stance that the Civil Guard would take remained uncertain. Both republicans and monarchists knew that whichever way Sanjurjo went, the guards were likely to follow, given their loyalty to him and their general commitment to obey the orders of their director general. As far as Sanjurjo was concerned, the April 12 elections had made his choice clear. That very night, he announced to a cabinet meeting that the monarchy could no longer count on the Civil Guard's support.[28] Both the abdication of the king and the declaration of the Second Republic occurred two days later. That there has been much debate about whether Sanjurjo formally declared his adhesion to the republic before or after the abdication speaks to how important it was to the Civil Guard that their leader not declare his loyalty to a government that was not in power, even for an hour.[29]

While the civil guards had followed Sanjurjo's lead in not opposing the republic, their enthusiasm about the new regime was mixed. Some guards reacted positively to the proclamation of the republic, while others stayed in their posts or sullenly watched over celebrations.[30] They had been put in an awkward position because in many towns the republicans and Socialists they had persecuted for decades were now in control of local governments and able to give them orders.[31] The *RTGC* addressed the coming of the republic with a tone of acceptance rather than celebration, encouraging guards to maintain their commitments to discipline, political neutrality, and order, especially with a perceived danger of communism lurking, while also reassuring them that none other than Sanjurjo was their leader and that the country continued to respect their work.[32]

THE REPUBLICANS:
FROM OPPONENTS TO SUPPORTERS

The republicans, long adversaries of both the Restoration system and the Civil Guard, suddenly found themselves in control of the Spanish state in April 1931. An important component of this state was the approximately thirty thousand civil guards stationed around the country in every town of any size.[33] The force still had a dual ministerial dependency, its primary mission was still the maintenance of public order in rural areas, and the *Reglamento para el servicio,* the *Reglamento militar,* and the *Cartilla del Guardia Civil* were all still in effect, little altered since the time of Ahumada.[34] With the coming of the republic, a major reform or dissolution of the corps was expected, but the influence of conservative republicans and then the institution's own evident utility to the republic meant that no sweeping transformation ever took place. The new liberties and hopes that the republicans gave to the working classes, in particular, had ushered in an unprecedented wave of strikes and protests, but the republic frequently deployed the Civil Guard, known for its propensity for violence, to police these mobilizations while taking no steps to reduce those violent tendencies.

The provisional government that took power in April 1931 was a broad coalition of widely differing political viewpoints, which included opposing perspectives on the Civil Guard. Some conservatives late to jump on the republican bandwagon, such as Miguel Maura, brought the Restoration's hardline approach to public order into the republic and supported maintaining the Civil Guard unaltered. In this view these conservatives were joined by Alejandro Lerroux's more broad-based Radical Party. Lerroux had steered his party to the right in the decades after the Montjuïc scandal, executing a strange about-face by replacing his anti–Civil Guard rhetoric with praise for the institution. Meanwhile, the center-left Acción Republicana (Republican Action), which was the party of the emerging republican leader Manuel Azaña, called for the reform or even dissolution of the Civil Guard. Since left republicans had been repressed under the Primo de Rivera dictatorship, they came into the Second Republic skeptical of the Civil Guard's loyalty and usefulness. As for the left-republican Radical Socialist Party and the Partido Socialista Obrero Español (PSOE, or Spanish Socialist Workers' Party), the largest party in the coalition, they favored the immediate disbanding of the corps.

This combination of forces meant that the provisional government looked to move quickly to modify heavily or even dissolve the Civil Guard. However, Maura refused to make any changes. He explained: "My companions, including the president [the conservative republican Niceto Alcalá Zamora], asked me to dissolve the corps, or, at the least, to modify it such that we would give the sensation that we had dissolved it. After long hours of study and reflection, I categorically denied not only to dissolve it but even to alter a single comma of the famous regulations. They are, in truth, a model of foresight, of organization, and of disciplinary spirit."[35]

It would not be long before other members of the government came around to Maura's position. After two incidents on the day of the republic's declaration, the Civil Guard and the new regime enjoyed a honeymoon period in which there were no cases of deadly violence involving the force. But the convent-burning incidents in May made the honeymoon short-lived. These events brought into focus the dangers of the Civil Guard to the republic as itself a cause of popular protest and violence, but also its necessity as a powerful tool for quelling unrest. This second lesson was the one that republican leaders took away from the events. They dropped plans to alter or dissolve the corps and did not hesitate to deploy it in the future.[36] Maura's successor as minister of the interior, the more center-left Santiago Casares Quiroga, echoed Maura's sentiments regarding the Civil Guard almost verbatim, calling the *Cartilla* and *Reglamento* "admirable, unshakeable things. It is not possible to take out even a comma. It is a magnificent work that of the Duke of Ahumada. I myself know some articles and concepts from memory."[37] In the end, there was no major shift in the government's approach to the Civil Guard and public order in general during the Second Republic because republicans believed, as much as any previous rulers, that they could not risk any breakdown in order without risking the survival of their entire regime.[38]

In fact, the provisional government took measures to strengthen its powers to maintain public order and to found a new police force that would assist in this task. On October 21, it promulgated the Ley de Defensa de la República (Law of the Defense of the Republic), which restricted the freedoms of speech, the press, and assembly granted under the Constitution by broadly prohibiting "acts of aggression against the Republic" and by granting the minister of the interior sweeping powers to ban strikes, protests, and associations.[39] Meanwhile, Maura spearheaded the development of an entirely new police force.

At the beginning of the Second Republic, there was the Cuerpo de Seguridad urban police force, as well as a detective force, the Vigilance Corps, which also operated in the cities.[40] Both forces were within the portfolio of the minister of the interior and therefore under civilian control. However, since the Cuerpo de Seguridad was a small force with light armament, the Civil Guard frequently operated in urban areas as well, as it was called in when there was any disturbance. The idea behind the new unit, known as the Sección de Asalto (referred to in this work as the Assault Guard), was that it would be an elite, quick-response force within the Cuerpo de Seguridad, equipped with flat-bedded trucks that would enable it to respond quickly to signs of disorder. With the Assault Guard maintaining public order in the cities, the Civil Guard could concentrate on rural policing. Maura also hoped that by arming the new force with pistols and batons rather than rifles, it would be less violent than the Civil Guard.[41] Being a civilian force entirely under the Ministry of the Interior, the Assault Guard would also avoid the ambiguities of the Civil Guard's dual ministerial dependency.[42]

As for civil guards, they had long complained that they were not intended for public-order duties in cities, yet they feared, with good reason, that this new corps was intended to supplant their institution gradually as the republic's primary force of public order.[43] But after an anarchist insurrection in January 1932, the Assault Guards were also armed with rifles, and the two forces increasingly came to see each other as allies in the fight against the republic's periodic bouts of unrest.[44] Nor did the republicans' hopes for a less violent force really materialize. Despite the Assault Guard's civilian structure, its officers were recruited directly from the army, and, especially after the anarchist insurrection, its own developing police culture began to look remarkably similar to that of the Civil Guard.[45]

In the early years of the republic, while the government was devoting resources to the new Assault Guard, articles and letters in the RTGC indicate that civil guards were also calling for practical reforms to be made to their own institution, but these suggestions went unheeded. There was agreement that guards needed to switch from the Mauser rifle to the less powerful and unwieldy short-barrel Mauser. This version had already been made the regulation weapon of the Civil Guard, but most still carried the older model. In addition, there were modernizers who went further and echoed the attitudes of some in the Cuerpo de Seguridad and especially the Vigilance Corps by arguing for a modernization of the Civil Guard's equipment and tactics in imitation of the latest developments in policing in the United States, Great Britain, France, and Germany, such as deploying tear gas for nonlethal crowd control.[46] One retired sergeant went so far as to suggest that article 7 of the *Cartilla* be clarified.[47] Another controversial suggestion was to stop carrying long arms entirely and only carry pistols and to trade bayonets and swords for batons.[48]

The republicans' top priority was ensuring the loyalty of the Civil Guard to the new regime. Therefore, they required that civil guards swear allegiance to the republic, which almost all of them did. Republicans also hoped to use the guards' commitment to honor as a way to guarantee their loyalty. Politicians knew that boosting the Civil Guard's honor would solidify its support as well, so they frequently sung its praises. There were also material incentives; over the course of the republic the Civil Guard benefited from several pay increases and expansions in size.[49] The creation of the Assault Guard was yet another way in which republicans hoped to strengthen their hold on power while reducing the violence of policing in urban areas. Yet much of the unrest was taking place in rural areas under the jurisdiction of the Civil Guard. In their obsession with public order and the consolidation of their power, and in their rush to appease the Civil Guard, republicans did not realize that there were calls for reforms emanating from within the institution, suggesting practical changes in regulations and equipment that might have made its policing less violent. When it came to the Civil Guard, republicans saw a zero-sum game of either order and stasis or reform and confrontation. After decades of struggle against the state's forces of public order, their political imagination could not envision the possibility of mutually beneficial reforms.

THE SOCIALISTS: OPPOSITION IN A NEW KEY

The Spanish Left was divided during the Second Republic between various socialist, anarchist, and communist parties and unions. As the Civil Guard struggled to adapt its policing to the new democratic context of the republic, so the new era only deepened internal divisions within working-class groups because they were unable to arrive at a consensus about how much to operate within the republican system in pursuit of social reform. This section will focus on how these divisions resulted in uncoordinated approaches to the Civil Guard that served to heighten tensions with the force without effecting any substantive changes in its organization or culture that might have helped reduce its violence. Both this section and subsequent chapters will focus on the approach of the Socialists to the Civil Guard, since their willingness to take advantage of the republic's new legal and extralegal opportunities for political contestation best exemplifies the new complexities in the relationships between the Civil Guard and the working classes brought about by the republic. More radical Socialist leaders deployed incendiary rhetoric and even violence against the institution as a way to harness the mobilizing potential of opposition to a force so hated by the working classes, provoking harsh responses by the Civil Guard. Yet some Socialist leaders were more reticent about alienating a force so fundamental to the authority of the republican state, which meant that in the end the Socialists only increased the tensions between the working classes and the Civil Guard without either significantly reforming or eliminating the force.

While anarchism had long been the most powerful working-class movement in Spain, in the early years of the republic the new regime gave the socialist PSOE the chance to be the party that advocated for workers within the republican system, and its membership grew rapidly in 1931. The Socialists, as they saw it, sought to transform Spanish society by taking political power away from the caciques and placing it directly in the hands of the people. To many of them, the Civil Guard was key to the survival of the old order, and so they opposed it with letters of complaint, newspaper articles, speeches, and protests. While the party leadership wished to proceed with caution to avoid open conflict with the institution, the possibility of using criticism of the hated Civil Guard as a way to mobilize rank-and-file members was hard to resist. While the Civil Guard was certainly not new to criticism, which it interpreted as an offense to its honor, the institution was not accustomed to the opposition being so open and widespread. Lacking a public press or representation in the Cortes of their own, guards had to rely on others to respond to their adversaries for them. The exception was when guards were policing protests, in which case violence could become a tool for asserting their own position.

Opposing the Civil Guard was part of a broader strategy by Socialists in 1931 to build their power, especially at the local level. The elections of that year had swept the PSOE into many towns' city halls, and the Socialists' union, the Unión General de Trabajadores (General Workers' Union, or UGT), was ex-

panding rapidly. However, the real power in many towns was still in the hands
of the caciques. Therefore, the Socialists launched an offensive against them,
constantly denouncing the old *caciquil* system in the press and in the Cortes.
Since they viewed the Civil Guard as the muscle that gave the landowners and
caciques their power, the Socialists also called for the dissolution of the corps,
regularly including this objective in their party programs.[50] The unpopularity
of both the caciques and the Civil Guard made them easy targets around which
the rank and file seeking radical change and some party leaders could unite in
opposition.

In contrast to the official government support, the long-standing animosity between the Civil Guard and most working-class people continued into
the Second Republic, and the mass politicization that accompanied the fall
of the monarchy gave these people the desire to express their grievances
against the institution, while the republic's freedoms of the press and assembly gave them the ability to do so. One way in which Socialist organizations
allowed workers to make their complaints known was by sending telegrams
to the minister of the interior, and his ministry appears to have received such
messages almost daily. The complaints were most commonly about the Civil
Guard using unnecessary force or detaining excessive numbers of people, and
an incident of Civil Guard violence could provoke a whole slew of telegrams.
While the veracity of most of the complaints cannot be determined, their sheer
number is further proof that the relationship between civil guards and townspeople was often fraught. At the same time, frequently these complaints were
only of a local nature, requesting the transfer of a particular station commandant or officer.[51] Once again, one sees the importance of the local commander in
shaping the Civil Guard's relationship with a particular pueblo. That most local
organizations concentrated their efforts on the transfer of particular guards
rather than the abolition of the institution as a whole was typical of the local
nature of Spanish politics in general.[52] Yet unlike landowners' requests for extra protection, which were often granted, calls for the transfer of a civil guard
or other such requests were almost never heeded—a fact that must have been
frustrating for the working classes and fed the Socialist argument that the real
power under the republic still lay with the caciques.

The nonviolent means through which the Socialists opposed the Civil
Guard, including telegrams, speeches, and newspaper articles, fit within Juan
Linz's classification of them as semiloyal to the republic.[53] That is to say, they

were willing to play by the republic's rules of political participation, but they were also willing to violate those rules if they felt doing so was the only way to advance their interests. While the republic generally allowed freedom of speech and of the press, "injuring" the armed forces, including the Civil Guard, not only physically but also verbally or in writing, was not permitted, and so by criticizing the Civil Guard, the Socialists were playing on the boundaries of legality.

Military prosecutors, acting on behalf of the Civil Guard, frequently pressed charges against authors who they felt were damaging the corps's honor. The injuries did not have to be direct—anything that suggested that the *Benemérita* was not living up to a part of its honor code, such as claiming that guards were the servants of a particular segment of the population rather than the benefactors of all people, could warrant proceedings being filed. Calls for the dissolution of the Civil Guard were also considered injurious because they implied that the force was not respected by everyone. But Socialists were prepared to meet these legal challenges. They wrote critical pieces anonymously, destroying the original manuscripts, and, if an editor was asked the identity of the author by an investigative judge, he simply claimed that the piece had been sent in the mail or that he could not remember. If the judge did discover the author's name, he or she, no doubt not coincidentally, often turned out to be a deputy of the Cortes who therefore enjoyed parliamentary immunity. In other words, deputies could essentially attack the Civil Guard in writing with impunity, but prosecutors still went through the motions of filing charges as symbolic gestures. Even if guards could not punish those who insulted them, they would not stand by and do nothing when they felt their honor had been offended.[54]

At the national level, Socialist opinion regarding the Civil Guard was not completely united. Some believed that rather than dissolving the corps entirely, the government should change its culture to make it a tool of the republic rather than of the cacique. As Julián Besteiro, leader of the conservative wing of the PSOE, famously said of the Civil Guard to Azaña, "It is an admirable machine. We should not eliminate it, but rather make it work in our favor."[55] The party's two other most prominent leaders, Indalecio Prieto and Francisco Largo Caballero, also seem to have thought that eliminating the Civil Guard might be unwise.[56]

Nevertheless, the Socialist Party as a whole, bowing to the influence of

prominent members more willing to pander to the rank and file, moved forward with its efforts against the Civil Guard. Most horrifying to the guards
themselves was a committee that Socialists in the Cortes formed on November 26, 1931, to investigate reports of abuses by the institution and consider
how it might be reformed.[57] Guards were offended by the suggestion that the
Benemérita might be in need of reform, and they feared that the committee
was actually intending to dissolve rather than simply alter their organization.
Adding insult to injury was the fact that the leader of the committee was Margarita Nelken Mansberger, a Socialist deputy for Badajoz Province from the
radical wing of the party whom guards would come to see as the antithesis of
everything for which they stood.

An examination of Nelken's life provides an example of what the civil
guards firmly believed that they were *not*. There was much for them to dislike
in her very background. First, her parents were of foreign origins, her father being German and her mother French; Margarita herself had been born in Spain.[58]
Second, she was not Catholic; her parents were Jewish, and she was an atheist.
Third, her wealthy background enabled her to receive an excellent education
and enter the intellectual elite of Madrid and Paris.[59] She was secular, urban,
and cosmopolitan, whereas guards were Catholic, rural, and insular. She had
studied music and art in Paris and quickly emerged as a prolific and respected
art critic. After returning to Madrid, she began to take an interest in social
activism and feminism, and in 1918 she founded Spain's first nursery for the
children of working mothers.[60] However, the Church, eager to maintain its
monopoly on social services, soon shut the operation down.[61]

Such disappointments made Nelken vehemently anticlerical. She accused
the Church of mismanaging its social services and of using them to push its
moral agenda. She believed that the Church's insistence on keeping sex within
the confines of marriage stifled women's freedom of expression. She herself
had two children out of wedlock and lived with the father of the second, even
though he was already married.[62] In essence, she was suggesting women also
be able to enjoy the kind of sexual freedom that was already tolerated for many
men like Sanjurjo in Spanish society. After his wife had died in childbirth, the
famous general lived a promiscuous lifestyle as a widower; he also had a child
out of wedlock, and he frequented brothels and contracted syphilis.[63] As for
the civil guards, whose sexual conduct, as well as that of their wives, was held

to a stricter standard by their regulations, Nelken's ideas of sexual liberation must have seemed particularly shocking, even though they appear to have had no difficulty turning a blind eye to Sanjurjo's licentiousness.

Around this same time, the poverty that Nelken witnessed in Madrid's working-class neighborhoods made her see women's liberation as part of the larger economic inequalities in Spanish society. She came to believe that freedom for women could only be attained by eliminating the repressive structures of society through a turn to socialism. As she explained in her bestselling book, *La condición social de la mujer en España* (*The Social Condition of the Woman in Spain*), "The feminist question in Spain is . . . a purely economic question." She believed that only when women no longer had to depend on men economically could they truly be free.[64] Given her new attraction to socialism, she toured Spain during the Primo de Rivera years giving lectures to workers. Along with the Church, she came to identify the Civil Guard as one of society's structures for oppressing the worker. She became the institution's most vocal critic, to the point where Sanjurjo wrote her a personal letter, expressing his disappointment at her position but also his confidence that her attitude would change as she got to know the professionalism of his guards better.[65] Given this context, one can imagine the alarm with which guards then reacted to the news that Nelken would lead the congressional investigation of their organization, especially since that organization, which has been called Spain's "masculine institution par excellence," was being challenged by a woman.[66]

Like virtually every other aspect of her life, Nelken's election to the Cortes had been controversial. Nelken joined the PSOE in 1931 and began writing a column commenting on the sessions of the Cortes for *El Socialista*, which made her well-known within the party.[67] When a vacancy for representing Badajoz Province became available in October of that year, the Socialists nominated Nelken so that the PSOE could have a female deputy, even though Nelken had never lived in Badajoz.[68] Nevertheless, her criticism of the Civil Guard on the campaign trail appealed to the province's large numbers of landless laborers, or braceros, and she won the special election by a large majority.[69] However, Deputy Diego Hidalgo Durán of the Radical Party contested the results, claiming that she was not a Spanish citizen, given that her father was German. A congressional committee was formed, and it determined that although it was true that she had never formally declared her Spanish citizenship, an exception would be made.[70]

Nelken's controversial election to the Cortes damaged her reputation. Azaña was outraged that a mere art critic (and a woman) could suddenly be propelled to such a prominent position.[71] Even many Socialists made demeaning comments about her.[72] They felt challenged by her outspoken nature and refusal to downplay her femininity in Spain's masculine world of politics.[73] Despite all the antipathy from political elites, she was an instant success with Badajoz's braceros, joining them in seeking to push the PSOE in a more radical direction, such as by insisting on the dissolution of the Civil Guard. She was moved by the extreme poverty she witnessed in the province and took to her new role as representative of its citizenry with the same gusto that she had previously deployed for women's liberation.[74] If Sanjurjo was the paternal protector of the civil guards, Nelken had become the maternal protector of the braceros.

Nelken had appointed herself enemy-in-chief of the civil guards, and they could not have found an opponent who would have been easier for them to despise. She had an international background whereas they celebrated themselves as uniquely Spanish. She argued that Catholicism was the root cause of Spain's ills whereas they saw it as an essential guide for righteousness. She advocated sexual freedom for women when they did not even have this freedom as men. And finally, she championed revolutionary socialism whereas they sought to defend order and the status quo. Once Nelken was a deputy for Badajoz, the province became a battleground of contrasting visions for Spain as guards sought to defend their honor against what they saw as a serious affront to it.

THE RIGHT:
SUPPORTERS OF THE CIVIL GUARD

The elites of town society continued to be the main supporters of the Civil Guard during the Second Republic. But the new regime challenged these elites' positions of power. While during the Restoration the cacique had been the epitome of the town elite, his power was undermined by freer elections. This development might not have been entirely negative for the Civil Guard, given its uneasy relationship with the caciques, except that it brought republicans and Socialists who had been critical of the institution to power in most towns.

Then there were the landowners. They needed the Civil Guard more than ever before to protect their persons and property against the protests and strikes that swept the country in 1931. Their methods for courting the favor of the Civil Guard did not change, but they took on greater significance when the praise of the propertied stood in such contrast to the insults of the workers. In addition, these landed elites took their support for the Civil Guard to the national level. Adapting to the new mass politics of the democratic system, right-wing politicians and newspapers defended the institution against attempts to reform or eliminate it.

There were three main ways in which local elites offered support to the Civil Guard during the Second Republic: they provided financial assistance, homages, and telegrams of praise. As discussed in chapter 2, the Civil Guard had always relied on local elites for some financial support, but this aid took on new importance during the Second Republic. As had been the case under previous regimes, since the republican government lacked enough funds to provide every town with a Civil Guard post and to support the numerous concentrations of guards in one province or another, local governments and private individuals were allowed to sponsor guards' housing.[75] If, as often occurred during the Second Republic, Socialists took control of a local government and withdrew official support, then the Civil Guard was forced to look to wealthy individuals to make up the difference. For example, when the towns of Llerena and Monasterio (both in Badajoz Province) decided that they were not going to provide guards a *casas-cuartel* any longer, local property owners offered free accommodations themselves, fearing that without the Civil Guard their persons and property would be unsafe and their town would descend into anarchy.[76]

Second, organizing an homage to the *Benemérita* was another tried-and-true way for local elites to strengthen their alliance with their town's guards that took on new significance because it could be done under a republican guise.[77] These ceremonies were supposed to demonstrate the much sought-after respect that a whole pueblo had for the Civil Guard, reinforcing the relationship between the two. With speeches by prominent figures in the town and the Church overseeing the ceremonies, the reality was that these events allowed townspeople to show guards who was on their side. Although the ceremonies were fairly simple affairs, they seem to have been key events for guards because they were always reported in the *RTGC* and were often attended by the command chief or another high-ranking officer. During most town celebrations, civil guards had to be on duty, but this one was especially for them. Often, the homages involved the donation of a new republican flag to a Civil Guard post, which allowed the organizers to conduct these events under a republican pretext, even though the emphasis was on the Civil Guard rather than the republic. A maid of honor (*madrina*) always presided and presented the flag to the station commandant, her femininity representing the pure soul of the pueblo that the masculine guard would protect. When she was able to praise the guards with the same terms of abnegation, duty, bravery, and order that they used to describe themselves, she affirmed that their mission to bring military values into civilian society was succeeding.[78] All this symbolism was presented as a show of support for the Civil Guard from the entire pueblo, but it was hard to miss the presence of the wealthy and the absence of workers in the audience.[79]

Third, following in the tradition of the caciques, local associations of land-owners and businessmen could attempt to sway the government in the Civil Guard's favor through letters and telegrams of support addressed to the minister of the interior. These gestures served to counteract telegrams of protest sent by the Socialists and to demonstrate to guards who was on their side. Frequently, salutatory telegrams were presented as emanating not just from the propertied but rather from people of all classes. For example, from July to October 1931, the minister of the interior received various telegrams from Guadix (Granada) either praising one Captain Alfonso Cimas or denouncing him for persecuting workers. Those denouncing him, unafraid to antagonize the Civil Guard since they were already attacking it, all mentioned that the telegrams were from explicitly worker organizations, such as the Socialist Party. In contrast, those defending him claimed to represent "all social classes," which seems unlikely, given the telegrams from the workers' organizations. The contrast suggests that property owners were more careful not to violate the Civil Guard's ethic of political neutrality by proclaiming that they represented only one segment of the town and revealing that the Civil Guard's support was indeed only partial.[80]

Whereas the Civil Guard needed the Right to maintain its sense of honor, property owners felt that they needed the Civil Guard to maintain their very existence. The minister of the interior received many telegrams from employer and Catholic groups, written with hints of desperation, pleading for the number of guards in one town or another not to be reduced.[81] When the municipal government of Berlanga (Badajoz) proposed removing its guards, "numerous residents" offered "anything necessary in order to avoid the absence of the Civil Guard, which would create the gravest risk to persons and things."[82] A withdrawal of "the only police force that merits confidence" also alarmed the right-wing agrarian unions of Melilla, who feared the absence of the "only guarantee that sustains the morale of rural workers."[83] The fears of the elites were not totally unfounded. In addition to their frequent deployments to protect property, guards occasionally shielded caciques in their *casas-cuarteles* against angry mobs.[84]

A final source of support was the national right-wing press. The Civil Guard's sense of honor had always demanded public adherence, and, with the coming of the republic, this support became a question of survival in the face of the calls by some Socialists and republicans for the institution's reform or dissolution. Guards had traditionally trusted that the services they performed would speak for themselves, but with the existence of their institution called into question on the national stage, guards needed positive media coverage. The institution's supporters were happy to take on this role as another way to strengthen their relationship with the *Benemérita*, in this case at the national level. The powerful right-wing press provided the vehicle through which to transmit this support. Papers knew how to flatter guards by eulogizing the very aspects of their organizational culture in which guards themselves took the most pride. For example, the center-right *El Imparcial* printed exactly what they wanted to hear when it said that the pueblo saw their institution as "the symbol of integrity, of valor, of discipline, of abnegation, and of patriotism."[85] Guards delighted when newspaper articles praised their institution, and the *RTGC* frequently reprinted these pieces. Invariably, the sources were papers of the Catholic Right, such as *ABC* and *El Debate*. The articles often appeared after an incident of violence involving the institution, so that the Right stood as its defender against potential criticism. The Cortes was also a powerful venue for supporting the Civil Guard not only because detailed summaries of its sessions were reprinted in all the major newspapers, providing free publicity, but also because agrarian and Catholic deputies could act as the Civil Guard's advocates when legislation concerning the institution was under consideration.

All told, civil guards were happy to receive these pledges of support and affirmations of their honor, whether in the Cortes, newspapers, or their local communities, but ultimately the fact that these praises emanated almost exclusively from the right-wing elements of society undermined their claims to political neutrality.

THE CIVIL GUARD:
OLD PRACTICES IN A NEW CONTEXT

While civil guards had to rely on civilian supporters and military prosecutors to reply to the intensified criticism that they faced at the national level under the Republic, they could respond directly to the surge in protests and strikes that accompanied the new regime. In this section, I will demonstrate how civil guards could make political claims of their own in the absence of specific orders during confrontational situations and of any training in crowd-control techniques. Even the RTGC remarked that "in cases of public disorders, doubts and uncertainties almost always arise over the modes, forms, or procedures to follow."[86] The basic guidelines that guards were to follow, their regulations, had remained essentially unaltered for decades, but the higher number of protests that guards had to confront and greater perceived challenges to their honor meant that they resorted to violence in these situations more frequently during the Second Republic.

Usually lacking any specific instructions besides to go monitor or dissolve a protest, civil guards had only the *Cartilla* and *Reglamento para el servicio* to guide them. The republic, eager to demonstrate its ability to maintain order, kept articles of the *Reglamento* intact that encouraged guards to move quickly to suppress with violence any sign of disorder, aggression, or insult on the part of a crowd. The *Reglamento* also took a hard line on those who injured the Civil Guard either verbally or physically, backed by the fact that such offenses fell under military jurisdiction and were defined broadly by the famous article 7 of the Code of Military Justice as "those [cases] that attack and show disregard for the military authorities and those that injure and libel . . . they tend to diminish the prestige or loosen the ties of discipline or subordination of the armed forces."[87]

While guards certainly did not want to be physically injured, just as important to them was avoiding the injury that their honor would receive if they were verbally insulted or had their authority challenged by a physical assault. The commonly heard chant of "Death to the Civil Guard!" touched upon guards' fears of lacking the respect of the public, of physical harm, and of having their institution dissolved altogether. Another favorite cry, "At them who are few!" played on their sense of isolation by challenging their trust in discipline and superior firepower to keep them safe when surrounded by a hostile crowd. The cry also reminded them that those who did not support their institution greatly outnumbered those who did. As for insults to guards' mothers, these were obvious provocations to men for whom honor was so important.[88] All told, the guards' focus on honor made them particularly sensitive to insults and willing to act with violence to suppress them. When guards used force against those who offended them, they were drawing upon a long tradition of deploying physical violence as a defense of one's honor to make the point that the honor of the *Benemérita* in particular must not be infringed.[89]

When a protest was illegal or seemed to be becoming disorderly (such as when insults were thrown at the Civil Guard), the reader will recall that article 7 of the *Cartilla* dictates that a guard's "first weapons should be persuasion and moral strength, resorting to those [weapons] that he carries with him only when he sees himself offended by others or [when] his words have not been enough. In this case, he will always leave in good stead the honor of his arms." Although this article was meant to prevent violence, it made guards reliant on having enough respect from the public to be obeyed, and, when this obedience was not forthcoming, it actually encouraged them to respond with violence. Sometimes persuasion did work, but the problem was that if protesters did not listen to the guards, then the guards were likely to punish the crowd severely for this lack of respect. If guards failed at their attempts to persuade, regulations required them to sound a bugle call of warning twice before using force to dissolve a protest.[90] Unfortunately, most Civil Guard posts did not have a bugler, so they were reduced to shouting their warnings, and often these could not be heard amidst the general din of a protest.[91] After the warnings, the guards were to open fire and were also to do so at any time if they were attacked. In other words, they did not have to wait to be attacked in order to use force; disobedience was enough to legitimize such action, once persuasion and warnings had been tried.[92] After the crowd dispersed (or, more likely, fled in panic), the last step was to arrest a large number of "ring leaders" to make clear that members of the crowd were the guilty parties, even if the guards had been the ones causing all the serious casualties. Very commonly in such instances, the casualty count at the end of the day would be one or two guards lightly wounded and several protesters dead and severely wounded.

Part of the problem was that the Civil Guard's regulations left few intermediate options between a violation of the law and the application of force.
This situation sparked a debate among guards about whether they should,
as one letter to the RTGC put it, "Ensure cold compliance with Article 7 of the
Cartilla or abandon the field?"[93] Given their commitment to exact obedience,
it seems that almost all guards would have, at least in theory, favored cold
compliance.[94] However, in practice, guards had the option of delaying the application of deadly force once the line of legality had been crossed, buying
protesters more time to disperse. The most common device for doing this was
firing shots in the air, which was not according to regulations because, so the
thinking went, every shot a guard fired was meant for a guilty party, but a stray
bullet fired in the air could hit someone who was innocent, potentially making
the guard liable for manslaughter.[95] Nevertheless, the practice was widespread,
belying the assertion that the guards followed their orders and nothing more.

Judging from the opinions expressed in the RTGC, the Civil Guard's culture
was at least open to those guards who chose to delay the application of force,
despite all the talk of blind adherence to the regulations. The guards' image of
themselves as humanitarian servants of the community served as a counter-
vailing force. The RTGC praised a Civil Guard detachment that, when attacked
with insults, rocks, and small arms fire on its way to retrieve a stolen sewing
machine, retreated instead of opening fire, leaving three of their number injured. It concludes: "Tell us if [these] few civil guards, whose powerful arms can
cause hundreds of deaths per minute, could have been more humanitarian."
When angry workers attacked two *parejas* in Arroyomolinos de León (Huelva),
they were beaten up and disarmed (although "it is very difficult to disarm a
pareja") when they tried to respond with persuasion rather than immediately
opening fire. The RTGC praised their "humanitarian sentiments," even if it
ultimately determined that their "prudence and philanthropy brought them
grim consequences."[96] In other words, being disarmed could still be considered
honorable if framed within the context of the humanitarian aspect of the Civil
Guard's mission.

The other factor depriving guards of intermediate options for crowd control was their weaponry, which was designed for military use and did not lend
itself to nonlethal coercion. The regulation Mauser rifle was built for soldiers
to have a long range, a rapid rate of fire, and plenty of stopping power, at the
cost of being heavy and bulky. Unfortunately, these same features made the

Mauser about the opposite of the ideal policing weapon, which would have a short range, high maneuverability, and the ability to deliver nonlethal force. Although guards were required to keep their barrels pointed in the air unless they were about to fire, the deadly potential alone of the Mausers could aid guards' efforts to persuade protesters to back down, even if such a tactic meant they were obtaining obedience through fear rather than respect.[97] Indeed, the Mauser was indicative of the orientation of guards to see conflicts with protesters who had crossed the line of legality more as battles than situations to be de-escalated, and, since they regularly carried 150 rounds of ammunition, they were ready for a prolonged firefight.[98] Their entirely military training and lack of any formal instruction in crowd-control techniques meant that seeing these situations in any other way was not even a possibility for most.

If, in the end, whether or not the Civil Guard's response to a protest turned violent largely depended upon how quickly it proceeded from warnings to the use of its deadly weapons, then the emotions, shaped by their culture, of the particular guards on the scene were at least as important in determining the outcome of the confrontation as their regulations. They always claimed that in every use of violence they were simply doing their duty, but fear seems to have often been a factor in cases when they turned to violence quickly. With the law giving them almost complete impunity, it was all too easy for guards to pull their triggers at the first sign of danger. In one embarrassing instance, when a group of suspected thieves failed to obey orders immediately to stop and get on the ground, civil guards opened fire, wounding two, before the suspects had time to reveal they were actually *carabineros* in the middle of an undercover operation.[99] Much depended upon the ability of the commanding officer on the scene, usually a noncommissioned or junior officer, to control the urge to apply disproportionate force. Here is where festering mutual animosity between a pueblo and its guards could come to have deadly consequences. For example, Socialists in a town in Córdoba Province praised the lieutenant of their section for avoiding a "day of mourning" when their sergeant, supposedly under the influence of property owners, had guards use their rifles "to calm hunger" during a bread march.[100]

Certainly, guards were aware that they had a dangerous job, and their speeches and writings were full of talk of sacrifice and a willingness to die in the line of duty. One corporal wrote in the *RTGC* that guards were "opposing gunfire and the explosion of bombs with their brave chests, generously and stoically shedding their blood in the holocaust of order, peace, and law, an august and silent mission that makes them worthy of high praise."[101] Nevertheless, death was not something that they sought out either. These were men interested in preserving their careers and their families, not the *africanistas* shouting slogans like "Long live death!" Yet what they feared was a loss of honor as much as a loss of life or limb.

Perhaps here is the place to return to the question of why the Civil Guard was so violent during the republic. The problem was essentially one of a disconnect between continuities on the part of the Civil Guard's organizational culture and shifts on the part of the political culture of Spain's working classes in particular. The Civil Guard's lethal armament and preexisting practices for policing protests, largely developed during the Restoration period, remained unchanged during the republic. The regulations and institutional habits that constituted that repertoire gave guards few options for responding in a nonviolent manner to disorder or insult. Their culture of intolerance for both disorder and insult did not help the situation. Therefore, put in the simplest terms, the Civil Guard's organizational culture contributed to making violence a possible outcome of a confrontation between guards and protesters, and the increased number of strikes and protests during the Second Republic meant that that outcome occurred more frequently.

Insofar as it also addresses republican policy decisions regarding the Civil Guard, this chapter covers ground well-trodden by previous works on the Civil Guard in the Second Republic. But rather than staying at the level of national policy making, the chapter examines the consequences of these decisions on sociopolitical claims made at the local level by Socialists, right-wing elements, and the Civil Guard itself. The picture that emerges is essentially one of institutional continuity in the midst of rapid political change. The new freedoms of assembly and speech introduced by the republic resulted in a dramatic shift to aggressive advocacy in the streets for further change, but it was hard for both republican and Socialist leaders to adjust their old habits after decades of opposition. Republicans quickly saw the usefulness of the Civil Guard for maintaining their newfound political power; however, in focusing their efforts on building a new urban police force, they failed to see that changes to the

Civil Guard's equipment and tactics might also be necessary for it to maintain order in a context of open and vigorous sociopolitical contestation in rural areas as well. While some of the voices with the most practical ideas about how to improve policing in this context came from civil guards themselves, if change to a military culture comes from senior commanders who embrace ideas emanating from below and get support from civilian leadership, then it is no surprise that these ideas remained unheard. Not only did the civilian leadership (the republicans in government) fail to think creatively themselves about how to reform the Civil Guard while maintaining its loyalty but they also kept in place a director general who was more interested in defending the military honor of the institution than in reforming it.

Meanwhile, Socialists leaders like Margarita Nelken criticized the Civil Guard in the mass press, in the Cortes, and through letters of complaint to please rank-and-file party members eager for radical change, but their remarks, which guards perceived as offenses to their honor, further soured relations between the Civil Guard and the working classes without achieving the reform or dissolution of the institution. Another consequence of this intensified criticism was that guards had to rely on landowners and other conservatives more than ever to provide support at both the local and national levels to reaffirm their institution's honor. The resulting appearance of favoritism also contributed to the increased animosity from the working classes. When these tensions at the local level resulted in violence, it would have profound implications for the political course of the republic at the national level.

SIX

CASTILBLANCO

The Ultimate Disrespect

At around 10:00 p.m. on New Year's Eve in 1931, a detachment of civil guards arrived in the town of Castilblanco to find all four guards who had been stationed there lying dead in the street, beaten to death with sticks, stones, knives, and the butts of their own rifles. How had these brutal murders occurred? The right-wing press deduced that they could have only been the work of semisavage peasants led by revolutionary provocateurs, while the Socialists believed that the social structures that created the oppression and poverty of the rural working class were to blame. More recently, historians have found an explanation in the increasing mobilization of rural workers as socialist and anarchist ideas and practices made their way from the national level down to Spain's more isolated areas.[1] This chapter considers this mobilization as just one of the factors leading to the outburst of violence, the others being the Civil Guard's police culture, the policies of the republican state, and the choices of individual actors.[2]

The deaths at Castilblanco had their origins in the dynamic between the increased mass mobilization in Badajoz Province under the republic and the Civil Guard's rigid organizational culture. As the Socialists mobilized Badajoz's landless peasantry to demand agrarian reform, the Civil Guard responded to the protests with harsh tactics. The object of protest shifted to the Civil Guard itself. The institution's normal operating procedures prevented incidents like Castilblanco in most cases, but in the tense atmosphere of the republic, a few key mistakes by individuals in Castilblanco were all that was needed to turn one town's anger into deadly violence.

The influence that Castilblanco had on the history of the republic resulted less from the incident itself than from the ways in which opposing forces sought to shape how it was perceived by the public at the national level. The leaderships of the two principal groups involved, the Civil Guard and the PSOE, did not want to see news of Castilblanco spark further violence, but the organizational cultures of both institutions, combined with the provocative actions of a few prominent figures, steered them to courses of action that only augmented tensions further. The freedom of the press allowed by the republic made shaping how an event was portrayed by third parties in the papers especially important for public relations. But Director General Sanjurjo, who was more familiar with the army's military values than public relations in a democratic context, was so shocked by Castilblanco's insult to the town's civil guards that he made controversial comments to reporters that squandered his chance to use the incident as a way to build public sympathy for the Civil Guard. Meanwhile, the Socialist leadership advised moderation, but some prominent figures, like Margarita Nelken, looking to please the radical rank and file, continued to repeat the party's line on the Civil Guard's role in the exploitative structures of rural Spain, destroying the Socialists' chances of improving relations with the institution.

THE LOCAL INCIDENT

The Origins of the Conflict

The origins of the Castilblanco incident are to be found in the conflict between the mass mobilizations enabled by the republic and the Civil Guard's duty to enforce the laws of the liberal state. The town of Castilblanco is located in Badajoz Province, one of the poorest in Spain and one where the latifundia system of land tenure was most prevalent.[3] A small number of landowners held most of the land in huge tracts and raised livestock or low-intensity crops like olives.[4] They needed large numbers of laborers for the olive harvest, but these laborers did not make enough during that time to sustain themselves for the rest of the year when they were mostly unemployed.[5]

During the Restoration period, protests over food, taxes, and unemployment, usually led by women, were common. However, in the early twentieth century, a new force for political mobilization began to emerge: unions, and particularly the Socialist UGT (and subsequently its agrarian arm, the Federación Nacional de Trabajadores de la Tierra [National Federation of Workers of the Land or FNTT]). Strikes gradually became the primary means for rural workers to express their grievances, making Badajoz a classic rural example of the shift to mass politics that was simultaneously taking place in urban areas.[6] The advent of the republic mobilized Badajoz's landless laborers, who hoped for immediate improvements in their social and economic conditions. Drawing on their new strategy of direct challenges to local socioeconomic structures, the number of strikes in the province soared, as did the number of property invasions as the poor gathered acorns on private lands.[7] These acts drew the poor into intensified conflict with the Civil Guard, which was charged with policing strikes and protecting private property.

At the national level, the Socialist leadership wanted to moderate the rank and file's impulse to direct action in order to allow the republic's agrarian reform measures time to take effect. There were forces pushing it in a more radical direction, however. Socialists needed to stake out a distinct position for themselves as they jockeyed with the left republicans for power within governing coalitions at the national, regional, and local levels. At the same time, Socialists needed to satisfy their membership base, especially since there was a danger that they would lose ground in Badajoz Province to the anarchist CNT, which was calling for the immediate occupation of large estates.[8] Some of the most radical Socialists, such as Margarita Nelken, responded to these pressures by sharpening their own rhetoric, using denunciations of the Civil Guard as a way to deflect the anger of the landless laborers. These Socialists judged that alienating the institution was a small price to pay for the mobilizing power that criticism of the force could have.

The resulting tensions between the Civil Guard and the Socialists in Badajoz reached their peak in Almendralejo, one of the province's larger towns. On November 7, 1931, some forty people occupied hunting estates in the area, and Civil Governor Manuel Álvarez Ugena, who was a member of Prime Minister Azaña's Acción Republicana, called in a concentration of civil guards—an example of the government's policy of deploying the Civil Guard despite the danger of it escalating the situation. On November 29, these guards were ordered to protect strikebreakers who were going to work during an olive harvest strike. Strikers threw rocks at the guards, and they responded by opening fire. The Civil Guard command chief, Lieutenant Colonel Pedro Pereda Sanz, requested that Álvarez Ugena send a military judge to investigate accusations that his men had been insulted. By December 17, the Civil Guard had arrested fourteen people, including the mayor, who was blamed for fomenting the protests. The FNTT then announced a general strike for the thirtieth and thirty-first of that month to demand the dismissal of both Pereda and Álvarez Ugena, the release of all prisoners, and the appointment of a special judge to investigate abuses committed against workers.[9] Minister of the Interior Casares Quiroga concentrated fifty civil guards in the province for the days of the strike and ordered troops from Madrid to supply food and guard public transportation in the provincial capital.[10]

What began as a clash between the pueblo of Almendralejo's idea of justice and that of the Civil Guard became a larger political struggle as soon as the general strike was declared. The Civil Guard had already injured several workers in Badajoz since the start of the republic, but only when it challenged the Socialists politically—by arresting their affiliates—did they fight back. The strike gave the restless rank and file a cause around which to unify, and, if successful, it would demonstrate that the Socialists were the ones effectively in control of the province, with virtual veto power over who was appointed to positions of authority there.

In the days leading up to the strike, the Socialist propaganda machine went into action to drum up support for it. *La Verdad Social*, the UGT organ in Badajoz, printed several articles criticizing the comportment of the Civil Guard in the province. Nelken, meanwhile, published a caustic open letter to Casares Quiroga in *El Socialista* in which she denounced the application of military justice in Almendralejo and accused the civil guards there of being defenders of the landowners and provocateurs.[11] Nevertheless, the strike was legal, and its leaders intended it to be peaceful.[12]

Local Tensions and Violence

It was within this context of local, provincial, and national tensions between civil guards, Socialists, anarcho-syndicalists, and republicans that the strike leading to the Castilblanco incident began. Meanwhile, within Castilblanco, local frictions between guards, newly mobilized rural workers, and town elites were the immediate causes of the incident. The Socialists, in their drive to extend their reach, had probably arrived in the town around the time that the republic began. They had established a *casa del pueblo* (house of the people), as local UGT centers were known, that connected the town to the national movement by receiving a copy of *El Socialista*.[13] While its residents most likely had only a vague idea of their union's doctrines and structures, the idea of the strike as a way for them to challenge Castilblanco's status quo was now on the table.

This status quo was one of poverty and stark socioeconomic inequality. Castilblanco (population approximately three thousand) was located in a district so remote that its official name was Extremaduran Siberia (Siberia Extremeña).[14] The road to the town was almost impassable for automobiles, and the soil was so poor that most people survived on hunting and raising goats.[15] The land-tenure problem was also extreme here; ownership of over half the land was concentrated in the hands of less than 2 percent of the property holders.[16] The mayor, Felipe Maganto, was a member of the Radical Party who had been in office since before the republic and was himself a security guard for a large property owner.[17]

Stationed in Castilblanco in part to protect these properties were four civil guards, José Blanco, Francisco González Borrego, José Matos González, and Agripino Simón Martín, who would also be the ones to face the nascent political mobilization of the townspeople. These guards were typical examples of the generation that served under the republic as well as of the relations guards often had with the towns they policed. Two of them, Matos González and Simón Martín, had previously been in combat while serving in the army in Morocco. In addition, González Borrego and Matos González were from Badajoz Province. González Borrego had been stationed in Castilblanco since 1926 after requesting a transfer back to Badajoz, and he was now engaged to a woman from the town, so he presumably had good relations with the pueblo.[18]

The story of the station commandant, Corporal Blanco, illustrates how the disconnect between the Civil Guard's culture of strict enforcement of the law and sensitivity to honor and a pueblo's more flexible sense of justice could create tensions that could be accentuated by both the mass political mobilizations that accompanied the republic and differences between individual guards. Aside from González Borrego, all of the guards in Castilblanco, including Corporal Blanco, had been in the town for a year or less. According to a local newspaper, Blanco was popular during his eight years stationed at a town in his native Galicia, but, judging from a letter he wrote less than a month before his death to his mentor for the corporal's exam, his relations with the townspeople in more restive Badajoz were anything but cordial.[19] He seems to have been a practitioner of James Q. Wilson's legalistic style of policing, of which the Duque de Ahumada would have approved. However, his predecessor in Castilblanco had had more of the watchman style. When Blanco began making daily arrests of people gathering acorns from private land, a customary practice in this area, the townspeople became angry and confused. There were several confrontations and one attempt to assault the *casa-cuartel*, but Blanco only redoubled his efforts. He concluded his letter by bragging that he was tidying up the town for the civil governor and the "people of order" by leaving the acorn gatherers "more docile than lambs."[20] Blanco steadfastly refused to adapt the strict adherence to the law that was part of the Civil Guard's culture to this Extremaduran pueblo's more informal idea of social justice. When it became obvious that he was not winning the respect of much of the town, he contented himself with only the approval of the town's elite by categorizing them as the "people of order." Less than a month after he wrote his letter, Blanco's failure to reconcile the cultures of the Civil Guard and the pueblo would cost him and his men their lives.

It was in this context of tension between the civil guards and the towns-people of Castilblanco that news arrived that the FNTT was to go on strike on the thirtieth and thirty-first of December 1931. Some three hundred people marched through town on the thirtieth without incident, shouting denunci-ations of *caciquismo* and the Civil Guard.[21] In framing their protest as a strike and in asking for more than simply bread, the townspeople of Castilblanco were shifting to a form of claims making that sought structural change rather than just material benefits.[22] The town's civil guards, meanwhile, stayed in their *casa-cuartel* on this first day, despite the fact that the strike was technically illegal since it had not been registered with the municipality. The people of Castilblanco, through their show of collective strength, had forced Blanco to allow them to bend the rules.

The next day, however, the choices of several individuals proved key steps in the chain of events that led to the Castilblanco deaths. The first decision was made by Mayor Maganto, who, perhaps fearing that the protest was really about challenging the local power structure as much as about the dismissal of the civil governor and command chief, ordered Blanco to dissolve it on the second day.[23] Blanco and his three civil guards followed the mayor's request, although not without some trepidation. Blanco made a second fateful decision by marching all three straight into the crowd, inexplicably ignoring the standard Civil Guard practice of having them stand to the side, while he went to ask the president of the *casa del pueblo* to dissolve the protest.[24] What mostly likely happened next is that a woman attempted to join the crowd and Simón Martín pushed her back with his rifle. Some of the protesters grabbed his rifle to stop him, and he responded by firing the weapon, killing a townsperson. The crowd, horrified, fell upon all four guards and killed them with whatever weapons they could find, with only one protester injured in the tumult.[25] The incident had all the characteristics of what Randall Collins calls forward panic. In a moment of extreme tension and fear, a panicked emotional rush trumps rational consideration of how to resolve the situation.[26] Yet when the panic subsided, the townspeople's contempt for the guards remained. A woman brought the dead civilian's body into her home, but, in a final show of disrespect, the guards' bodies were left in the street for hours.[27]

Expanding Socialist influence in Badajoz and the tensions that process engendered between townspeople and the Civil Guard were the causes of the strike in Castilblanco, but it was the choices of a few individuals that provided the immediate conditions for such a bizarre eruption of violence. Despite their strict military culture, civil guards had to make adjustments to the informal structures of town life. Corporal Blanco took pride in taking his regulations' mandate to enforce the letter of the law literally. However, in so doing, he created the exact problem for himself that the sociologist William Foote Whyte also observed in Boston's North End in the 1930s: "The policeman who takes a strictly legalistic view of his duties cuts himself off from the personal relations necessary to enable him to serve as a mediator of disputes in his area."[28] If there had not been such a stark contrast in the way in which Blanco and his predecessor had interpreted their duty to protect private property, Castilblanco's residents may not have been resentful enough to turn against their civil guards with violence. Even on the day of the strike, if Maganto had not called out the Civil Guard, if Blanco had not sent his men into the crowd, or if Simón Martín had not gotten involved in a scuffle, the deaths would have been avoided. In the tense atmosphere of the Second Republic, the poor choices of just a few enlisted guards and the spontaneous fury of a crowd were enough to cause a tragedy that was to have consequences at the national level.

THE NATIONAL AFTERMATH

Sanjurjo, the Civil Guard, and the Supporters

Castilblanco was not the first instance in which political protesters had killed civil guards. Yet in the aftermath of the Castilblanco incident, for the first time since 1874, some civil guards contemplated rebellion, a fact that leads to the question of how the incident could have pushed them to consider such a radical violation of their commitment to serving the government in power. Like at the local level, the answer again lies in the incompatibility between the Civil Guard's rigid culture of honor and the republic's game of mass politics. To begin with, guards' desires to take their own private revenge on Castilblanco's residents did not create good publicity. The townspeople there had not just killed but dishonored their guards. Such an obvious refutation of the idea that the pueblo respected the Civil Guard led its members to conclude that outside forces must have been at work, and their fears that Margarita Nelken would dissolve their beloved corps made a conspiracy theory all too easy to develop. From there, one individual again drove events forward; in this case, it was Director General Sanjurjo, whose own sense of military honor led him to make impolitic statements to the papers. His remarks were welcomed by the right-wing press, however, which wanted to score political points on the Socialists while solidifying conservatives' relationships with the Civil Guard. Castilblanco was a key moment in the history of the republic because it helped to increase the anxiety and fear that Spain's disparate counterrevolutionary elements felt toward their perceived enemies, and these emotions would eventually enable them to unite during the Civil War.[29] As for the Civil Guard, the reaction of Sanjurjo and his supporters began a realignment of its values by suggesting that rural workers were not worthy of at least ostensibly equal treatment and that the corps's ultimate loyalties lay with the *patria* rather than the government in power.

Since the civil guards were the republic's only rural policemen, they had to be the ones at the Castilblanco crime scene, even though it would have been difficult for them to have a dispassionate response to the deaths of their comrades. After doing some investigating, the guards that Lieutenant Colonel Pereda Sanz had dispatched to the town began making arrests, detaining some fifty people in the town hall.[30] The guards could not resist retaliating in some way for the four deaths, which they considered to be the ultimate insult to their institution's honor. They forced the prisoners to remain standing with their hands in the air on the town hall balcony for an hour and a half, hitting anyone who lowered his arms with their rifle butts.[31] Guards had reacted similarly if not more brutally in other incidents in the past, such as in the repression of the Jerez uprising of 1892. In the context of the republic, however, their opponents responded to such actions not with a bomb but rather with a media campaign that allowed them to turn public attention away from the murders and construct a counternarrative of Castilblanco in which guards were once again the victimizers rather than the victims.

At the national level, the Civil Guard's director general was its public face, and his reaction to an event like Castilblanco would speak for the entire corps. In letting Sanjurjo remain in the post, the republic allowed a man more adept at defending his military honor than tactful public relations guide how the incident shaped perceptions of the Civil Guard. On January 4, Sanjurjo arrived in the city of Badajoz for the fallen guards' funeral and to meet with their families.[32] Thousands of people attended the event, and the dignitaries present consisted of the usual display of the Civil Guard's supporters. But it was Sanjurjo who received the most attention from the press.[33] He gave a tearful speech at the burial in which he explicitly called the Civil Guard's cult of honor a religion.[34] In a subtle warning to those like Nelken who called for the dissolution of the corps, he added, "Pity Spain the day in which there are no men capable of making the sacrifice as do those who pertain to this institution!"[35] At the same time, he promised that "the Civil Guard, without a spirit of revenge and for which there is no doubt about the nobility of their hearts, will continue doing its duty exactly and at all costs."[36] He could already sense the danger of Castilblanco causing the guards to take further acts of revenge, but he himself was not yet ready to step fully outside the bounds of legality.

After the ceremonies, Sanjurjo's sense of honor could no longer permit him to restrain his remarks in an interview he granted the local newspaper. He prided himself on not being a politician, but it was at moments like this when he would have been wise to watch his words, for the interview was quoted in other papers across the country. He began the interview by declaring that "in a corner of Badajoz Province there is a Riffian hideout. General Sanjurjo's subordinates [that is, the civil guards] have the mission of bringing the rule of justice to it." He went on to describe the town as "the most deplorable possible. I didn't know that such savage towns still existed in Spain."[37] It seems that his visit to Castilblanco prior to the funeral to see the guards' corpses had had a profound effect on him. In drawing a comparison between the townspeople and the Moroccans that many Spaniards viewed as racially inferior, he was contributing to the idea that the kind of brutality seen in Morocco could be employed against the rural poor in Spain as well. His statement envisioned policing rural Spain as a fight to pacify supposedly uncivilized people, rather than as an effort to win the respect of all citizens.

Sanjurjo's next statement was even more provocative, shifting from blaming local "savage" townspeople to theorizing about a national conspiracy: "The incident had been premeditated. Of that there is absolutely no doubt in my mind. Everything had followed a plan. The attack on the *Benemérita*, the destruction of that post, were a deed agreed upon by the leaders of the movement." Even as he demeaned them, he also refused to believe that the residents of a pueblo could have so disrespected the Civil Guard all by themselves. Therefore, there must have been a conspiracy directed from the outside, and Nelken was the perfect suspect since she had been criticizing the Civil Guard and she was one of the organizers of the strike. Indeed, her newer kind of attack on the institution's honor upset him even more than the town's physical assault: "We are not pained by the sacrifice of our lives; since its creation this institution has answered the call of duty without regard for distance or effort. What pains us is that this loyalty to our mission is not recognized and that preaching against our discipline and our sentiments is given free rein."[38] He even pointed to Nelken directly, remarking on "the danger to the social peace posed by the continued hostility manifested by some political organizations [i.e., the Socialists] against the *benemérita* institution. The absurd thing is . . . that an office of information has been created against the Civil Guard and that this office is led by Margarita Nelken, who is not even a Spanish citizen, but rather German. That is to say, she comes from the country that has the best-organized espionage in the entire world."[39] His outrage at being challenged by a woman and, supposedly, a foreigner had made him into a conspiracy theorist.

While Sanjurjo's official speech may have urged his men to be restrained, his off-the-cuff remarks, which seemed to reveal his true feelings, were also broadcast nationwide in the press. He believed the Civil Guard was the only bastion holding back social revolution, and so any undermining of the *Bene-mérita* must be halted at all costs. In other words, defending the Civil Guard (and thereby, in his mind, the social order) was more important than defending the republic. Here one sees the seeds of the redefining of the Civil Guard's idea of loyalty that Sanjurjo would use to justify his *pronunciamiento* less than a year later.

This talk of a crackdown to restore order or even to take revenge appealed to some civil guards who feared that they might meet a fate similar to that of their comrades in Castilblanco. There were rumors that guards were ready to rebel then and there. One guard recalls that his comrades in the Fourth Division (Seville) were prepared to take this step against a government that "tolerated the insults and infamous injuries" to their institution.[40] They concluded that "we had to adopt an attitude consistent with the magnitude of the Extremaduran tragedy. We could not and should not remain in suicidal and cowardly passivity." In their desire to avenge Castilblanco's insult to their honor, they fantasized about extralegal acts of revenge. One of them wanted to shoot "all the authors, accomplices, and accessories, and, above all, the political instigators, without waiting for the end of the trial . . . [thereby] taking justice into our own hands." In the end, they decided that they would put their trust totally in the hands of Sanjurjo regarding what course of action to take.[41]

Upon Sanjurjo's return to Madrid, he had a meeting with the field officers there. They, too, were ready to rebel against the government, which they blamed for Castilblanco. However, despite his bravado at the funeral, Sanjurjo was not yet prepared to take this step. According to Esteban-Infantes, he explained that if the Civil Guard rebelled, it would do so alone and would seem to be doing so only for its own benefit, rather than for that of the *patria*.[42] Even as Sanjurjo made the political calculus about whether or not to rebel, he was sure to keep in mind public opinion and introduced the idea of the need to defend the Spanish nation in order to maintain at least the pretense of political neutrality.

Sanjurjo was not the only one reaffirming his confidence in the Civil Guard. The Right mobilized as always to show its support through favorable press, religious ceremonies, and financial assistance.[43] For instance, the conservative Valencian paper *Las Provincias* had effusive praise for Sanjurjo and the

Civil Guard, asserting that "his labor is among the most significant and patriotic that has been done in Spain" and that "without Sanjurjo and without the Civil Guard, the nation would not survive in these times."[44] Funerals for the fallen guards were held around the country, but seem to have been more about demonstrating the Right's support of the Civil Guard than mourning the dead at Castilblanco. Perhaps the best example was a mass in Bilbao to which guards were invited.[45] According to left-republican Vicente Fatrás, after the service, both the clerics and guards joined in a pro–Civil Guard demonstration in which the crowd shouted not only "Long live the Civil Guard" but also "Death to the Republic."[46] Contributions to the families of the deceased civil guards were also a symbol of support. The Castilblanco incident received so much attention that the Civil Guard was able to give about twice as much money to each Castilblanco family as to those of the other guards who died in the line of duty in 1931 and 1932.[47]

The fact that an incident in one of Spain's most far-flung corners could provoke such a nationwide uproar speaks to the symbolic importance of the Civil Guard as a synecdoche for the question of how the institutions and practices of the monarchy would adapt and be adapted to the new republic. The incident's aftermath was an opportunity for the institution to earn sympathy from the public by highlighting the sacrifices that it was making for the republic. However, the consequences of leaving Sanjurjo in place as director general became clear when he let the *africanista* military culture of which he had been a part shape his response, demeaning the townspeople that guards lived amongst while seeming to place his concern for honor above his loyalty to the republic. Meanwhile, the Civil Guard did receive much sympathy from the public, but its sources were exclusively the right-wing press, the Church, and the propertied classes—hardly sending a message that the whole society was behind the institution's efforts.

The Socialists Take Back the Narrative

That four civil guards had been killed during a Socialist strike was embarrassing for the movement and threatened to undermine both its campaign against the Civil Guard and its public image more generally. Socialists would have to defend themselves in three key arenas of democratic contestation: the press, the parliament, and the courts. At first, party moderates took the lead in the Cortes by presenting a muted response acceptable to their republican allies, but more radical critics of the Civil Guard were already returning to their old talking points in the press. By the time the alleged murderers of the four guards were put on trial, the old Civil Guard practice of torturing prisoners enabled the Socialists to reverse the dominant Castilblanco narrative, turning the town's residents into the victims. The Socialists may have succeeded in neutralizing the political advantage that the Civil Guard and its supporters stood to gain in the aftermath of the incident, but their continued criticism of the institution, without regard for its sensitivity to insult, ensured that any chance of détente between the two was lost, setting the stage for further conflict.

The responses to Castilblanco by the Socialists in the press followed a pattern similar to those of the Right. Initially, Socialists also denounced the killings. Francisco Largo Caballero denied that his party had ever had violent intentions against the Civil Guard and even claimed that Castilblanco's *casa del pueblo* had not been admitted to the UGT.[48] Nevertheless, after a few days, some Socialists began to search for ways to divert attention away from the fact that the civil guards had died during one of the Socialists' strikes to their own understanding of the underlying causes of the republic's violence.[49] Whereas the Right saw the causes of the incident in the combination of the savage nature of the villagers and the incendiary rhetoric that the republic permitted, the Socialists looked to socioeconomic structures, blaming poverty and, as usual, *caciquismo*. Yet in their eagerness to seize control of the narrative in the press, Socialists wound up repeating, even in the wake of these deaths, talking points that guards had already found offensive. The result was an increased tension between the two groups that began to approach the level of animosity between the Civil Guard and the anarchists.

Some Socialists seized the opportunity presented by Castilblanco to reiterate their denunciations of the Civil Guard. For instance, Nelken, in an editorial published in *El Socialista* just days after the incident, stopped just short of arguing that the murders were justified. She claimed that when some townspeople had asked for work, Corporal Blanco told them that "the work that he would give them would be the rod." She continued, "We are the first to recognize that the death of those four civil guards of Castilblanco constitutes a shameful act of barbarism, but we cannot help but also recognize that beasts will be beasts, and that the man treated like a beast and induced to be a beast cannot, in the moment, respond in any other way."[50]

At this point, while rebellion was little more than a fantasy for civil guards, they could make at least a token effort to silence people who criticized them like Nelken. Military prosecutors filed charges against several Socialists, including Nelken, for insulting the Civil Guard in the press, but, probably not coincidentally, all of the authors were deputies in the Cortes, and the body never granted a suspension of their parliamentary immunity. Nelken was the most common target of these accusations; she had at least three cases opened against her for articles in *La Verdad Social* and *El Socialista*, written both in the lead-up and aftermath of the FNTT strike.[51] All told, such accusations appear to have been little more than nuisances to the accused, given their parliamentary immunity, but they did create at least the illusion that something was being done to defend the Civil Guard's honor against insult.

Meanwhile, democratic governance and a free press meant that an event as shocking as Castilblanco would also be debated in the parliament and the courts, and the press would relate all that transpired to the public. These forums brought the different interpretations of the incident into dialogue with each other, highlighting the agendas and motivations behind each one. In the Cortes, the debate within the PSOE about how aggressively to target an institution like the Civil Guard that was part of the republican state reduced the Socialists to a tepid response that simply repeated standard talking points. There was even more division among the republican parties, whose reactions ranged from strong condemnation of the Civil Guard by the Radical Socialists to an equally strong condemnation of the Socialists by the Radicals. Although Prime Minister Azaña could still find near consensus in suggesting that the institution should at least be respected as part of the republic, how long such agreement would be possible was an open question.

The Cortes was in recess until January 5, 1932. On that day, the Castilblanco media frenzy was at its height, and how the issue would be addressed in the Cortes was awaited with anticipation.[52] In fact, tensions indicative of the disunity within the PSOE erupted even before the debate began. That morning, Nelken gave an impassioned speech to the Socialist parliamentary group in which she spoke of the poverty of Castilblanco's residents and the abuses of the Civil Guard. Manuel Muiño retorted that she was a dangerous provocateur of Badajoz's workers. It was agreed that Andrés Saborit, who did not represent Badajoz, would speak for the Socialists in parliament that day.[53]

The raucous debate before the full Cortes captured how both the various republican parties and the Socialists used Castilblanco for their own political ends and how even Nelken's own party rejected her challenge to the patriarchy of the Spanish political system.[54] Radical Diego Hidalgo began the discussion with rhetoric as harsh as any in the right-wing press, more focused on discrediting the Socialists than the Castilblanco incident itself. He called for the application of the Ley de Defensa de la República and argued that the Socialists should have protested to the government or the Cortes rather than launching a strike. He then went on to suggest that the strike had been provoked by two or three Socialist leaders, among them the deputy for Badajoz Nicolás de Pablo, who Hidalgo claimed had been stripped of his post in the provincial government.[55] Later in the debate, the Carlist Joaquín Beunza accused two other Socialist deputies for Badajoz, Nelken and Muiño, of being the instigators.[56] Nelken tried to defend herself, but members of her own party instead escorted her out of the chamber.[57] Meanwhile, women gathered outside the congress to denounce Nelken as a foreigner and demand her expulsion from the country, while also raising cheers for the civil guards who were guarding the building. [58]

As for the Socialist who was allowed to speak, Saborit reiterated his party's talking points, arguing that the strike was peaceful and that structural problems, such as *caciquismo*, poverty, and poor communications, rather than particular individuals, were responsible for the crime.[59] The Radical Socialist Eduardo Ortega y Gasset went further than the Socialists and took the opportunity of the death of four civil guards to criticize their institution and call for its reform.[60] Some of his points echo suggestions that some guards had made in the *RTGC*, such as that the Civil Guard was the only gendarmerie in Europe still armed with rifles, that military jurisdiction should not be applied to such cases, and that "we have to concern ourselves with the mentality of the armed force with which we have to defend the public order." He even proposed that the force's revered *Cartilla* be changed.[61] However, he also, as Azaña put it, raised for discussion "the prestige of the institution, as if these guards had been not the killed, but rather the killers."[62]

Ortega y Gasset's speech sparked a debate among several deputies over whether or not crimes against the Civil Guard should be tried by court-martial. At this point, Azaña felt the need to intervene as a voice of moderation. He pointed out that the deputies had turned Castilblanco into a political question but that it was not the fault of any political party. He denounced those who used the Castilblanco dead as a political weapon, observing that to attack the

Civil Guard was to attack the republic, of which the institution was now an obedient part.[63] This position suggested that left republicans had fully accepted the Civil Guard as a necessary component of a republic that was not afraid to assert its authority. The fact that everyone except the Radicals applauded the speech, considered one of Azaña's best, demonstrates that at this point there was still room for the full acceptance of the Civil Guard into the republican system.[64]

At the July 17 to 19, 1933, trial in Badajoz of those accused of the murders at Castilblanco, competing interpretations of the incident also collided, but this time the Socialists and the military were the ones to confront each other. For the military, the trial was an open-and-shut case of bringing twenty-two residents of Castilblanco to justice not so much for the murder of the civil guards as for offending their honor. As for the Socialists, the trial was about working within the republican system (in this case, its courts) to point out to a mass audience the continuities between that system and the monarchy. The Socialist team of defenders had little chance of winning the case, but they could highlight that the Civil Guard had tortured prisoners, that a court-martial was trying civilians in peacetime, and that the real problem was *caciquismo*. In sum, the two parties presented sharply contrasting beliefs about the source of political violence under the republic. For the military, that source was provocateurs and disorderly elements who refused to respect the armed forces. For the Socialists, that source was a repressive social structure in which the state, including institutions like the Civil Guard, colluded with the rich to suppress the poor.

The prosecuting attorney, Ricardo Calderón, accused twenty-two people of insulting the armed forces, intending to insult the armed forces, illegally demonstrating, and profaning corpses.[65] While not typical in legal systems based on English law, in continental Europe, such prohibitions on insulting key national institutions like the armed forces are common, but the extent and severity of enforcement of these provisions can vary widely. In Spain at that time, the punishment could be as severe as death. In the case of Castilblanco, given that, as one of the defense attorneys put it, "No one can affirm with surety who injured or killed," Calderón did not present any murder charges, but that did not matter since he could still ask for the death penalty for six of the accused for insulting the armed forces.[66] He requested prison terms for the rest, including six life sentences.[67] In Spain's inquisitorial military justice system, Calderón had only to guard against the arguments of the defense since the military investigative judge had already laid out the evidence and recommended a guilty verdict. And Calderón had what appeared to be a strong case anyway: many of the defendants had already confessed, some had been found with blood on their clothes and/or with weapons, and there were plenty of witnesses.

As for the defense team, since many of the defendants had made incriminating statements during their initial interrogations (although almost all were later retracted), it was forced to undermine rather than strengthen the credibility of its clients' statements. The defenders pinned their hopes on a photograph that they had obtained from a Badajoz newspaperman of the prisoners being tortured by being forced to keep their hands in the air. All of the defense attorneys were able to highlight major inconsistencies in each of their clients' testimonies and suggested that they had fabricated their stories under torture. The attorneys highlighted how both defendants and witnesses stated that they had been tortured by a wide variety of methods usually involving being beaten while tied in a distorted and painful position.[68]

The defense team went beyond seeking to prove the innocence of its clients by also bringing the Socialist Party's alternative view of guilt and justice into the courtroom, which saw the republic as the defender of the pueblo rather than necessarily the enforcer of a legal code inherited from the monarchy. The defenders began by arguing that it was impossible to determine which particular individuals had killed the civil guards, for they had not been killed by individuals but rather by the crowd, even the entire pueblo, as a collective act.[69] They then suggested that guilt actually lay not on individuals but on a social phenomenon: *caciquismo*. As for the Civil Guard, no echo of Azaña's vision of the force as in the service of the republic was to be found here. Instead, the defenders stated that the Civil Guard "was in Castilblanco a force of protection and blind obedience to the abuses and injustices of the cacique."[70] They argued that the Civil Guard was so dangerous that the pueblo's actions were actually a form of self-defense; after all, Civil Guard Simón Martín had fired first, and the protesters felt that they had to respond by killing all the guards because the Civil Guard's discipline was such that if one fired, all the others would follow suit.[71] Such assertions may have appealed to Socialist readers of the book that the defense lawyers published of their statements, but they can hardly have been likely to convince the officers who made up the court-martial.

The court found all but one of the Castilblanco defendants guilty and handed down six death sentences and six life sentences, with the rest receiving short sentences that they had already served. Were the twenty-one found guilty the ones who killed Castilblanco's four civil guards? We will never have a precise answer. But the Castilblanco trial was never about determining who the murderers were. For the prosecution, as the charge of "insulting the armed forces" suggests, the trial was about avenging the insult to their institution's honor more than the deaths of the four civil guards. For the defense, it was an attempt to recast the residents of Castilblanco as the victims in the incident rather than a realistic hope that they would be acquitted. The trial proved an example of the republic's continuation of the military's role as the legal defender of the Civil Guard's honor. At the same time, the Socialists' defense of the accused also constituted one of the most strident criticisms yet of the Civil Guard's place in the republic.

Readers will observe the similarities between this trial and that of Montjuïc more than thirty years earlier—the military court, the charge of "insulting the armed forces," the accusations of torture, and the efforts to present the accused as victims. Clearly, the numerous scholars who have emphasized the continuities in the approaches to public order of the monarchy and the republic have a point. But the differences are even more striking. Whereas radicals like Lerroux used Montjuïc to experiment with mass mobilization in urban areas like Barcelona in the 1890s, these techniques were much more developed and widespread by the 1930s. After all, the Castilblanco protest was not an old-style peasant uprising but rather a strike organized by a labor union. With the advent of the republic, Badajoz's landless laborers were demanding a voice in how they were treated by the state, including the Civil Guard, but the corps had not undergone a parallel transformation. Instead, each station commandant still had wide discretion in balancing his mandate to enforce the letter of the law with the pueblo's more informal structures. Therefore, the underlying cause of these four guards' deaths was not just the failure of their commander to find that balance but also the townspeople's new sense that they could do something about the Civil Guard's presence in their town.

The Restoration and the republic both had to balance their obligations to allow the exercise of constitutional rights with the need to maintain order. The

Restoration was quick to suspend those rights, but, in the Montjuïc case, cracks in its efforts to shield the military (including the Civil Guard) from criticism appeared first internationally and then in provinces not under a state of emergency. For the republic, the challenge was even more difficult, not only because it had a mandate to allow freedom of speech but also because previous events like Montjuïc had primed left-wing groups to criticize the Civil Guard—and these criticisms began to appear just days rather than weeks after the events. As for the Civil Guard, the use of old investigative practices and the impolitic words of a director general with previous ties to the monarchy meant that, like Montjuïc, what should have been a cross-class propaganda victory for the Civil Guard begat only more division. This spiral of violence, repression, public outcry, and polarization seen after Castilblanco was to be repeated on a much larger scale in October 1934. Yet by New Year's Day of 1932, the bloodshed of the week of December 31 to January 6 was just getting started.

SEVEN

ARNEDO

From Victims to Perpetrators

A s the Cortes deputies were leaving the chamber after the Castilblanco debate, Socialist Deputy Amós Sabrás Gurrea, in tears, announced that he had just received a call from another Socialist deputy for Logroño Province, José Orad de la Torre, saying that "something truly horrible has happened." While confusion and dismay reigned in the hallways of the congress, reporters turned to Minister of Justice Álvaro de Albornoz for more information, but he responded sarcastically, "Now they're going to be talking every day of killings by the Civil Guard."[1] Returning to his office after the debate, Prime Minister Azaña wrote in his diary that reporters were waiting at his door to ask him "if it's true that some event has occurred. 'I don't know anything,' I responded, 'ask Interior.' A little later [Minister of the Interior] Casares enters the office and tells me that, in Arnedo, the Civil Guard has clashed with the pueblo and has killed six or eight. Just what we need."[2] Another instance of political violence involving the Civil Guard was indeed about to give Azaña more headaches, and Albornoz had not been far off when he remarked that there would be killings by the Civil Guard every day. There had already been six other incidents in the previous four days in which guards had killed a total of ten civilians and injured dozens more. Like Castilblanco, however, Arnedo was something exceptional, this time not because guards were killed but rather because of the number of people that guards killed and the way in which they did so.

At Arnedo, as at Castilblanco, the entrenched police culture of the Civil

Guard, the rising challenge to the status quo presented by Socialist mobilization, the efforts of the republican state to balance these forces, and the decisions of key individuals all came together both to precipitate the incident and
give it polarizing implications at the national level. Locally, newly mobilized
workers making demands set the stage for the incident (although here in an
industrial rather than agricultural setting), but it was ultimately contingent
upon the spontaneous decisions of the civil guards present. It is unclear exactly
what happened that day, but it is evident that, in the chaos of the moment, the
guards' automatic response, dictated by their organizational culture and their
sensitivity to honor, was an excessive use of force.

While a combination of local structures and contingent events led to the
Arnedo incident, its repercussions would serve to drive a wedge between the
republic and the Civil Guard as a whole. The reactions of both the Socialists and
the government sought to advance their visions for the republic without turning the Civil Guard against it. Socialists replicated their pattern of denouncing
the force while also joining the republicans in the government in adopting a
moderate official stance. The government, meanwhile, contemplated beginning
a reform effort while also not actually taking any steps to alter the system by
which the civil guards at Arnedo got away with murder. In the end, the reforms
that did take place had much to do with the individual foibles of Azaña, on the
one hand, and the Civil Guard's high-profile director general, Sanjurjo, on the
other. When Sanjurjo's concern for honor over political expediency led him to
imply that defending the republic was not his top priority, Azaña had to dismiss him. The blow wounded the general's honor enough to push him to join a
rebellion against the government that August. While most guards were not yet
ready to follow suit, the subsequent reforms that Azaña enacted, which guards
interpreted as insulting, planted the idea that their honor might be better maintained through violent rebellion in the name of order and the *patria* rather than
through loyalty to the government in power.

THE LOCAL INCIDENT

The Origins of the Conflict

As at Castilblanco, the stage for Arnedo was set by a Socialist mobilization
that sought to challenge entrenched power structures and usher in a republic

in which the Socialists themselves would hold the reins. While it is impossible to know exactly why the civil guards opened fire that day, characteristics of both the individual actors present and of their organizational cultures more generally may have influenced the guards' spur-of-the-moment decision. The Socialists intended for their strike to be peaceful, but their leaders could not resist employing provocative Socialist rhetoric against caciques and civil guards as a way to work up the crowd. As for the civil guard in command at the scene, prior disciplinary infractions suggest that he was not the best candidate for ensuring that peace would be maintained.

As in Badajoz, worker mobilization in Arnedo had begun during the Restoration period. Yet unlike Castilblanco, by the time of the Second Republic, Arnedo was in the process of becoming an industrial town through its growing shoe manufacturing industry, and it was somewhat larger, with a population of over five thousand.[3] The town was located in Logroño Province (also known as La Rioja) in northern Spain, which was more industrial and lacked the severe land-distribution problem of Andalusia and Extremadura. That is not to say that Arnedo was a rich town. Although its shoemakers made a bit more than agricultural laborers, they could still only afford the most spartan existence. In the first decades of the twentieth century, businessmen were developing the town's shoe industry, but many of their employees still worked on farms part-time.[4] One of the largest factory owners was Faustino Muro Rubio, who had shrewdly risen from sandal maker to industrialist in the 1900s. As in rural Badajoz Province, unions were beginning to make inroads into La Rioja around the same time. After the Primo de Rivera dictatorship eliminated the CNT's presence there, the UGT, which had long been seeking to establish itself in Arnedo, was in a position to expand rapidly in 1931.[5] Muro, meanwhile, had begun a years'-long fight against unionization back in 1911, enduring a prolonged strike four years later that required a concentration of civil guards. Since Muro also had political power by being a member of the city council, he can be considered a cacique. This influence aided his efforts to prevent unionization. By 1931, his sandal factory's workers had still not achieved this goal.[6]

Municipal elections in April and May 1931 swept republicans and Socialists into Arnedo's town hall, but elites like Muro would not relinquish their socioeconomic power so easily. Accounts of the exact sequence of events differ, but it seems that two months earlier, Muro had fired one of his 170 workers, and a republican commission wrote a letter of complaint to the civil governor, saying that the dismissal had occurred for political reasons. The civil governor noted that Muro had encouraged his workers to vote for monarchist candidates in the April elections.[7] Fifteen more of Muro's workers threatened to walk out if he did not hire back the first employee, but his aversion to labor organizing was so great that he simply fired all of these workers as well.[8] The mayor, two civil governors, and an arbitration board all met with Muro to try and get him to rehire the workers, but he would not budge. The negotiations stretched on through the rest of 1931, with Arnedo's growing UGT branch, which had opened in June, taking up the workers' cause.[9] On January 5, 1932, regional Socialist leaders were scheduled to meet with various officials, including the following: the civil governor, Ildefonso Vidal Serrano; the chief of the Civil Guard's Logroño Command, Rodrigo Palacios; and the Radical mayor, José María Fernández Velilla Herrero. They gathered in Arnedo's town hall to negotiate a resolution to the dispute. The Socialists organized a strike for the same day to support their demands that the workers be rehired and that the eight-hour day be respected.[10] Here was an opportunity for the UGT to demonstrate its new presence in the town and to show that the caciques' authority would no longer go unchallenged.

On the evening of January 4, in preparation for the strike, regional leaders deployed rhetoric that, while typical of Socialists at that time, also implied that a confrontation might occur. The speakers there did remind the six hundred some people assembled that the strike was to be a peaceful one, with Orad de la Torre even saying that "everyone should be in the street accompanied by their women and children in order to give the sensation that we want peace."[11] Still, such precautions suggest that the leaders anticipated that there could be trouble with the forces of public order. Orad de la Torre promised that he would be "always at the head of the strikers; the first breast that would be put in danger would be his." The speakers' own language also became rather bellicose as they tried to use the crowds' anger as a motivational tool. Several spoke of bringing the fight to the factory owners, and Jesús López Ortega, president of Logroño's *casa del pueblo*, even asserted that "the movement ought to begin peacefully, but . . . if the owners want war, with war we will respond." As for Muro, one speaker asserted that when workers ask him for bread, "he seeks to answer them with the shrapnel of the Civil Guard."[12] These leaders simply could not resist applying their party's stock revolutionary language to local circumstances as a way of stirring up the crowd, thus heightening the atmosphere of tension, even if their intentions were actually no more than a peaceful strike.

Twenty-four civil guards policed the strike in this atmosphere of both long-standing tensions and provocative rhetoric, and the individual who led them was not exactly the Civil Guard's finest. The number of guards present was so much larger than at Castilblanco because Arnedo was a section headquarters and additional guards had also been concentrated there from nearby towns.[13] The section chief was 2nd Lieutenant Juan Corcuera Piedrahita. Although he had previously been praised for his energy in arresting murder suspects, he appears to have been lackadaisical in his command of the Arnedo Section as his career wound down (he was fifty-one years old). He had received two days of house arrest in 1927 for ordering the station commandant of a town in his section to arrest some murder suspects instead of leading the pursuit himself.[14] In 1930, the command chief reprimanded him for not reviewing his section's documentation and for only doing 6 percent of the paperwork himself, demonstrating "an apathy and neglect inappropriate for the section chief."[15] He does not appear to have been popular with Arnedo's citizenry either. One resident recalled that he frequented the casino, rubbing elbows with the mayor and a factory owner.[16] There is an interesting parallel here between Muro and Corcuera. Both had risen in socioeconomic status over the course of their careers, the former from worker to factory owner and the latter from enlisted man to officer, but they seem to have preferred to reinforce their new status as members of Arnedo's elite rather than strengthen their relations with the town's less fortunate.

Choosing Violence

On the day of the strike, Socialist leaders continued to employ language that may have made these civil guards feel threatened, but ultimately the deadly outcome was the result of the poor leadership of one individual officer and an organizational culture that led the guards quickly to violence. The strikers began picketing around 7:00 a.m. on January 5, and they brought the town to a virtual standstill, even blocking agricultural workers from going to tend the fields.[17] At 2:30 p.m., about eight hundred strikers, including many women and children, gathered in the plaza in front of the town hall to hear more speeches and await the arrival of Civil Governor Vidal Serrano. The speeches echoed those of the previous evening, urging peace while also threatening violence. Along with more denunciations of Mayor Fernández Velilla Herrero, Orad de la Torre urged the strikers to ask those shop owners who did not join the strike to do so and to hint that, if they did not, windows may be broken. A leading Socialist from another town in the region echoed the Civil Guard's own language of duty and sacrifice as he steeled the crowd for the possibility of violence, declaring that "all have the duty to sacrifice their bread, the bread of their children, and even their lives, if necessary, in defense of their legitimate rights."[18]

Upon the arrival of Vidal Serrano, the Socialist leaders joined him in the town hall to begin the negotiations. These negotiations were short, however, because Vidal Serrano brought news that a labor arbitration board had decided in favor of the workers. The factory owners therefore agreed to rehire them and respect the eight-hour day.[19] Around 4:00 p.m. on January 5, the Socialist leaders announced the victory to the crowd gathered in the plaza in front of the town hall, and it erupted in jubilation.[20] It then split up into several groups as strikers paraded around the streets of the town to celebrate. After about an hour, two of the groups reconverged on the plaza, shouting, "Long live the strike!" "Down with the caciques!" "Down with the mayor!" and "Death to the Civil Guard!"[21] The guards were posted in front of the town hall, and, perhaps feeling threatened, Lieutenant Corcuera ordered his men to clear the plaza. As they used their rifles to push the crowd back, Civil Guard Alejandro Fernández hit a girl in the head. Several members of the crowd responded by shoving him to the ground (some witnesses say he simply tripped), and they kicked a sergeant when he came to Fernández's aid.[22]

Then the shooting began, but accounts differ as to who fired first. The civil guards claimed that they answered shots fired from the crowd, whereas townspeople said that Corcuera gave the order to fire as soon as he saw the tussle over Fernández. Carlos Gil Andrés, who wrote a book on the Arnedo incident, summarizes the confused testimonies that the guards gave of what happened next according to the now-lost investigative report of José Calviño, civil governor of Vizcaya: "Of all the guards present only eleven confessed to having used their rifles. Two of them excused their action saying that they only fired in the air, four that they only did so at random, without aiming and without knowing if they caused casualties, and the five others stated that they only pulled the trigger against an individual 'who was brandishing a pistol,' shielded from behind a column some fifteen meters away."[23] A few witnesses confirmed that it was only the guards from out of town that fired. As soon as the shooting started, the crowd fled in panic in all directions as the guards gunned down several as they made for shelter in a pharmacy across the plaza.[24] Most witnesses agreed that the shooting continued for no more than a minute, with guards firing blindly in all directions until Lieutenant Colonel Palacios came out of the town hall and ordered them to cease fire. In that amount of time, the guards had killed six (one man, four women, and a two-year-old boy) and injured more than thirty others (a civil guard was also shot in the leg).[25] Five victims later died of their wounds, bringing the final death toll to eleven.

In the Arnedo incident, it was the civil guards who experienced forward panic, which is characteristic of police atrocities.[26] All three main causes of the Civil Guard's violence during the republic—inappropriate weaponry, a general increase in protests and strikes, and an organizational culture predisposed to violence—can be seen at work in Arnedo. The UGT brought workers out into the streets to contest their town's power structures as never before. There seems to have been no reason that the Civil Guard could not have policed this mobilization peacefully. But its culture of sensitivity to insult, combined with its lethal weaponry, its limited playbook of responses, and the poor leadership of one individual commander with a mediocre record led to a very different outcome. Although some of the Socialists' rhetoric had been provocative, witnesses agree that the demonstration was entirely peaceful, and so Lieutenant Corcuera had no reason to order its dissolution, which caused the tussle between Fernández and the crowd.[27] Perhaps the cries of "Death to the Civil Guard!" made Corcuera feel that his men's honor and safety were being intolerably threatened. While regulations did allow his men to fire without warning if attacked, their Mausers made the number of casualties particularly high when discharged into a crowd at close range. Whether or not Corcuera gave the order to fire, he clearly did not take firm control of the situation, nor were his men rigidly disciplined and obedient, as some Civil Guard historians have claimed, because they fired randomly and some may not have fired at all.[28] The spontaneity of their actions suggests that they were not guided so much by a reasoned decision based on their regulations as by a reflex conditioned by the culture of their organization. All told, the fact that Colonel Palacios was able to bring the shooting to an end as soon as he exited the town hall suggests that, had Corcuera demonstrated firmer leadership, things might have gone quite differently. Absent such guidance, in the moment of confrontation the guards had to select from the options provided by their limited training in an instant, and they chose opening fire all too easily.

Was Arnedo revenge for Castilblanco, as some historians have asserted?[29] The spontaneity and confusion of the actions of Corcuera and his men suggest not, although their jumpiness was no doubt influenced by the fear that swept the Civil Guard in the wake of Castilblanco and Sanjurjo's response to it.[30] In other words, Arnedo demonstrated the limitations of the Civil Guard's culture as it confronted the frequent popular mobilizations of the Second Republic. These mobilizations caused guards to feel increasing anxiety about the opposition, real or imagined, that their institution, their honor, and even their lives faced. Although the Civil Guard emphasized discipline and obedience, its strict hierarchy meant that the poor leadership of one inept officer, coupled with this anxiety, could have disastrous consequences.

THE NATIONAL AFTERMATH

The Socialist Response

While the Socialists had had to manage the bad publicity generated by the fact that the Castilblanco incident had occurred during an FNTT strike, Arnedo provided free propaganda that bolstered their argument that they were fighting against the violent repression of local elites and the Civil Guard. In the event's aftermath, they followed a familiar script of mobilizing financial resources, charismatic leaders, and the press to highlight their version of the story. But while they could attract national media attention to the Arnedo funeral, moderate leaders, reluctant to criticize the Civil Guard, prevented the party from presenting a unified narrative. Instead of coordinating with republicans to enact meaningful reform of the Civil Guard, Socialists wound up limiting themselves to propagandistic stunts that were high on drama but low on substance.

At the local level, Socialists took the lead in supporting the victims and their families, whereas the government did not feel obliged to join in this effort in the way that it had after the Castilblanco incident, since the victims were not representatives of the state. Rejected by the national government, on January 17, Mayor Fernández Velilla Herrero put out a call for donations to local governments around the country.[31] The Socialists responded enthusiastically,

presenting a total of over twenty thousand pesetas to the families of the victims.[32] However, all these donations provided the victims' families with far less
that the approximately forty-three thousand pesetas that the family of each
civil guard killed in Castilblanco had received from the government alone.[33]

The Socialists' support for their fallen comrades also extended beyond
monetary assistance into all their usual forms of mobilization: letters of complaint, strikes, rallies, and speeches. Many worker organizations, especially
from northern Spain, sent telegrams of protest that demanded the dissolution of the Civil Guard.[34] In addition, the UGT, joined by the CNT, staged a regional protest strike on January 7 that almost completely shut down La Rioja.[35]
Speaker after speaker before the crowd in Logroño harshly denounced the Civil
Guard and Sanjurjo.[36]

The event that most directed the spotlight at the Socialist cause was the
funeral for the Arnedo victims in the town itself. The event, with perhaps two
thousand workers from around La Rioja and beyond in attendance, was as
much a spectacle as the one for the dead at Castilblanco had been, but this
time the Socialists were at the center of attention.[37] Numerous deputies from
the party were in attendance, and now it was Margarita Nelken's charismatic
presence that stole the show, as had Sanjurjo's at the Castilblanco funeral.[38] At
the cemetery, Nelken gave a speech "in the name of socialist women . . . in the
name of all the female workers of Spain" that invoked her womanhood as a tool
for accentuating the pathos of the moment as she spoke of the two-year-old
child who had been slain. Her speech was remarkably similar to the one that
Sanjurjo had given at the Castilblanco funeral. She likewise called these victims "martyrs" and included a call for peace: "Neither revenge nor hate before
death, which is, perhaps, the only truth in life."[39] She never mentioned the
Civil Guard, but doing so was unnecessary. The actions of Lieutenant Corcuera and his men had already done more to undermine the corps's reputation
than anything she could have said. At the end of her speech, overcome with
emotion, Nelken nearly fainted and had to be helped out of the cemetery.[40]
In Badajoz, Sanjurjo's tears had been signs not of effeminate weakness but of
a Homeric honoring of fallen comrades. Nelken's dizziness, in contrast, was
interpreted as effeminate; her femininity provided her with her appeal. As the
only prominent woman in the PSOE, she was in a unique position to be able
to use these dead, many of whom were women, to bolster the Socialist cause.

For some Socialists, like Nelken, who had not backed down after Castilblanco, Arnedo allowed them to renew their efforts to rally the Socialist Party behind the reform or dissolution of the Civil Guard. Since the Socialists were also in the government, however, not all of them had the luxury of taking such an oppositional stance, given the need to compromise with their republican partners. At the same time, even Socialist members of the government had to be forceful in their condemnation of these deaths during a strike by their own party's union. Therefore, Francisco Largo Caballero visited Azaña on the morning of January 6 and announced that the Socialists were ready to resign in protest. After being calmed down by Azaña, he agreed with the prime minister and Minister of the Interior Casares Quiroga to carry out the reforms of the Civil Guard that Miguel Maura had previously blocked, restructuring the institution to reduce its autonomy. Azaña explained, "When I did the reform of the army I thought to do it to the Civil Guard, and in the same sense: decapitating it, so that such an important force was not in the hands of one person."[41] That evening, the UGT issued a statement that was much more moderate than those of its locals. It contained only limited criticism of the Civil Guard, asserted that "one ought to feel the same pain in the case of Castilblanco as in that of Arnedo," and reassured the public that the UGT "has demonstrated its animosity toward violence and disorder."[42]

As it had for Castilblanco the day before, the Cortes provided a forum in which the different interpretations of the Arnedo incident could vie with each other for general acceptance. The lack of unity among the Socialist parliamentary group about how to respond to Arnedo continued when the deputies met prior to the Cortes session on the afternoon of January 6. Deputy Juan-Simeón Vidarte described the meeting as "even more tempestuous than that of the day before" because some deputies regretted the moderate stance that their party had adopted on the fifth and suggested that they call for an immediate dissolution of the Civil Guard. However, José Orad de la Torre ultimately dominated the session with an account of what had happened in Arnedo. He embellished his report with anecdotes that seem to have been invented to heighten the drama of the story while glorifying his own role and emphasizing the Socialists' lack of any culpability.[43]

Amós Sabrás began the Arnedo debate in the Cortes itself with a report on what had happened in the town on the previous day based on the account that Orad de la Torre had just given to the Socialists, complete with some of his embellishments. Sabrás also read a telegram to the congress that requested that Casares Quiroga order the guards concentrated in Arnedo to moderate their actions because they were threatening workers and hitting them with their rifle butts. The telegram supposedly had been sent by Orad de la Torre that morning, but Casares Quiroga said he had not received such a telegram, and there were no other reports of aggression by the Civil Guard at that time. Despite all this, Sabrás ultimately bowed to the moderate stance of the Socialists' national leadership and concluded by assuring the congress that he did not think that the incident stained the prestige of the institution as a whole, especially if it cooperated with the investigation.[44]

Arnedo was the Socialists' chance to reverse the negative publicity generated by Castilblanco, and they sought to do so through all their usual methods of financial assistance, speeches, and denunciations in the Cortes. There was even hope that the event could provide them with the momentum they needed to push through a reform of the Civil Guard. However, the republic never did reform the institution to the extent that the Socialists desired. Split between radical rhetoric that appealed to the rank and file and their need to cooperate with republicans as part of the government, the Socialists missed their chance to make the "admirable machine" of the Civil Guard, as Julián Besteiro had put it, "work in our favor."

The Government Response

If the Socialists had to present a stern response to this attack on their strikers without alienating their allies in the government, the government itself had to show that it was responding to the incident without alienating its largest force of public order. It attempted to do so through its own interventions in the Cortes and three different investigations. The Arnedo deaths also stood to give the government the momentum it needed to steer the Civil Guard in a less violent direction, but, in the end, the guards at Arnedo went unpunished and no changes were made to ensure that such an incident would not happen again.

At the debate in the Cortes on the day after the incident, Casares Quiroga gave the government's response to Sabrás. He spent most of his speech defending the Civil Guard, his position as its commander-in-chief leading him to turn to the same arguments about hostile masses and humanitarian civil guards that were common on the Right. He reminded the congress that there were different versions of the story, and they would have to wait for investigations to determine the cause. He then went on to reason that the fact that the crowd had converged on the plaza from two directions might have given the impression that it had "hostile intentions," and he even suggested that, far from being aggressive, Lieutenant Corcuera had urged some stores not to go on strike out of a humanitarian concern that townspeople be able to acquire basic items.[45]

After several other speeches, the communist-leaning José Antonio Balbontín brought in an extreme view of the Civil Guard as an institution that "only exists in order to fight, battle, and kill peasants where large property owners are concentrated," prophesizing that whether the government dissolved it or not, "it will be dissolved [eventually] by the revolutionary pueblo."[46] Azaña felt the need to intervene once again at this point. The moderate position he had taken the day before now served him in good stead, for he was able to deliver a consistent message even though guards had been the aggressors rather than the victims at Arnedo. As he had defended the Civil Guard against Ortega y Gasset's attacks the day before, he now defended it against Balbontín's, echoing the corps's own rhetoric in order to do so: "The Civil Guard has, through the spirit of the institution, blind obedience to the constituted power." Azaña argued that the only thing that mattered in the Arnedo case was whether or not there had been aggression against the guards; that is to say, whether or not they had obeyed their regulations.[47]

The prime minister recalled the reaction to his remarks in his diary:

> The speech was better than yesterday's. Today even the Radicals have applauded me. The ovation was enormous, and the government has been left, not only victorious, but fortified. The political effect in the Cortes, profound.
>
> Ortega [y Gasset] says that these two speeches of mine are my "consecration" as prime minister.[48]

Historians agree that Azaña's rhetorical skill in these speeches was so successful that the government actually emerged stronger from these two incidents that had initially threatened to cause a governmental crisis.[49] However, the underlying issues remained the same. In his desire not to alienate the force, Azaña himself had subscribed to the Civil Guard's view that all it had to do to operate under the republic was follow its own regulations. Taking advantage of the Arnedo incident to push through meaningful reform without also turning the Civil Guard against the regime would be a delicate balancing act indeed.

But first, the government had to determine exactly what had happened and to punish the guilty parties.

On the same day as the debate in the Cortes, two judicial inquiries were announced, one civilian and the other military, in addition to a special investigation for the Ministry of the Interior led by Vizcaya's civil governor, José Calviño.[50] These efforts were a test of whether or not the state would continue to permit the Civil Guard's violent excesses to go unpunished. As it turned out, the guards at Arnedo did indeed walk free because the republic had left unaltered the regulations that gave their organization broad powers to employ deadly violence as a means of crowd control. The government had also left intact the law that placed the force under the legal jurisdiction of the military.

Calviño's civilian report was quite damning of the Civil Guard's role in the events and especially that of Lieutenant Corcuera. Calviño concluded that Corcuera was unjustified in giving the order to dissolve the crowd and that the guards' use of deadly force was also unjustified, whether or not there had been any aggression against them and whether or not Corcuera had given the order to fire. At the very least, Calviño argued, the guards should have given warnings before opening fire, and Corcuera should have given the order to cease firing as soon as it became clear that the crowd was in no way resisting.[51]

The military also submitted an investigation of its own to the Ministry of the Interior. Its interpretation of the event contrasted sharply with Calviño's. It concluded that the crimes of insulting and committing aggressions against the armed forces had been committed. Therefore, it recommended that a criminal investigation be opened. Major Carlos Muñoz Merino, a military prosecutor, did so, but he could not find enough evidence to bring a case against anyone in the crowd. Instead, he did the opposite and filed charges against Lieutenant Corcuera for eleven counts of manslaughter and twenty-four of assault and battery.[52] Since this all-military trial precluded the presence of a star Socialist legal team, Corcuera's court-martial received none of the publicity of the Castilblanco case. Given the way that the Civil Guard's regulations were written, Muñoz Merino had a difficult task in proving Corcuera guilty. He had to demonstrate that there was neither insult nor aggression toward the Civil Guard, since either one of these might have justified Corcuera's actions according to the regulations. Given the contradictory nature of the evidence, Muñoz Merino needed to rely on speculation to make his case. He argued that, since the strike had been peaceful up to the time of the incident, there was no reason to believe that the crowd had suddenly become aggressive in the plaza.[53]

The military court announced its decision on February 24, 1934. The judges focused on whether or not someone from the crowd had fired first, and since the contradictory testimonies could not give them a definite answer to that question, they unsurprisingly concluded there was not enough evidence to find Corcuera guilty.[54] The Civil Guard regulations' hard line on insulting the force had meant that a civil guard like Corcuera was in effect immune from any conviction related to deaths like those of Arnedo, even though in this case, unusually, one military prosecutor had broken the military's tradition of always defending its own by filing charges against the lieutenant. Calviño's civilian report had also demonstrated quite a different understanding of when it was appropriate for a guard to employ force, but as long as the corps's regulations remained unchanged and the military would always interpret them, there was little chance of guards being held legally responsible for their actions in any real sense. The government was unwilling to risk losing the Civil Guard's loyalty by altering these fundamental components of its identity.

The Seeds of Rebellion Germinate

While Azaña defended the Civil Guard in the Cortes and the state's military judicial apparatus shielded its members from punishment, the government was more willing to meddle in matters of the institution's organization and personnel. Unfortunately, these efforts wound up creating more dissatisfaction with the republic than increased loyalty and reduced violence. Once again, organizational cultures combined with the emotionally charged reactions of individual leaders to produce this outcome. On the one hand, Sanjurjo shared the Civil Guard's sensitivity to insult but took it to an extreme. On the other, Azaña's superficial reform efforts were more vindictive than substantive. They were indicative of the republicans' failure to divine what guards would or would not find unacceptable to their honor.

Despite the confidence that Azaña expressed in the Cortes about the Civil Guard's loyalty, he had his doubts. He knew that Sanjurjo was not planning a coup, but the prime minister was concerned that the general might eventually be won over by those who saw him as a potential "restorer of social order."[55]

These concerns were more products of the fallout from Castilblanco than Arnedo, but it did not help that Sanjurjo had written in his January 7 general order that he hoped "everyone knows that if our dead touch our souls, we are also pained by those that fall before us in the fight of blindness, trickery, and ignorance with the strict line of duty."[56] This statement seems almost to praise rather than apologize for the Arnedo killers by suggesting that the victims at Arnedo were simply collateral damage caused by the guards' duty to obey their orders blindly. He could not conceive of civil guards failing to do their duty; therefore, he fit Arnedo into his conspiracy theory, concluding that "the events of Arnedo demonstrate that the attacks on the Civil Guard are the beginning of an organized plan against the institute."[57]

For these reasons, just two days after his Solomonic speech, Azaña decided to dismiss Sanjurjo from his post as director general. Although Sanjurjo, according to Azaña, had previously expressed interest in being relieved from the difficult assignment, now "his amour propre would not suffer" the indignity of being made to appear to have abandoned the Civil Guard when it was attacked.[58] Azaña sought to ease the blow by making Sanjurjo the director general of the Carabineros instead, even though the command of this smaller force was less prestigious.

Sanjurjo's transfer took place on February 3.[59] In his farewell general order to the Civil Guard, he spoke to his men as a father leaving a son on his own. As usual, honor provided the framework for the entire piece, and, amidst his effusive praise for the honor of the institution as a whole, there was an ambiguous message about where its ultimate loyalties should lie. He praised obedience to and sacrifice for the government, but he also suggested that "if some day you have doubts, if on some occasion you falter, do not hesitate to ask for the help or counsel of your old director general."[60] In other words, he was suggesting that someday civil guards might have to make a choice between their duty to the republican government and their loyalty to Sanjurjo and his conception of the *patria*, between two different understandings of their honor's source.

Azaña's transfer of Sanjurjo turned out to have a touch of irony because it was primarily meant to prevent the general from becoming the focal point of a conspiracy, but the move so offended Sanjurjo's honor that he became open to talk of a coup, which he had previously frowned upon. His desire to rid himself of a government that had so offended him was not his only motivation, however. He was concerned about anarchism, efforts to give Catalonia autonomy, and the Socialists' "constant injurious attacks on the Civil Guard and announcements of its dissolution: events like those of Castilblanco."[61] By the summer of 1932, Sanjurjo had joined a group of generals hoping to oust the left republican–Socialist government but not to end the republic. Their plan was not particularly well thought out; it was hoped that if Sanjurjo took Seville and another general seized parts of Madrid, then the Azaña government would be forced out, as in the *pronunciamientos* of the nineteenth century. The conspirators felt that they had to act quickly because the government already had thorough knowledge of their plans and Catalonia was about to be granted its autonomy. Therefore, they decided that the uprising would begin on August 10 of that same year.[62]

Despite the plot's low chances of success, Sanjurjo thought that his prestige alone would be enough to carry the day.[63] In a sense, he turned out to be right, for he was successful in persuading both the Civil Guard and army units in Seville to rise up on the tenth.[64] Although Sanjurjo was attempting to overthrow the government, he tried to maintain the myth of his political neutrality in the manifesto he released that day. He presented the republican period as a time of violence and chaos and stated that the goal of the rebellion was "above all, that social peace and discipline be restored, in benefit of all classes."[65] He had deemed what he understood to be the defense of public order as more important to maintaining his honor than staying loyal to the government in power.

The uprising in Madrid and other cities failed, leaving the rebels in Seville alone, and Azaña began mobilizing forces from around the country to converge on the city.[66] Sanjurjo, however, was undaunted. His plan was to go out himself and meet any units that arrived to oppose him, trusting that his personal honor and courage would win them over without a fight. Clearly, his experiences as a prominent general had not shaken his belief that setting a personal example of bravery was the best way to lead. Unfortunately for Sanjurjo, the commanders of the Ninth Infantry Regiment did not share his confidence, and they withdrew their support for the rebellion. Although the Civil Guard's Seville Command continued to stand with the former director general, Sanjurjo realized that the game was up, and he fled Seville in a taxi with a few confidants.[67] The fugitives made for Huelva, but they were discovered by civil guards and *guardias de seguridad* at the entrance to the city and arrested.[68]

Sanjurjo was immediately jailed in Madrid, where he awaited trial in a military prison. A confession he gave and the manifesto he had released left little doubt of his guilt, and so the Sixth Chamber of the Supreme Court gave him and a few other leading conspirators only a summary court-martial on August 24. The defendants could not contest the evidence that the prosecution presented that day. However, when the prosecutor stated that the defendants' actions had deprived them of the military virtues of honor and patriotism, they were outraged. One of them retorted, "I have been a prisoner of the Moors. Various times they put the mouths of their rifles on my chest to kill me, but ... they never insulted me! And here today it has been said that we do not have honor."[69] The court found Sanjurjo guilty of military rebellion the next day, sentencing him to death.[70] The rapidity of these proceedings stands in stark contrast to the two-year ordeal that both the accused in the Castilblanco incident and Lieutenant Corcuera were going through. The government seems to have felt the need to act quickly to make an example of Sanjurjo.

Still, Azaña commuted Sanjurjo's sentence to life in prison on the same day that the Sixth Chamber announced its verdict.[71] He explains his reasoning in his diary:

> I have considered the subject as a political case in that it ought to become most useful to the Republic. To execute Sanjurjo would oblige us to execute afterwards six or eight others that have incurred the same punishment, and those of Castilblanco. It would be too many bodies in the path of the Republic. *Pronunciamientos* must be discredited by their own failure and by the discredit of their instigators. Shooting Sanjurjo, we would make a martyr of him, and we would found, without wanting to, the religion of his heroism and his gentlemanliness. . . . A more exemplary punishment is Sanjurjo failed, alive in prison, than Sanjurjo glorified, dead.[72]

Azaña grasped that Sanjurjo's honor was more important to both him and his followers than his life, and so the harshest punishment would entail destroying that honor. Therefore, Azaña ordered the general stripped of all the honors he had earned and sent to a prison for common criminals rather than a military prison.[73] While allowing the military justice system jurisdiction over civilians in some cases was controversial, military prison promised to be a place where Sanjurjo could feel at home and be respected. To be placed among ordinary criminals, among those whom the civil guards saw as their true enemies, was horrifying to him.[74]

Azaña's crushing of the rebellion gave him enormous political capital, and he felt the time was now right to "decapitate" the Civil Guard, punishing it for its involvement in the rising. Within a month of the rebellion, he had reduced the size and functions of the office of the director general and the general staff, changing their names to inspector general and general inspection; appointed a brigadier general instead of a major general to be the new inspector general; and placed the corps solely under the Ministry of the Interior, ending its dual dependency on the Ministries of the Interior and War. He also eliminated the institution's rank of major general and its post of subdirector general, the highest positions that a Civil Guard officer had been able to attain.[75] Finally, he dissolved the Civil Guard's Fourth Division, the one that had sided with Sanjurjo in Seville (and had also considered rebelling after Castilblanco); however, this action did not translate to any change on the ground since supervision of the two commands in Seville was simply transferred to the Twenty-Eighth Division.[76]

These changes were typical of Azaña's approach to military reform. While he was careful not to take things too far, he could not resist letting a touch of vindictiveness creep into his decrees. The alterations may appear to have been only cosmetic, but the civil guards interpreted them as a deep offense to their honor because the changes reduced their control over their own institution, eliminated the highest position they could attain, reduced their corps's prestige, and weakened their links with the rest of the military.[77] At the same time, the reforms did nothing to address the Civil Guard's violence—the real threat it posed to the republic—and nothing to provide guards with nonlethal weaponry, to improve their regulations and training regarding nonlethal crowd control, or to modify a judicial system that gave them almost complete impunity. Sanjurjo had rebelled in part because Azaña had offended his honor; now the prime minister's actions threatened to send the Civil Guard on a similar path.

The aftermath of Arnedo and the subsequent Sanjurjada, as the August 1932 rebellion became known, gave Azaña his chance to reform the Civil Guard in a way that would maintain its loyalty to the republic while adapting its policing methods to the needs of a democratic society. However, although some civil guards expressed openness to practical reforms, the measures that Azaña did take had a more punitive character and demonstrated a profound misunderstanding of the Civil Guard's military culture. While Sanjurjo certainly had to be dismissed as director general, he interpreted his transfer to the Carabineros as an insult rather than a compromise. Azaña's reforms to the Civil Guard's structures appeared cosmetic, but they diminished the very thing that was most important to civil guards: their prestige. The effects of Azaña's choices were soon evident when Sanjurjo launched his coup attempt. While he did not manage to gain much support, the fact that Seville Command did back him unquestioningly, favoring a charismatic leader who appealed to the values of their military culture over their duty to the government in power, did not bode well for the future of the republic.

Both Castilblanco and Arnedo were incidents with national repercussions that were caused by unique local circumstances, although these circumstances themselves were shaped by larger trends. In both cases, Socialists were struggling to undermine the entrenched power structure of the old *caciquismo* system. Nevertheless, the outcomes of the two strikes were far from predetermined. Despite the Civil Guard's ethos of discipline, its behavior at Arnedo was as spontaneous as Civil Guard Simón Martín's fatal scuffle at Castilblanco. Trained to respond to any verbal or physical insult, lacking clear instructions from their superiors, and on edge in the aftermath of Castilblanco, when they felt threatened, the guards at Arnedo turned to a tactic that certainly was part of their police culture: opening fire.

As at Castilblanco, divisions within the Socialist ranks blocked them from presenting a unified message after Arnedo. They consistently supported the victims of both Muro and the Civil Guard, but they employed stock revolutionary rhetoric during the strike and afterward that focused on making the funeral and Cortes debate into national media spectacles that would bolster their own image. Meanwhile, the Socialist leadership backed the government's moderate approach, which sought to avoid offending the Civil Guard. The prime minister's only substantive response to the incidents was transferring Sanjurjo, a move that smacked more of payback than a desire for reform. As it happened, Azaña's decision fulfilled his fears of rebellion by making Sanjurjo into a conspirator. In his reaction to the Sanjurjada, Azaña again sought to punish more than reform, only adding to the corps's resentment toward the republic.

Given the tensions created by the regime's rapidly changing sociopolitical landscape, the Civil Guard's fraught relationship with the working classes, and its difficulties with nonlethal crowd control, it may have been inevitable that some incidents akin to Castilblanco and Arnedo would occur with the coming of the republic. However, the true tragedy of the two events lies in the fact that reactions on all sides only served to increase the likelihood that such cases would occur again. The root problem was a failure to be concerned with the cultures of the other interested parties and with making a reduction in violence the first priority. By criticizing the civil guards for being servants of the caciques, radical Socialists offended the thing guards cherished most—their honor—without ever actually effecting much reform. Meanwhile, in their stubborn refusal to admit wrongdoing under any circumstances, guards scapegoated "instigators," like Nelken, instead of considering possible weaknesses in their own culture, regulations, and tactics; most republicans and many Socialists did not question those structures either. As these debates over what the place of the forces of public order in the new republic should be continued, they set in motion a series of events that culminated in the uprising of October 1934, which was the most serious outburst of violence the republic and its forces would have to contend with prior to the Civil War.

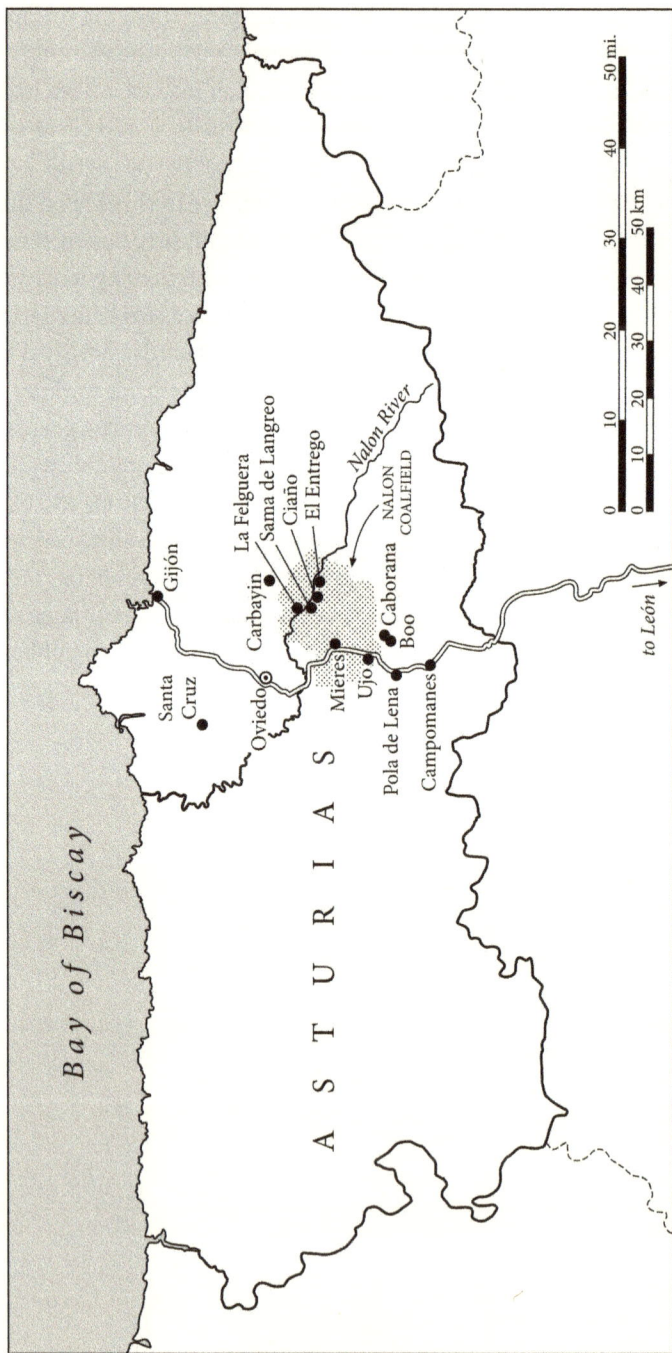

Map of the Asturias Region indicating the locations discussed in the chapter.

EIGHT

ASTURIAS 1

Military Glory

T he civil guards at Oviedo Command headquarters were anxious on the night of October 4, 1934. There were rumors that the appointment of members of a right-wing Catholic party to the cabinet might spark an uprising. Sometime after midnight, the command chief, Lieutenant Colonel Juan Moreno Molina, received a call from the station commandant in the town of Posada de Llanera. Two of his men had been shot and one was dead. Moreno Molina immediately dispatched reinforcements.[1] By morning, reports were flooding into the command headquarters and Civil Governor Fernando Blanco Santamaría's office of attacks on Civil Guard posts as towns throughout the province's mining areas rose up in rebellion. Communication with some posts had been cut. Hundreds of rebels were said to be assembling on the outskirts of Oviedo. Moreno Molina turned his attention from sending reinforcements to preparing for his own position to be attacked. Blanco Santamaría managed to declare a state of war and ordered Army Colonel Alfredo Navarro Serrano to send a request for more ammunition and air support before all communication with the city was cut off.[2] It had become clear that this was not just another protest or even an insurrection. This was a war, a concerted attack on the symbols of governmental power in Austrias, the Civil Guard prominent among them, the likes of which the institution had never seen before. The Civil Guard would have to both draw on and adapt its culture to this unprecedented situation, which would have a greater impact on the course of the republic and the institution's relationship with the new regime than any other single event prior to the outbreak of the Civil War almost two years later.

With a total of 111 civil guards killed in all of Spain (along with at least 1,051 civilians and 173 members of other government forces), the Socialist-led insurrection of October 1934 was the most violent series of attacks that the Civil Guard had ever had to face in its history up to that point, thus necessitating two chapters' worth of treatment here.[3] Rarely in European history has a police force faced such a direct and deadly assault.[4] The uprising was also by far the most violent episode of the Second Republic period—the month of October 1934 accounted for over half of the total deaths by political violence. Yet only in the Asturias region did the revolt reach proportions that one might call a war—the around one thousand deaths there made up over 80 percent of the rising's total death toll.[5] This insurrection was certainly not the first time that Civil Guard posts had been attacked in Spain, and guards responded, as they always had, by defending their *casas-cuarteles*. But these more concerted attacks raised new questions about what following their code of honor meant. When a *casa-cuartel*'s walls were weakened by dynamite and guards began to run out of ammunition, there was no clear answer to the question of when they could surrender with honor. Those who sought glory through a refusal to surrender that virtually sought out death took an approach to honor more familiar to the Spanish Legion than to the Civil Guard, but it was this approach that was praised in the Civil Guard press and echoed in military tribunals, leading to its more widespread adoption by the Civil Guard in July 1936.

These two chapters present Asturias in the last months of 1934 as, first, another case study in how the interactions between the Civil Guard's culture, mass political mobilizations, governmental policies, and individual choices amplified the political violence of the Second Republic. Second, they treat the revolt as a key point in a shift in the Civil Guard's culture and its relationship with the republic that culminated in many guards themselves violently rebelling against the government in 1936.

Armed rebellion was itself a form of mass political mobilization. Since the attack on and the defense of a Civil Guard post were already practices within the cultures of both workers and civil guards, distinct patterns emerged as dozens of posts were assaulted in Asturias. Station commandants felt the need to uphold their honor by defending their posts even when they had no chance of holding them. At the same time, this defense was not necessarily a fight to the death. Assailants were willing to protect women and children, and guards were willing to surrender after they had put up a fight. Within this general pattern, the isolation of these small units and the unprecedented scale of the attacks also meant that there was considerable variation in how individual command-ers chose to respond. Afterward, the Civil Guard's militarization ensured that those who fought to the last would set the new standard of how to respond to such a situation, while military courts made known that failure to combat rebelliousness on the part of the Left would not be tolerated.

THE ORIGINS OF THE CONFLICT

The National Origins

In the wake of the Castilblanco and Arnedo incidents, the consolidation of the republic continued to be hindered in part by frequent instances of political vi-olence that were often perpetrated by its own forces of public order. The level of political violence in 1932 remained almost identical to that of 1931 and actually increased in 1933.[6] The most serious episode of violence in 1933 that involved the forces of public order was Casas Viejas. This incident lies outside of the purview of this book because the Assault Guard rather than Civil Guard was the primary force involved, but many of the same patterns at play in Castilblanco and Arnedo can be observed there as well, and in its aftermath lie the origins of Asturias rebellion. As part of a broader anarchist uprising in January 1933, on the morning the eleventh of that month, the townspeople of Casas Viejas (Cádiz) joined the uprising and killed two of their civil guards. That same af-ternoon, Civil and Assault Guard reinforcements arrived and conducted door-to-door searches. The occupants of one hut shot dead the assault guard who came to search them. The remaining guards besieged the hut, and an all-night shootout began that ended with the government forces burning down the hut, killing eight inside. Angered by the death of their comrades, the assault guards then shot fourteen prisoners on the same site.[7]

This massacre made clear that the republic had failed in its Assault Guard to create a force that would keep order in a more peaceful fashion than the Civil Guard.[8] As with the civil guards at Arnedo, the fact that these assault guards' comrades had taken casualties and poor leadership of the ranking of-ficer present were factors contributing to the violence. In this case, the Civil

Guard lieutenant on the scene repeatedly urged restraint, but the Assault Guard captain, Manuel Rojas Feijespán, ignored his advice.[9] The republican government's obsession with maintaining order played a role as well; even if Azaña did not actually utter the infamous instructions to "shoot them in the belly," the director general of security does seem to have given orders to repress the rebellion harshly.[10] The larger point, however, is that Casas Viejas revealed that the organizational culture of the Assault Guard was not substantially different from that of the Civil Guard. The Assault Guard's officers had been detached from the army and many of them had served in Morocco. In addition, although there were frequent articles in support of nonlethal weaponry and other modernizing reforms in police journals at the beginning of the republic, by 1933 the Assault Guard's equipment was just as militarized as the Civil Guard's (at Casas Viejas, they were armed with a machine gun and grenades as well as rifles).[11] Now facing the second anarchist revolt in as many years, these assault guards also saw themselves as part of an existential struggle for order in which the deaths of their comrades were worthy of revenge, even revenge that took the form of murder in cold blood.

If Azaña's response to the Castilblanco and Arnedo incidents wound up fortifying his government, Casas Viejas had the opposite effect, undermining his coalition by leading the Socialists to question their participation in that government. Ultimately, however, the machinations of President Alcalá Zamora caused the fall of the Azaña government in the summer of 1933, sparking new elections.[12] It was during the election campaign that the true effects of the Casas Viejas incident were felt. The Socialists refused to campaign as a bloc with the left republicans while the Radicals criticized the left republicans constantly for their handling of the incident. As a result, the Radicals and the CEDA (Confederación Española de Derechas Autónomas, or Spanish Confederation of Autonomous Rightist Parties), which was a coalition of conservative Catholic parties, did well in the November 1933 elections.

The Socialists' horror over the republic's conservative turn at the polls is hard to overestimate. While different factions of the party had previously been at odds regarding how much to cooperate with the republic, most agreed that having the CEDA enter the government would be intolerable. Castilblanco and Arnedo had roots in the Socialists' efforts to bring about their vision of the republic throughout Spain, but now they were fighting to prevent the country from moving further from that vision. The focus of the Socialist press shifted from criticism of *caciquismo* and the Civil Guard toward a new enemy that was perceived to be a more immediate threat: fascism. The international context is important here because fascism's success in Italy and Germany had become as frightening for the Left as communism's success in Russia was for the Right. Engelbert Dollfuss's dictatorial rule in Austria particularly alarmed Socialists because, although Spain's fascist party was minuscule at the time, they saw the CEDA as part of a similar "clerical fascist" movement.[13] Some of the rhetoric of the CEDA's leader, José María Gil Robles, as well as of its youth arm, did echo fascist tropes.[14] President Alcalá Zamora agreed with the Socialists that the CEDA should not be part of the government, and so he had Lerroux's Radicals lead minority governments that excluded the CEDA.[15] Meanwhile, Gil Robles hoped to provoke the Socialists into a rebellion that could be easily crushed while also convincing the president to appoint him to be prime minister. In September 1934, Gil Robles held a rally at Covadonga, the mythical site of the beginning of the *reconquista*, which was in the Socialist stronghold of Asturias. Sure enough, the Socialists countered with a general strike in the province.[16]

In the end, however, it was difficulties with coalition partners and in-fighting within the Radical Party that meant that, by the next month, Alcalá Zamora had no choice but to accept a new government under Lerroux that in-cluded three CEDA ministers, Gil Robles among them. News of the new govern-ment leaked on October 4, and the Socialist leadership ordered a general strike to begin the very next day.[17] Was this to be a protest, an insurrection, or a revo-lution? The implications of the long-standing divisions within the leadership were greater than ever when it gave mixed signals as to the object of the strike and made few preparations besides stockpiling some weapons and distribut-ing propaganda pamphlets.[18] As it turned out, most of Spain simply did not participate on October 5, although there were strikes and skirmishes in some provinces, and the Catalan government attempted to declare itself a state within a federal republic.[19] Those who did rebel faced a government that was willing to unleash the brutal potential within the Civil Guard's organizational culture.

The Local Origins

The rebellion was most serious, and the repression harshest, in Asturias. Na-tional politics provided the spark that ignited revolution in Asturias, but a strong sense of community in the face of serious socioeconomic tensions explains why it was the only region where a revolution was attempted in earnest. Asturias was Spain's most important coal-mining region, and while the miners were far from a unified group, their shared opposition to local elites did create a sense of community. The miners believed that various groups of outside identities—bosses, the clergy, and the forces of order—were colluding to oppress them socially and economically. When the right-wing parties took power in 1933, the miners began to feel that there was no longer hope of the republic improving their situation. They came to the conclusion that they would have to expel the outsiders and take control of their community for themselves.[20]

The forces of order, and especially civil guards, were the first targets both because they were the armed representatives of the government in power and because workers regarded them as the instruments of the domination of their communities by outside elites. In addition, by that time attacking a town's *casa-cuartel* had become a standard insurrectionary practice. The association of the Civil Guard with the local elites, in this case, the mining companies, was particularly strong in the coalfields.[21] While the mining companies had their own police, they needed civil guards to combat more serious unrest. Therefore, they sometimes paid for the construction of *casas-cuarteles*, particularly as Socialist-dominated local governments cut municipal funding for housing guards.[22]

Conflict between miners and the Civil Guard had a long history in Asturias. As early as 1897, guards killed two and wounded seventeen more during a food riot in the large mining town of Mieres.[23] The participation of Asturias in the nationwide general strike of 1917 significantly worsened the atmosphere of tension. Although the strike began peacefully in Asturias, the region's military governor ordered the government forces to hunt down strikers "like wild beasts."[24] Confrontations between the two groups caused several deaths.[25] The most infamous element of the repression was the "train of death," a train that ran the length of Asturias and was filled with guards who had orders to fire on all subversives whom they passed.[26] After the strike was over, three hundred were detained in Oviedo's Model Prison (Cárcel Modelo), and many were tortured.[27] Drawing upon the propaganda techniques that it had refined during the "crimes of Montjuïc" events in the 1890s, the left-wing press again seized on the brutality of the repression as a way to vilify the regime, describing "horrible crimes," "infamies," and women driven mad with terror.[28]

With the arrival of the Second Republic, wildcat strikes became common and tensions with the forces of order were again on the rise.[29] By 1934, civil and assault guards were being deployed frequently to combat an intense period of strikes and protests, which contributed to the spiral of tit-for-tat violence.[30] As in Badajoz, criticism of the Civil Guard also served as a cause around which the local community could unify.[31] In an incident on September 1, *guardias de seguridad* killed a worker during a protest by a Socialist women's group in the large mining town of Sama de Langreo, but a participant remembered them as civil guards.[32] *Avance*, the region's incendiary Socialist organ, expressed outrage that the civil governor had deployed these forces to Sama without its mayor's knowledge or consent and concluded that "Sama de Langreo has lived through a few hours of war. It was the invasion of a foreign army."[33] Workers felt more endangered than protected by the forces of order, and they prepared to fight back against what they saw as a military occupation of their community.

While the miners of the Asturian coalfields had a longer history of political mobilization than the farm laborers of Castilblanco or the factory workers of Arnedo, many of the causes of their conflict with the Civil Guard were the same. Tensions with the institution were long-standing because of its association with the powerful mining companies. The Asturian workers were also just as resentful of its interventions in their local affairs as Castilblanco's residents had been. The corps's frequent use of violence and mass arrests in response to the increase in strikes and protests that accompanied the Second Republic did irreparable damage to its reputation. By 1934, there was no hope of winning the miners' respect; both sides were preparing for armed confrontation. Yet once again it was the efforts of Socialists at the national level to carve out a political space for themselves in the republic that proved the spark that ignited this major eruption in political violence. Convinced that a CEDA-dominated government would spell the end of the republic's usefulness to the Socialist cause, party leaders gave in to the radical impulses of the rank and file. On October 5, 1934, the miners deposed area civil guards from their positions of authority as a matter of course—they were the local representatives of a state that the miners believed brought them only oppression. But the scale and violence with which the miners expelled the guards could not have been imagined even a year earlier.

THE SHIFTING BOUNDARIES OF HONOR: PATTERNS IN HOW CIVIL GUARDS RESPONDED TO VIOLENT ATTACK

The Asturian rebels inflicted casualties on thirty-two Civil Guard posts in this first phase of their attack. Here, I will concentrate on the Fourth Company (Sama), which encompassed almost all of the major mining areas, 50 percent of the posts that sustained casualties in Asturias, and 70 percent of the total Civil Guard casualties in the region.[34] Of this company's twenty-three posts, all of which fell to the rebels, I will examine in detail a handful that illustrate the range of possible responses to the assault.

Defending his post against attack is not part of the normal duties of a policeman; therefore, military rather than police culture becomes more relevant to analyzing these responses. Yet the similarities between the responses of many of Fourth Company's posts suggests that an attack was not entirely unexpected either, and indeed expectations had already emerged within the cultures of both the civil guards and the miners about how such an event should unfold. What the civil guards were defending was their honor more than their building, and so they would refuse an initial offer to surrender and instead put up a vigorous defense of their *casa-cuartel*, but ultimately they were willing to surrender after causalities had been taken and the building destroyed. However, the variations on this pattern are also revealing. A few officers looked to their training in the army to seek glory through death defending the *patria*, while a handful of others felt it was not their duty to lose their lives in a siege that they could not break. In other words, there was no universal consensus on what a civil guard's honor required of him in such a situation, with some considering such a fight beyond their duties as policemen and others believing that they had a soldier's obligation to fight to the death.

In the aftermath of the rebellion, the fact that guards were under military jurisdiction ensured that they were judged according to the military's definition of honor. Those who fought until resistance was no longer possible were lauded, and those who chose not to seek any glory at all were punished. The majority who put up a fight but then surrendered were not questioned. These guards had not abandoned the idea of the Civil Guard's policing as a negotiation between their duty to enforce the law and their need to accommodate the realities of the communities in which they worked. In this extreme situation, their duty was to hold their posts against the reality of a pueblo in revolt, and so they chose to fight but did not hold out until the bitter end. However, those who did fight to the death introduced an idea of honor that officers had already been exposed to in the army but that was new to the Civil Guard: glory through death in battle. Therefore, the continuity in the Civil Guard's idea of honor was strong, but a rupture was beginning that would continue into the Civil War of 1936.

A Combat Ritual: The Typical Response

There were three main groups of elites whom miners sought to expel from their communities on October 5, 1934, usually through death or imprisonment: civil guards, priests and monks, and mining company managers.[35] However, the nature of the confrontations with each of these groups was unique. Arrest and murder of religious and mining company personnel was sporadic and often did not involve armed resistance. Many priests and monks tried to escape by disguising themselves as workers, while nuns were not subject to violence since they did not present a threat to the vision of a community ruled by the working-class male.[36] In contrast, guards were fellow men who stood armed and ready to resist the miners' revolt. Therefore, a town's *casa-cuartel* or other police installation was always the first target of the uprising's revolutionary violence.

The procedure of these fights with the Fourth Company's posts seemed to follow a predetermined pattern since taking a town's *casa-cuartel* was already a standard revolutionary practice. Examples of assaults on Civil Guard posts can be found going back to the Second Carlist War, and the ritual was solidified during the three anarchist insurrections that took place in 1932 and 1933. Most guards defended their honor by putting up a vigorous defense of their post, but when they had taken casualties and their building had sustained severe damage, they felt they could surrender with dignity. Table 2 illustrates the patterns in more detail. Rebels, outnumbering guards from between about five to one to one hundred to one, would surround a post in the early hours of the morning. Around 4:00 or 5:00 a.m., they would begin their assault, often pausing several times to give the guards a chance to surrender, promising that prisoners would

TABLE 2. The Civil Guard Posts of Fourth Company (Sama) in the Insurrection of October 5, 1934

CASA-CUARTEL	TYPE OF POST	NO. OF GUARDS[a]	NO. OF REBELS	GUARDS KILLED[b]	GUARDS INJURED[b]	NO. OF REBELS KILLED[c]
Sama de Langreo	Company	62	500–2,000	38	1	4
Caborana	Section	8	—	—	—	—
Boo	Post	5	—	—	—	—
Cabañaquinta	Post	9	—	—	3	—
Moreda	Post	10	200	—	5	1
La Rabaldana	Post	7	300	3	3	—
Santa Cruz	Post	—	—	—	4	—
Turón	Post	—	—	—	—	—
La Felguera	Section	—	400+	1	—	—
Barredos	Post	10	—	—	1	—
Campo de Caso	Post	—	—	—	—	—
Ciaño	Post	5	200	4	—	1
El Entrego	Post	6	100	4	2	—
Laviana	Post	11	500	4	3	1
Sotrondio	Post	11	500	2	3	
Ujo	Section	6	—	—	1	1
Campomanes	Post	5	60+	12	7	7
Murias (Mieres)	Post	—	1,300 (Mieres)	1	2	—
Pajares	Post	4	—	—	1	—
Pola de Lena	Post	6	100+	—	—	2
La Rebollada (Mieres)	Post	14	1,300 (Mieres)	—	4	—
Riosa	Post	—	—	—	—	—
Santullano	Post	5	—	2	3	—
TOTALS	—	—	—	71	43	17

NOTES:

[a] The number of guards at the post on October 5, 1934, not including reinforcements that arrived during the revolt or other government forces present.

[b] For the sake of consistency, all data in these columns are from Aguado Sánchez, *Revolución de octubre de 1934*, 506.

[c] For the sake of consistency, all data in this column are from González Calleja, *Cifras cruentas*, 234–35.

[d] D = dynamite, O = other explosives, P = pistols, R= rifles, S = shotguns.

TIME OF ATTACK	REBEL ARMS[d]	DAMAGE TO CUARTEL	NO. OF SALLY ATTEMPTS	SURRENDER[e]	FATE OF COMMANDER
2:30 a.m.[f]	DOPRS	Severe	3	Yes	Cross of San Fernando
9:00 a.m.– 4:00 p.m.	—	—	1	Yes, Torrens	6 months prison
—	—	—	—	Yes, Torrens	Life in prison
—	D	—	1	Yes	—
—	DS	—	3	Yes	—
4:00 a.m.	D	Destroyed		Yes	—
4:00 a.m.	D	Destroyed	1	Yes, Torrens	—
—	—	—	—	—	—
	D	Blown up	Some flee	Some do	
2:00– 6:30 a.m.	DOPS	Burned down	—	Yes	—
—	—	—	—	Flee to Nava	—
3:30 a.m.	DOPS	Burned down	—	Yes	—
3:30– 8:00 a.m.	DOPS	Severe	1	Yes	—
4:00– 8:00 a.m.	O	—	—	Yes	—
3:00 a.m.	DPS	Severe	3	Yes	—
5:00– 9:00 a.m.	D	—	—	Yes	Death sentence
10:30 a.m.	DORS	Roof collapses	—	Yes	—
—	—	—	1	Yes	—
—	—	—		Abandoned	—
5:00 a.m.	PS			Immediate	6 years prison
—	—	Some	2	Yes	—
—	D	—	—	Yes	—
4:00–9:00 a.m.	D	Destroyed	Moved buildings	Defeated	—
—	—	—	—	—	—

[e] Torrens = Civil Guard Lieutenant Gabriel Torrens Llompart facilitated the surrender.
[f] The fight lasted until 2:00 p.m. on the sixth.
SOURCES principally Taibo, *Asturias, octubre 1934*, and Aguado Sánchez, *Revolución de octubre de 1934*. Please note that this table represents a synthesis of sometimes differing accounts and that limited information is available for some posts.

be treated fairly. The guards usually refused, but they sometimes did allow their families the chance to leave the *casa-cuartel*. The miners' shotguns and pistols made little headway against the guards' rifles, but dynamite proved a surprisingly effective weapon, destroying the flimsy walls of the *casa-cuartel* and forcing the guards to attempt an evacuation. It was during these almost always unsuccessful efforts to break out of their encirclement that the guards sustained many of their casualties.[37] Trapped and defenseless, they would then surrender.

In analyzing the testimonies of rebel leaders who participated in the attacks on the *casas-cuarteles*, what stand out are their repeated attempts to allow the civil guards to surrender. These efforts may have been exaggerated to make the rebels look more humane, but it stands to reason that they would have encouraged surrender in order to spend less precious ammunition and time on subduing the guards. If the guards, realizing their hopeless situation, had surrendered without a fight, they would have been spared their heavy losses. But there was a consensus that their honor would not permit such a course of action.[38] While their understanding of honor certainly included the notion of sacrifice, this meant the hardships of daily patrol and the remote possibility of death at the hands of a criminal or protester. Death in pitched battle was not part of the bargain. However, when they did face such a possibility, they risked their lives in order to uphold the honor of the institution. Only after they had taken casualties, their *casa-cuartel* was no longer defensible, and escape was not possible did most guards feel that surrender was acceptable. They may not have won glory fighting to the death, but they had demonstrated that they were no cowards either.

While there were exceptions, both sides tried to fight in a humane manner, such as by respecting white flags. When negotiating surrenders, the guards of several posts wanted guarantees that they would not be killed, which certainly suggests a level of mistrust, but ultimately almost every post did surrender, and some entrusted their families to the rebels even as they continued to fight. In other words, the animosity between the two groups, while intense, had not reached a point at which either side felt that annihilation of the other was the only solution. The miners' goal was not necessarily to kill the guards but only to remove them from their position of authority in the community. Unlike in the cases of mining company employees and clerics, all but one of the rebels' fifteen executions of civil guards occurred immediately following the attacks on the *casas-cuarteles*, suggesting violence in the heat of the moment rather than long-standing hatreds.[39]

There was a gendered component to the script that the two sides followed as well. Guards faced the unique and often-awkward situation of having their wives and children with them in the *casas-cuarteles* even as they entered combat, which was considered to be a purely masculine sphere. Contemporary sources on the fighting do not present a homogenous vision of what the role of families was in these situations. In some cases, the defense of their families was portrayed as giving the guards an extra motivation to fight, and wives could have a role in the fighting by lending moral support and by caring for wounded guards. In this way, wives could be portrayed as fulfilling traditional gender roles even in this extreme situation. For example, the cover of the November 1934 *RTGC* depicts a woman handing ammunition to two guards who are furiously defending their *casa-cuartel*.

Even if a combat role was considered inappropriate for women, their presence did put them in danger, and there were at least two posts in the Fourth Company where the wife of a guard was killed.[40] Brian Bunk notes that conservative propaganda pieces written after the revolt celebrated one of these women, Julia Fraigedo, for being killed while actually taking part in the fighting in Ciaño.[41] Yet he emphasizes that "her actions did not signify that she was unwomanly because her deeds personified the protective ideal of Spanish womanhood. . . . She was not being celebrated for defending the police barracks but rather for fighting and dying beside her husband."[42] While women were thus sometimes portrayed as making a positive contribution to the defense of a post (and the families inside), women and children could also be depicted as weakening the guards' resolve, their terror and weeping causing the surrender of a post.

Either way, the unusual presence of women and children in the masculine world of combat could aid the defense of guards' honor in such a setting. Wives in particular either provided support for that defense, reaffirming its legitimacy, or women and children provided an excuse for guards to surrender with honor. Both guards and rebels understood that women should not participate directly in the fighting, and ceasefires were sometimes negotiated so that families could leave the *casas-cuarteles*, even if the guards intended to keep up the fight.[43]

A Fight to the Death: The Glorified Response

There were several posts in Fourth Company that did fight to the death, adopting a militaristic understanding of honor as death in battle rather than negotiation with the community. This section will focus on the two most such famous
examples from Fourth Company, incidents that occurred at Sama de Langreo
and Campomanes. In both of these cases, the attitudes of the commanding
officers were crucial. The Civil Guard's rigorous discipline meant that guards
followed officers' decisions to keep up the fight even as the situation grew desperate, but guards surrendered when these officers were killed. To the miners,
these officers had exceeded the boundaries of the combat ritual, and so they
responded with increased violence as well. These confrontations were the most
celebrated by the Civil Guard's supporters in the aftermath of the rebellion,
paving the way for future encounters to be similarly bloody.

The Langreo district, which included Sama, was one of the largest mining
areas in Asturias, with around forty thousand inhabitants, over eleven thousand of them miners.[44] It was located at the western end of the Nalón coalfield
on the road to Oviedo. The Civil Guard post there, headquarters of the Fourth
Company, was under the command of José Alonso Nart, a thirty-six-year-old
captain who had served for several years in Morocco before joining the *Benemérita*.[45] If Corporal Blanco's fate at Castilblanco was a lesson in the dangers
of a guard stepping into an unfamiliar local world, Captain Nart's story is an
example of the dangers of the practice of guards obtaining postings in their
native regions that Ahumada had been unable to end. As the leading civil guard
in this restive district, Nart had ordered searches for stolen dynamite and personally led the protection of the mines and offices of one of the largest mining
companies, Duro Felguera, in the years prior to 1934.[46] But since he hailed from
a family of civil guards based in Gijón with interests that extended across the
region, he could hardly present himself as a neutral enforcer of the law in these
situations.[47] As his guards monitored the miners of Sama de Langreo, Nart attended society events in Oviedo and bourgeois weddings in Gijón.[48] He himself
seems to have owned a mine in Asturias, and his mother owned an estate in
La Felguera, just cross the Nalón River from her son's headquarters in Sama.[49]
Less than five months prior to the uprising, when the La Felguera town council
moved to close his mother's estate, Nart tried to block the move by threatening

one of the councilors.[50] Although a causal effect cannot be proved, these class tensions between Nart and the miners whom he policed may have contributed to the violence of the rising in Sama.

On the day of the rebellion, October 5, since trouble had been expected, Sama did have more than its usual complement of civil guards. With men concentrated from nearby towns and provinces, Nart had a total of sixty at his disposal. In addition, a section of assault guards and a police station were nearby. Equipped with a machine gun, the guards there were able to resist the miners all day even though the *casa-cuartel* was no more than a large row house. The defenders attempted to escape the confines of the *cuartel* twice, and twice they were beaten back.[51] They also refused various requests for their surrender, although they did pause to permit the evacuation of the women and children inside.

By the morning of the sixth, the guards were very low on ammunition, food, and water, and dynamite explosions had made the air suffocating. They had already held out longer than any other Fourth Company post. If Nart had decided to surrender at that moment, no one would have questioned his actions. However, he chose the path of glory through death by making a last-ditch attempt to escape to the mountains that had no hope of success. Indeed, he and his party of volunteers became scattered during the attempt, and all were killed.[52] The defenders who remained surrendered just minutes after Nart's death, which indicates that it was his determination that had led them to sustain the fight for so long in the first place.

It appears that some miners believed that the guards had overacted their part in this ritual by holding out in such a long and bloody fashion, voiding the need to play by the combat ritual's unwritten rules. As the surrendering guards left the *casa-cuartel* with their hands in the air, some of the rebels opened fire with their shotguns, killing between five and ten and thereby exacting their own revenge for the deaths of several of their comrades in the fight.[53] In total, thirty-eight civil guards were killed at Sama and one injured, but Nart did win his glory—in 1945 he was posthumously awarded the Cross of San Fernando.[54]

Campomanes was more of a village than a town like Sama, but its location was of crucial importance in that it was in the middle of the narrow pass through the mountains that connected Oviedo with León and, hence, the rest of Spain. The five civil guards there were attacked by sixty rebels on October 5 when their station commandant refused to surrender.[55] After he and another guard had been killed and the miners' dynamite had collapsed the *casa-cuartel*'s roof, the remaining defenders surrendered.[56]

Meanwhile, León's civil governor had received a telegram from a town just across the border in Asturias that read: "I am unable to communicate with Oviedo. Many trucks with armed revolutionaries passing by here for León."[57] The governor sent eighteen guards by car to investigate, equipped with one machine gun and under the command of Lieutenant Fernando Halcón Lucas.[58] Halcón came from a military family, and during his time in the army he had served for several years in Morocco, winning two medals there. Unusually, he had remained in the army for nine years before joining the Civil Guard only seven months before the October revolution.[59] Along his way to Campomanes, he picked up various other civil and assault guards, bringing his total to thirty-five. His party came under attack as it approached the town and found itself stuck in the middle of the road with the machine gun malfunctioning. Halcón had half his men stay near the vehicles while he took shelter with the rest in a factory.[60] The rebels' siege of the factory intensified as reinforcements arrived from other towns, but the guards still made two trips to their vehicles for more ammunition, taking casualties along the way. Halcón ordered three volunteers to slip out of the factory and use the nearest telephone or telegraph that they could find to call for more reinforcements.[61] The message these men got through to León triggered the mobilization of the two infantry regiments that were garrisoned there.[62] Meanwhile, dynamite killed all but one inside the factory in Campomanes.[63] After seeing that the factory had fallen, the remaining guards in the street fled.[64] By the time the army arrived on the scene the next day, soldiers found that Halcón's body had been mutilated.[65]

The story of Campomanes is in many ways similar to that of Sama. As in Sama, the fact that the guards at Campomanes kept fighting for so long seems to have been largely a consequence of their commanders' determination not to surrender; once these leaders died, the others capitulated quickly. The officers' refusal to give up was not shared by the average guard, who felt that a vigorous fight was enough to maintain the Civil Guard's honor. In both cases, the rebels also punished the guards for exceeding the limits of the combat ritual—at Sama they killed prisoners; at Campomanes they mutilated Halcón's corpse. At Sama, preexisting animosities between Nart and the miners may have also played a part. Perhaps it is also not a coincidence that both Nart and

Halcón had served in Morocco—they may have acquired their taste for glory there. This pursuit of glory turned out to be deadly but not useless. The fight in Campomanes delayed the rebels' efforts to establish a southern front that would stop the government troops advancing from León. While Halcón did not receive a posthumous Cross of San Fernando, he is also remembered with pride by the Civil Guard historians.

Surrender and Collusion: The Dishonorable Response

Civil guards like Nart and Halcón demarcated the upper boundary of what actions their institution considered honorable when the Fourth Company was put to the test by the frontal assaults of October 5, 1934. Others defined the lower boundary through actions that were deemed dishonorable. The arbitrator here was the military justice system, which convicted four of the Fourth Company's guards of, variously, negligence, crimes against military honor, and military rebellion.[66] In these instances, the guards surrendered with little or no fighting. Even if resistance was futile, the courts-martial (composed primarily of officers in the regular army) ruled that a substantial fight was required, preferably until the casa-cuartel was no longer defensible or ammunition had run out and there was no hope of escape. A close examination of the most prominent such trial, that of Lieutenant Gabriel Torrens Llompart, chief of the Ujo Section, permits a reconstruction, through counterexample, of the minimum requirements for defending the Civil Guard's honor in a combat situation.

The fight at Ujo began in a similar manner to that of others in the coalfields. The assault on the casa-cuartel commenced around 5:00 a.m. with the heavy use of dynamite. After suffering one wounded, Torrens surrendered the post around 9:00 a.m., but, according to one of the rebels directing the attack, he could have kept fighting because they found unopened boxes of ammunition and grenades inside the casa-cuartel.[67] What would cause serious trouble for Torrens, however, were his actions after his surrender. The rebels informed him that he and his men would be killed unless he aided them in obtaining the surrender of other casas-cuarteles, and he agreed to cooperate. Three other Fourth Company posts had been fighting vigorously against the rebels and refused multiple offers to surrender, but when Torrens spoke to the commanders of each one, they agreed to give in.[68] Given the hierarchical nature of the Civil Guard and its high degree of solidarity, when an officer of their own institution told them that their efforts were futile, guards felt they could surrender with honor. Just as Nart and Halcón had been able to push their men to resist beyond the call of duty, Torrens was able to persuade guards to give up more quickly than usual. After these successes with the Civil Guard, Torrens became a kind of negotiator-in-chief for the rebels, parlaying later in the conflict with both Brigadier General Carlos Bosch Bosch's column in the south of Asturias and General Eduardo López Ochoa's column coming down from the north.

Ultimately, it was the army that would be the judge of Torrens's actions when he was court-martialed after the rebellion was over.[69] At the trial, the prosecutor focused his statement on Torrens's failure to make honor his first priority. But the vision of honor the prosecutor outlined was that of the army's idea of death in battle. The investigative judge had already established an expectation of a fight to the death when he had asked Torrens, "Why did you not defend the building until its collapse, as was your duty, evacuating at that point the families of the guards and continue it [the fight] with your subordinates in the place of honor until losing your life[?]" The lieutenant had to admit in response that "effectively he recognizes that he could have resisted until the last moment without effecting the evacuation and leaving them [his men] to become prisoners." The prosecutor therefore portrayed Torrens's actions as a disgrace "for all who believe that honor is the first of the duties that one must complete," because the lieutenant chose to save his life when he should have understood that "to die killing is to live with honor even though one's life ends."

Torrens's defender, Civil Guard Lieutenant Pedro Martínez García de Ribadesella, also made honor central to his argument, describing his client as "a modest soldier who . . . always had as his motto the cult of honor." At the trial, Torrens had a new story to prove this claim, explaining that he had attempted a sally from the *casa-cuartel* in order to allow the families inside a chance to escape. Unfortunately, according to him, his men were surrounded by rebels outside of the building and captured. This narrative allowed him to avoid surrendering at all (thus conforming to the idea that rapid surrender could not be honorable) and made an apparently foolish decision to leave the *casa-cuartel* seem like a humanitarian effort to save women and children. The story played on the notion that the presence of family members at these fights was detrimental to the male sphere of combat.

The defense also tried to argue that Torrens had not willingly aided the rebels by dropping the idea of political neutrality. One of his men assured the prosecutor that Torrens read right-wing newspapers like *El Debate*, and García de Ribadesella declared that his client "detests socialist ideals." Torrens himself seemed to think that his prior uses of violence would prove that he did not sympathize with the rebels. He recounted how he had shot a worker in the leg when the man ignored a traffic stop. García de Ribadesella also proudly presented as evidence of Torrens's lack of sympathy for the rebels that he had fired on workers during the June 1934 general strike and bragged that *Avance* had "injuriously censured his conduct."

The judges were not convinced by the defense's efforts. Instead, they concluded that Torrens had surrendered the post "without having exhausted all means of defense" and without negotiating any conditions. The original copy in Torrens's handwriting of the letter demanding the surrender of General Bosch's column also convinced them that he had aided the rebels willingly. They found him guilty of crimes against military honor for his surrender and of military rebellion for cooperation and leadership in the uprising. He received a death sentence, which was later commuted to life in prison by the Supreme Court.

Torrens's case highlights the shifts in emphasis within the Civil Guard's culture brought about by the exceptional circumstances of the October 1934 uprising. Torrens and García de Ribadesella sought to ground their defense in the humanitarian component of the Civil Guard's conception of honor, but the judges of the court-martial, five out of six of whom were not civil guards, would have none of it. They preferred the prosecutor's more militaristic definition that emphasized death in battle. Even the defense's story about Torrens being overwhelmed by the rebels suggests that it held the idea that there could be no honorable surrender. In addition, its celebration of Torrens's distaste for socialism and previous violence against workers is indicative of the move away from the Civil Guard's ideal of political neutrality toward explicit antagonism with the working classes.

Multiple Responses in One Casa-cuartel:
The Curious Case of the Oviedo Command Headquarters

Stepping outside of the coalfields, the case of the Oviedo Command headquarters also deserves consideration because the different definitions of honorable conduct discussed above all manifested themselves in this one large *casa-cuartel*, allowing for close comparison between them.[70] While the guards present there were prepared to defend the building, in this case the senior officers felt that full military combat was not the role of the Civil Guard. Some of their junior officers saw the situation differently, urging offensive actions and putting the protection of honor above the protection of life. As in the case of Torrens, the military courts would decide which definition of the Civil Guard's role would be given precedence, and they chose a fully military pursuit of glory.

Different ideas of what defending a *casa-cuartel* should entail emerged as soon as the rebels had the Oviedo Command headquarters thoroughly pinned down on the sixth. Sixty-one-year-old Colonel Juan Díaz Carmena and the aforementioned Lieutenant Colonel Moreno Molina ordered guards to remain in the building and hold out for as long as possible, even though the third officer, Major Gonzalo Bueno Rodríguez, urged sallies to aid outlying posts. The colonels' orders suggest that they saw the Civil Guard's role in combat as being entirely self-defense. When the rebels brought a captured artillery piece to bear on the building, the colonels decided that such a situation was no place for a police force like the Civil Guard to be in. Therefore, on the eighth, they asked Army Colonel Alfredo Navarro for permission to evacuate to the army's adjacent Pelayo Barracks, but Navarro ordered them to stay in place unless defense of the *cuartel* could not be maintained. An hour later, the Civil Guard colonels concluded that this was already the case. Although some of the bolder officers may not have agreed with this decision, they supported their commanders and gave their unanimous consent to the evacuation.

When the rebellion was over, the two colonels were court-martialed for negligence (and, in the case of Díaz Carmena, crimes against military honor as well). One of the principal questions in the case was whether or not they had disobeyed Colonel Navarro's order in abandoning the *casa-cuartel* so quickly, before they had run out of ammunition and supplies. A team of engineers evaluated the amount of damage that the building had sustained, and it concluded that the building was very flimsy and that it had been hit by ten to twelve cannon balls. Colonel Moreno Molina emphasized that one ought to "keep in mind that the Civil Guard's *casa-cuartel* is not a military position—well, the building is already given the name '*casa*' [house]—and one can evacuate it if the defense necessitates it." The judges were not convinced; they concluded that since the *casa-cuartel* had only been attacked by one piece of artillery and the only casualties were five injured, the structure was never really in danger.

While Nart and Halcón led their men to continue fighting even after most units would have surrendered, the Oviedo commanders' lack of enthusiasm for involving the Civil Guard in military combat had a trickle-down effect as well. In fact, the low morale of the guards was also a factor contributing to the colonels' decision to evacuate. At the trial, their defender attributed the low morale to the artillery bombardment, the lack of reinforcements, and the constant fighting. He also portrayed the presence of women and children as detrimental to masculine combat by noting the demoralizing effect of the terrorized and weeping families inside the *casa-cuartel*. But again the investigative judge was unimpressed. He maintained that the low morale was caused in part by the poor leadership of the commanding officers: "With other more decisive and energetic chiefs there would not have been such a disagreeable spectacle of attacks and nervousness among the personnel that had to complete such an elevated and honorable mission."

Contrasting ideas of honorable leadership were also apparent in the evacuation to Pelayo. The colonels' plan was to have a main column go first with the remaining supplies and a second follow quickly with the rest of the men. Major Bueno again seized the opportunity to be in the lead and volunteered to head the first column. It came under machine-gun fire as it made its way between buildings, and Bueno and two sergeants were killed.[71] These men had died while facing danger in combat, but the colonels were not eager to follow suit. The three corpses lay in the street while the colonels quickly slipped through in a car without harm as part of the second column.[72] Although a retrieval of the bodies would have been of no practical value, at the trial the judges deemed avoiding the dishonor of having them lie in the street important enough to be worth the risk, as did the junior officers who had volunteered to lead a retrieval attempt. Yet once again the two Civil Guard colonels, now joined by Colonel Navarro, had considered prudence the better part of valor.

Once the guards were inside the Pelayo Barracks, ambiguities over what the military status of the Civil Guard was caused problems as well. The major who was in charge of the building's defense offered command to Colonel Díaz Carmena as the senior officer (Navarro was already occupied as military governor), but Díaz Carmena refused, arguing that a guard could not command army forces since his institution was not under the jurisdiction of the Ministry of War. In fact, the guards were under the Ministry of War at that moment since the civil governor had declared a state of war. While they may not have understood that this was the case, the larger issue was that apparently some officers envisioned the Civil Guard as an essentially peacetime policing force while others saw it as fully ready to take on a combat role if necessary.

On the eleventh, General López Ochoa's column lifted the siege of the Pelayo Barracks.[73] But, like Torrens, colonels Díaz Carmena and Moreno Molina (as well as some of the army officers) still had to answer for the choices that they had made before a court-martial. The tribunal found both guilty and gave Díaz Carmena a life sentence for crimes against military honor and Moreno Molina four years for negligence. As in the other cases that this section has considered, the judges ruled not only on the guilt or innocence of these two officers, but also, by extension, on whether or not the expectations of the Civil Guard were closer to those of a police or military institution. The colonels' plan of action was that of virtually every Civil Guard post when attacked: defend the casa-cuartel. But when the rebels brought artillery to bear, they transformed the fight (as least in the minds of these colonels) into a full-scale military siege of a kind that the Civil Guard was simply not prepared to counter. Even inside Pelayo, these officers felt that holding one's ground was the honorable and prudent course of action for the guards and that military command should be left to army officers. Other more junior officers, and the court-martial, thought differently. They believed that honor and prudence (and even survival) were not compatible. Cases such as the younger officers' eagerness to retrieve the bodies of their fallen comrades indicate they believed that the defense of honor, rather than of life, was to be the primary consideration in their decision making and that honor had to be asserted through offensive action.

October 1934 in Asturias was certainly not the first time that the Civil Guard had fought against an uprising, but never before had it faced such a concentrated assault. The attacks were a test of how this militarized police force's honor code would guide its actions in military combat. Suddenly, guards' casas-cuarteles seemed more like the blockhouses of the Rif than posts for rural policing. Even though the scale of the attacks was unprecedented, civil guards did follow a script that had been developed for generations through conflicts with Carlists, anarchists, and now Socialists. In every town that rose up, the Civil Guard post, as the key symbol of the central state's imposition of its authority over the locality, was the first target. The guards dutifully played their part, defending that authority and their honor along with it. As usual, the rebels' pistols and shotguns were no match for the guards' rifles. However, the miners' dynamite and overwhelming numbers reversed the usual balance, making the guards' defensive efforts largely symbolic. After their *casas-cuarteles* were rendered indefensible and escape had proved impossible, guards felt that they had demonstrated their valor and that they could surrender.

There were variations on the theme, however, and much depended on the attitude of the individual station commandant. Some officers, like Captain Nart and Lieutenant Halcón, preferred to fight to the death in hopes of winning glory, and their units did indeed suffer the highest casualties. Others, such as Lieutenant Torrens and the colonels in Oviedo, believed that putting up some fight without exhausting all means of defense was sufficient. As it appears that each officer acted in a way that he believed was honorable, the matter came down to a question of differing definitions of honor.

Courts-martial made matters somewhat clearer in the aftermath of the conflict. Judges found guards like Torrens, Díaz Carmena, and Moreno Molina guilty of not upholding their "military honor." Meanwhile, the tone of the Civil Guard press in the months that followed was one of celebration rather than sadness.[74] For example, in the November 1934 issue of the *RTGC*, a list of fallen guards bore the title "Glory to the Heroes," and the Civil Guard was described as the "vanguard of the army."[75] After this attack on the Civil Guard by seemingly the entire pueblo, maintaining a peaceful coexistence with that pueblo would no longer be a concern. Henceforth, for many guards, as for the army, honor would mean glory in battle.

The interactions among the four factors on which these case studies have concentrated—the Civil Guard's organizational culture, the mass mobilizations of the Socialists in particular, republican governmental policy, and the choices of individual actors—all played a part in explaining why both the insurrection of October 1934 in Asturias and its aftermath were two of the most violent and polarizing events of the Second Republic period. On the surface, the cause of the violence during the revolt itself is easily explained: rebels attacked Civil Guard posts, and guards defended themselves. However, the pattern that these combat rituals fell into had been shaped by the Civil Guard's history of conflict with Asturian miners and the institution's culture of honor, which guards felt demanded that they put up a fight until further resistance was no longer feasible. There were also a few individual officers who chose to fight to the bitter end following a more militaristic vision of honor as glory through death in battle that was reminiscent of the vitalist approach of the *africanistas* in the Spanish Legion. Afterward, these individuals were glorified, while courts-martial showed little sympathy for those who did not put up much of a fight. Through these tribunals, the republic was permitting the army a part in defining what honorable conduct for a civil guard would mean in such an unprecedented situation. Therefore, the state was complicit in this introduction of an understanding of the institution's honor as an absolute confrontation rather than a nonlethal negotiation with citizens. This new current in the corps's thinking stayed with it as it entered the even more turbulent year of 1936.

NINE

ASTURIAS 2

The Double-Edged Sword of Revenge

he account that Ignacio Lavilla, editor of *Avance*, gave of meeting Major Lisardo Doval Bravo, the civil guard in charge of the repression following the Asturias revolt, is nothing short of chilling. As a prisoner, Lavilla described how guards escorted him through a passageway to a large office. There Doval stood, with a map of Asturias spread out before him. He told Lavilla that he wanted him to point out where Amador Fernández, president of the Socialist miner's union in the region, was hiding. Lavilla noticed that "Doval had a tic that he used to impose more respect. An earlobe trembled when he became enraged. He always had a deep frown; there was forever an expression of contained violence on his face." After a few more hours in his cell to think it over, Lavilla was brought before Doval again but refused to divulge the information. Doval unleashed his violence, hitting Lavilla a few times himself before ordering the guards to finish the job. Lavilla remarked that "the disciplinary rigor of the guards was absolute. They were young [and] silent. They struck without warning, coldly and unfeelingly."[1]

The cinematic nature of Lavilla's description was indicative of the symbolic power that Doval was trying to achieve through his repression. In many ways, it followed a pattern set by so many previous examples, such as Montjuïc in the 1890s, that it had become part of the Civil Guard's policing culture. Extrajudicial executions, mass arrests, beatings, and torture were the order of the day. Yet this repression also had a severity and scope not seen previously. Since the scale of the assault on the guards had been unprecedented, the scale of the repression was naturally magnified in turn. However, the sadistic tortures perpetrated by Doval and his team were more than simply an expanded version of previous repressions. Earning the respect of all classes was no longer a concern. Instead, Doval's team sought to take its revenge on the workers of Asturias and systematically terrorize them. Guards hoped to sow enough fear in them to ensure that they would never put their honor at risk again. For the first time, guards deemed the working-class population of an entire region to be enemies. It was the Radical-CEDA government that enabled the corps to take this approach by declaring a state of war, creating a special investigative team with almost unlimited powers, and appointing a particularly brutal officer to lead this group. Whereas the miners of Asturias had challenged the Civil Guard's right to enforce the law of the republican state in their communities, guards now tested whether there were any limits on their authority under the republic or if they had an unfettered ability to take the administration of justice into their own hands.

These efforts failed to prevent further opposition to the Civil Guard. On the contrary, the atrocities had more profound national repercussions than ever, sparking renewed criticism of the institution in the 1936 electoral campaign that contributed to the polarization process and the Civil Guard's shift away from its ideal of political neutrality. The institution was adapting to the increasingly polarized politics of the Second Republic by embracing a more openly antagonistic stance toward the working classes. Yet the Civil Guard could not prevent the republic's working-class organizations from using the mass media to inform the public of its methods and thereby to tarnish its reputation, deepening resentments on both sides.

ASSEMBLING DOVAL'S TEAM

Within a day of the rebellion's launch, General Bosch's battalion from León and General López Ochoa's two battalions in Galicia were mobilizing to take back Asturias from the miners. It was the first time in Spanish history that workers and soldiers would face each other in a conventional battle.[2] Incredibly, the rebels were able to halt Bosch's advance northward in the narrow valley near Campomanes and keep him pinned down there, even as the government troops received continual reinforcements.[3] Meanwhile, López Ochoa's advance from the west was more successful. The real boon for the government began on the tenth, however, when legionaries and *regulares* (as the Spanish military units composed of Moroccan troops were known) from Morocco under Lieutenant Colonel Juan Yagüe Blanco arrived by sea in Gijón. López Ochoa was then able to use these veteran fighters to retake Oviedo.[4] By the eighteenth, López Ochoa, who was in overall command of field operations, reached an agreement with the remaining rebels whereby they would surrender in exchange for promises that the colonial troops would not occupy the coalfields and that there would be no reprisals.[5] Government forces moved into the coalfields the next day, ending the military phase of the insurrection.

While the guards' defenses of their *casa-cuarteles* may have borne a vague resemblance to colonial warfare, for *africanista* officers like Colonel Yagüe and General Francisco Franco, who was the special director of overall operations from Madrid, the similarities were clear. Since they considered the workers of Asturias to be rebels, as the Moroccans had been, these officers felt that rules of colonial rather than continental European warfare should apply. Both the legionaries and *regulares* had become accustomed to practicing a brutal kind of warfare in Morocco, and their commanders made little effort to discourage them from doing the same in Asturias.[6] Widespread looting was the most characteristic feature of their behavior.[7] There were also a number of killings, sometimes aided by local civil guards who could identify targets.[8]

Guards perpetrated their share of killings as well—55 percent of all the executions by government forces—but they would do so for purposes of calculated revenge rather than looting. In many cases, the junior officers who ordered the killings had been posted in the region and were easily able to identify their victims. In fact, the two largest massacres by the Civil Guard were the direct results of the two largest battles it had fought during the rebellion: Oviedo and Sama. Beginning the very day of its liberation by López Ochoa's men, Captain Nilo Tella Cantos set up a "Hall of Justice" in the Pelayo Barracks and, after brief questioning, ordered the execution of an estimated forty-three prisoners there.[9] In the Nalón valley, guards from the Sama, La Felguera, and El Entrego posts, led by Lieutenant Rafael Alonso Nart, the brother of the captain who had been killed during the rising, selected at least twenty-one prisoners they believed were most involved in the uprising. The guards then tied their prisoners up at a site near the town of Carbayín and killed them with swords and other weapons before tossing the bodies into a mass grave.[10] Several of the guards involved, including Nart, of course, had been personally affected by the revolt, but the murders also represented a more general act of revenge by the guards of the valley against their recent attackers.[11]

Such an uncoordinated and lethal repression could not be allowed to continue indefinitely. At the same time, conservative newspapers were putting pressure on the government in Madrid to ensure that workers would never attempt a revolution again.[12] The panic that Barcelona's bourgeoisie had felt during the Restoration about the social order being upended was now spreading around the country. Therefore, the government set ambitious goals for a more formalized repression: rounding up the leaders of the revolt, finding all 11,465 weapons that had been removed from a captured arms factory, and getting back all 14,425,000 pesetas that had been taken from the Bank of Spain in Oviedo.[13]

Therefore, while there were societal pressures for a harsh response, it was the Radical-CEDA government that set the stage for a particularly brutal repression in the months following the revolt. It moved quickly to declare a nationwide state of war, ban all socialist organizations, reinstate the death penalty, and crack down on private arms possession.[14] As for who would lead the repression, the government considered the Civil Guard the natural choice because it was a military force with experience in rural counterinsurgency and criminal investigation. The Civil Guard knew the coalfield communities better than any other government institution. However, eighty-six members of the corps had just been killed in the region, more than in any other single conflict in its history up to that point.[15] The Civil Guard was in no position to carry out its duties in a neutral and humanitarian fashion.

Diego Hidalgo, now minister of war, wanted an officer with toughness and knowledge of the region to lead a special investigative team in Asturias. General Franco suggested Doval, whom he had known since their days as cadets together at the Infantry Academy. As was the case with the Civil Guard as a whole, Doval was in one sense the ideal candidate for the job. He had been hardened by several years of service in Morocco (receiving a Cross of Military Merit), and he had extensive experience with criminal investigation and political repression alike. He knew Asturias well, having served in the region for about ten years, and had participated in the harsh repression of the general strike there in 1917. During the 1920s, he had earned a medal or note of thanks in his service record for apprehending criminals or suppressing disorders on an almost yearly basis.[16]

In another sense, however, the choice of Doval boded ill for Asturias's workers. His work repressing strikes and protests had given him a reputation for cruelty and violence.[17] He had quelled the 1930 general strike in Gijón so ruthlessly that the CNT had tried to kill him in revenge.[18] On April 18, 1931, just four days after the republic began, the municipal governments of Oviedo, Gijón, and Mieres had all demanded his transfer for ignoring whatever regulations he found inconvenient.[19] Previous chapters have explored how the Civil Guard was willing to bend the law when it came to questions of honor, but it appears Doval was willing to ignore it completely. He had held the ideal of loyalty to the government in power in similar disregard. It was only in April 1934 that the Amnesty Law had released him from the penal colony of Villa Cisneros in the Spanish Sahara, where he had been banished for participation in the Sanjurjada.[20] In other words, Franco had found in Doval the experience, ruthlessness, and politics he was looking for. As for Hidalgo, he was so impressed with Doval during an interview in Madrid that he gave the major special powers, effectively making him the dictatorial governor of Asturias.[21]

From October 23, Doval took charge of the repression in Asturias, shifting the Civil Guard's method of revenge from killings to torture. The means at his disposal were a mobile division composed of five columns of one hundred civil guards and twenty-five assault guards, with access to an infantry and machine-gun unit and the other civil guards posted around the region.[22] These were men picked from among the many guards who were enthusiastic about Doval's project. He received telegrams from guards across Spain requesting to join the unit, eager to do their part in avenging their institution.[23] He looked for men who had similar experience in war and repression.[24] Captain Tella Cantos, who was also a decorated veteran of the Moroccan wars and who already had a poor reputation in Asturias, continued at the Model Prison of Oviedo as the head of its investigative office.[25] Meanwhile, Captain Antonio de Reparaz Gallo led the effort to track down the most prominent leaders of the revolt. As for Doval, he personally took charge of an abandoned convent known as Las Adoratrices that he had converted into a detention center.

OLD METHODS ON A NEW SCALE

Doval's basic methods for tracking down arms and fugitives were straightforward. The first step was obtaining information about whom to arrest, which was readily provided by local elites and others in some way harmed by the revolution who served as anonymous informants.[26] Then, Doval's teams systematically swept through the mining towns, arresting thousands and detaining them in makeshift facilities, such as those mentioned above.[27] They used motor vehicles to come up on a town quickly, taking any fugitives hiding there by surprise. Army Colonel Antonio Aranda Mata, who observed Doval's work, described the next step: "The work is quite simple: with admirable patience and meticulousness, the forces go through each house," and, if a wanted man was not found, his relatives were detained until he turned himself in—and he had to do so with a rifle. Aranda concluded that while the technique seems excessive, "It gives some admirable results."[28]

Without question, Doval's men carried out a systematic program of torture inside their detention facilities.[29] As previous chapters have demonstrated, torture was an investigative technique that was part of the Civil Guard's police history and culture, and these men were under pressure to make large numbers of arrests and weapons confiscations quickly. However, the goal of the torture seems to have been to terrorize the population into never challenging the Civil Guard's authority again as much as to gather information. Most prisoners were never charged with any crime; they simply received a frightening beating and were then released after just a few days.[30] Given that an estimated ten thousand or more people were detained between October and December 1934 in Asturias, it is safe to say that a substantial portion of the region's working-class population went through this experience. If the goal had been to punish and make an example of the revolt's leaders, then such vast numbers would not have been necessary. As for the investigative aspect of the operation, although the guards had some success learning the locations of weapons, most wanted men were found during the mass roundups rather than through leads gained during interrogations.[31] Of course, the prosecutions that did occur took place under military jurisdiction, with the crime of "military rebellion" being charged in connection with a popular revolt for the first time, although prosecutors also employed the old catch-all charge of "crime against the military honor" of the security forces. With the death penalty reinstated, the courts sentenced dozens to this fate, but only six were ever executed thanks to a later amnesty.[32] Nevertheless, again, punishment of individual rebels was not the civil guards' primary goal. They felt that their institution had been insulted by the community of Asturian workers as a whole, and so they desired to punish that community collectively. While the courts could never handle such a massive operation, the guards could at least exact one night of their own style of revenge on each prisoner, terrifying him enough, they hoped, that he would never try to stand up to them again.

The torture methods that Doval and his men employed were not especially sophisticated. In fact, ordinary beatings were the most common technique. In addition to verbal abuse, prisoners frequently complained of broken ribs, knocked-out teeth, testicle mutilation, and wrist injuries from being tightly handcuffed during the beatings. Between these sessions, guards kept them in crowded and damp cells with little food or water. The goal of such treatment was often to force prisoners to sign prewritten confessions or denunciations of other suspects. Mock executions were employed if the beatings were not enough to obtain the confession.[33] Such treatment was too much for some to bear. There were several reports of mental breakdowns and attempted suicides among the prisoners, some successful.[34] In a few cases, the beatings themselves proved deadly as well.[35] More commonly, guards sent prisoners to the hospital (but only if absolutely necessary) or left them with chronic injuries or permanent scars.[36] In other words, the guards were making little effort to hide their work. Only knowledge of what was going on inside the detention centers would make Asturians fearful enough to give up hope of another revolt.

Doval also added a psychological element to his work to further terrorize the population. Even his choice of a former convent as his main detention center was symbolic. As was often the case with the *casas-cuarteles*, two markers of nineteenth-century liberalism's legacies were brought together—the abandoned convent and the Civil Guard. Lavilla described the building as having a dungeon-like quality, including "very high ceilings, an absence of furniture, stone floors, [and] dampness."[37] No wonder that for many commentators, Las Adoratrices provoked comparisons to even earlier historical periods—they described Doval's work as "medieval" and "inquisitorial."[38] Juan-Simeón Vidarte even saw a kind of perverse poetry in the convent being a place "where previously God was invoked, and now it recalled Dante's Inferno."[39] Inside the building, Doval played loud music that echoed through the halls along with the screams of the prisoners being tortured.[40] Such descriptions suggest that Doval was intentionally seeking to mythologize his work in Las Adoratrices. The medieval setting, the psychological manipulations, the guards' reputations for coldness, and his own infamous personality combined to create horror stories that were ripe for telling to the friends and families of the over five hundred prisoners who passed through the facility.[41] In a sense, Doval was indeed seeking to win respect for the Civil Guard, but it was a respect that was synonymous with fear, not admiration.

The methods of Doval and his team were nothing new, indicating continuity in the Civil Guard's practices as a force of political repression. Guards followed their institution's unofficial investigative technique of beating confessions and denunciations out of prisoners. In so doing, guards exacted their own punishment on prisoners for insulting their institution before they handed the suspects over to the judicial system. The motivation of revenge can be seen most clearly in the actions of Rafael Alonso Nart. Although he perpetrated the Carbayín massacre on the same day as Doval's arrival in Asturias, afterward he continued to conduct raids and make arrests in the Langreo area as he searched for his brother's killers.[42] According to a left-republican deputy from Sama, Doval allowed Nart to remain there for over two months, detaining in the basement of the local *casa del pueblo* some eighty people whom he blamed for his brother's death, torturing them "until the guilty ones were punished."[43]

Although idea of the Civil Guard taking justice into its own hands was not new, the scale of Doval's operation in Asturias was unprecedented. Its ambition matched the scale of the Asturias rebellion, with the number of arrests in the thousands. The way in which his team systematically sought to terrorize its victims, scarring them both physically and mentally, suggests that this time guards were trying to do more than make an example out of a few revolutionary activists. The guards were also trying to instill fear in as many working-class Asturian families as they could. No longer did they maintain the fiction that their deeds would earn them the respect of most of the population. Now the Asturian working class was the enemy, and it had to be forced into submission.

In other words, Doval's program of terrorizing the population was part of a larger effort to strip miners of all political power within Asturias's mining communities.[44] For example, as workers lined up to be rehired by Duro Felguera, a civil guard who had escaped Sama during the revolt reviewed each worker, conducting "an analysis of the revolutionary responsibility of each one."[45] In December, the civil governor formalized this process by requiring workers to hold a photo identification card approved by the police or Civil Guard in order to be eligible for employment.[46] Finally, workers seeking to be rehired were required to hand in a firearm in order to do so.[47]

Government policies, political pressures, and individual leaders contributed to the Civil Guard's shift to this more openly repressive role. It was the Lerroux government that gave the Civil Guard the lead part in the repression, despite its obvious resentments, because its local knowledge made it too valuable a tool to pass up. The government also made a particularly harsh officer the special commissary and, at least initially, did not put him under any oversight. Conservative sectors of society also put pressure on Doval to severely punish the revolutionaries and aided him in doing so. Nevertheless, the fact that Doval's actions were the logical extension of long-standing elements of the Civil Guard's culture leads one to believe that the basic pattern of mass arrests and torture would have been followed even if another officer had been appointed to the position, although Doval took these practices to a new extreme.[48] The repression in Asturias provided a hint of what the guards' organizational culture made them capable of when they were given free rein to take revenge on those they believed had challenged their honor.

POLARIZING NATIONAL REPERCUSSIONS

October 1934 saw the Socialists move outside of the legal bounds of political contestation, but Doval also paid little heed to the law during the repression. Since his work lacked legal grounding, he sought support for it from the public. He had some success in doing so, at least among the conservative sectors of society, and ultimately it was his ambition, rather than his methods, that proved to be his undoing. Meanwhile, left-wing groups began to construct a counternarrative that presented Doval's efforts as nothing short of demonic. It was the government's assignment of the Civil Guard, and Doval in particular, and its toleration (at least initially) of the team's brutal methods that allowed this new interpretation to emerge. In enabling Doval's excesses, the Radical-CEDA government forfeited its ability to argue that it had stayed faithful to the republican rules of the game while the Left had not. The ability to portray such right-wing governments once again as the enemies of the republic enabled left-wing parties to find common ground and take the reins of power for themselves.

At first, the government's strategy was simply to have the broader public know as little about the repression as possible. It used censorship to ensure that only favorable coverage of its forces got through, and it had banned the papers of the workers' parties anyway. While the remaining papers had limited coverage of the repression, they were filled with exaggerated stories of atrocities perpetrated by the rebels.[49] At first, these reports were effective in turning public opinion against the miners.[50] After the deaths of so many guards, all the usual means of showing support for the institution and its work were also set in motion—letters and articles of praise, donations, and homages.[51] Doval's efforts earned him special praise. His papers contain seventy letters of congratulations and thanks written between October and December 1934. The letters came from all over Spain, including quite a few from Asturias.[52]

Doval understood that the republic's mass press would ensure that the whole country would be watching him (to the extent that the censors allowed). Therefore, he tried to take advantage of this publicity to strengthen his already extraordinary power in Asturias. He may have aspired to become the director general of security or even the inspector general of the Civil Guard.[53] His strategy was to hold frequent press conferences when high-profile arrests were made, assuring the public that "as long as a single rifle remains in the province, I will not leave Asturias."[54] But weeks went by and he had still not located the fugitive he wanted most: Ramón González Peña, the supposed *generalísimo* of the revolt.[55] Captain Reparaz and his men eventually confirmed that he was in the house of a religious family friend by keeping it under observation while disguised as miners. However, early on the morning of December 3, it was Doval who led a team of ninety civil and assault guards in the raid on the house, taking a photo of the handcuffed prisoner for the newspapers.[56] Doval promptly received another flood of congratulatory telegrams from around the country, and Oviedo residents staged a large celebration in front of his office.[57]

Doval may have sought positive publicity, but he could not keep the darker aspects of his work a secret forever. Just weeks into his assignment, challenges to his narrative were beginning to emerge, particularly in England and France. Some of these documents found their way into Spain, usually in the form of pamphlets that reprinted investigative reports. These pamphlets sought to shock the reader through the sheer number of accounts of executions and torture that the reports contained, repeating the familiar form of writing about Civil Guard atrocities that radical groups had been following since at least the Montjuïc case in the 1890s. The primary goal was to undermine the government that had permitted such atrocities to take place, but the propaganda certainly did not help the Civil Guard's reputation either, particularly since Doval made such a charismatic villain.

In early November, a left-republican deputy, Félix Gordón Ordás, brought dozens of cases of executions and torture from around northern Spain directly to the attention of President Alcalá Zamora since Prime Minister Lerroux had refused to allow Gordón Ordás to present his evidence in the Cortes.[58] Doval's team reacted angrily, accusing Gordón Ordás of using his report to boost his own political career and arresting a mailman who had brought newspapers containing his accusations into Asturias. José Valdivia, the director general of security, sent an inspector to investigate all this, but Doval blocked the inspector's efforts as well, claiming that his special status placed him under the exclusive supervision of the minister of war. Captain Reparaz, writing during the Civil War, recalled how resentful the guards in Asturias were about the increasing scrutiny. He wrote that "the [masonic] lodges influenced things in Madrid. The government recommended 'much caution' in our labor," advice that in his opinion forced the guards to treat important prisoners "like distinguished guests in the prisons."[59]

Ultimately, it was Doval's refusal to have his power challenged rather than his cruelty that ended his reign in Asturias. Angered by Doval's rebuke of the inspector and envious of his power, Valdivia convinced Lerroux to order him transferred to Morocco on December 8 to become the chief of general security there.[60] Yet the major enjoyed the support of conservatives to the end. The very day of his transfer, members of "good society" in Oviedo marched in protest and regional newspapers praised his work.[61] Censors prevented ABC, which thought Doval's methods so excellent that they should have been extended to the whole country, from publishing a scathing editorial that claimed his dismissal was proof of the Lerroux government's "weakness."[62] Meanwhile, the political squabbling only continued when Doval reached Morocco. Over the objections of the liberal-minded high commissioner, Doval attempted to reorganize the Moroccan police, the *mejaznias*, according to the Civil Guard model and, therefore, to place them under military control.[63]

Back in Asturias, Doval's transfer did not mean that the repression was over. Captain Tella, for instance, continued his work at the overcrowded Model Prison, but word began to spread about what that involved as well. An extensive report by Socialist deputy Fernando de los Ríos, based on interviews with inmates at the Model Prison, was published in the French press, and soon after, 547 prisoners managed to sign and smuggle out an open letter to the attorney general of the republic denouncing their systematic maltreatment. The piece contains dozens of examples, with horrific beatings so severe that they caused serious injury or death again being the most common theme.[64] Soon after Doval's departure, Tella and Nart were ordered to join him in Morocco.[65] Reparaz interpreted all this as just one more example of the ingratitude with which the Spanish government and people repaid a civil guard who had worked so selflessly for them. He even remarked, in a sarcastic reversal of the Civil Guard's usual sensitivity to insult, that "my modest personality shared the honor of the libel and injury that were so prodigiously dedicated to my chief [Doval]."[66] Despite these investigations and transfers, no one was convicted of any crime related to the repression during the reminder of the period of right-wing governments.[67]

However, when Alcalá-Zamora called new elections for February 1936, the counternarrative of the repression did threaten to win a coalition of left-wing parties enough votes to end that period. Since elections could only be held if the country was not under a state of emergency, all constitutional guarantees were restored a month before the election. The Right's stories of rebel atrocities were central in its electoral propaganda, but now stories of atrocities perpetrated by government forces could dominate the propaganda of a new coalition of left republicans, Socialists, and communists known as the Popular Front. Amnesty for political prisoners became the main policy point around which the disparate members of the Popular Front united. Once again, the Left was using denunciations of the Civil Guard's actions as a rallying cry, mixing renewed calls for the dissolution of the corps with the main message that the right-wing forces that had given the Civil Guard free rein to behave so cruelly had to be removed from office.[68] This propaganda portrayed victims in an almost religious way as martyrs to the revolution in the face of the forces of reaction, which included the Civil Guard.[69] Some even went beyond sympathizing with the victims to praise the act of rebellion itself. The strategy worked. Public outrage over the repression was one of the main reasons why the Popular Front was able to coalesce to win the elections of February 16, 1936.

Margarita Nelken, who contributed her own book to the propaganda frenzy, provides an example of how the tone in some of these pieces had radicalized relative to that of the first three years of the republic.[70] Nelken had fled to France and then the Soviet Union after being involved in the uprising in Madrid. Impressed by the Soviet example, she allied herself with the most radical positions within the PSOE in her book, unafraid of deepening her party's divisions. She explained why October 1934 had been justified at a time when moderate Socialists were regretting the decision to rebel and argued that the uprising's failure had been caused by the hesitancy of these moderates.[71] She came to the conclusion that the republic had really been nothing more than a continuation of the oligarchic systems of the monarchy and that only a revolution could effect real change.

Naturally, Nelken also took the opportunity to reiterate her criticisms of the Civil Guard, arguing that it was an essential tool in maintaining the status quo. She accused guards of electoral manipulation and of being "the enemy incarnate, ferocious in their hatred and in their acts, of the working class." Her tone was even more confrontational than it had been in 1932. For instance, rather than lamenting Castilblanco, she actually praised the killings as being "the one time that the workers, fired upon by the Civil Guard during a peaceful protest, had had the courage to respond. . . . In Castilblanco, the Civil Guard continued to be at the orders of the same property owner as under the monarchy, and continued being, as under the monarchy, a corps made up of intangible, unassailable beings, of demigods above all responsibility."[72] Of course, she also criticized the Civil Guard's actions in Asturias, reprinting several of the reports on the atrocities.

While the failure of the October 1934 uprising tilted the Socialist leadership as a whole away from revolution and back toward electoral coalition building, the Civil Guard's own actions had aided radical leaders like Nelken in encouraging the rank and file to demand more sweeping and immediate changes than ever before. Brian Bunk argues that commemorations of the Asturias rebellion polarized Spain into conservative and leftist camps with competing narratives that sought to dehumanize the other side. The resulting hostile political environment created the conditions for civil war. Portrayals of the Civil Guard's actions in Asturias contributed to this process. Conservatives praised and rewarded the institution for its part in fighting back against the rebels. Bunk notes the importance of October in giving conservative men the idea that their homes and families were under siege by the Left, which led them to want to defend the domestic sphere with violence.[73] The story of the guards in Asturias gave credence to this line of thought because they actually did have to use violence to defend their homes and families against revolutionaries. Meanwhile, working-class groups saw those who rose up and attacked the guards as the heroes. During the 1936 election campaign, these groups mobilized as never before to pile on denunciations of the Civil Guard for the atrocities it had committed during the repression, desperate to end the string of center-right governments that they saw as nothing short of despotic. The result was a febrile political atmosphere in which tensions were so high that they frequently spilled over into violence. Such was the environment that the guards most feared, one where both their lives and the honor of their institution were in danger. But it was an atmosphere that, through the aftershocks of their actions during the repression, was partially of their own making.

As was the case with Castilblanco, a comparison between the repression of the Socialist-led revolt in 1934 in Asturias and that of the anarchist movement in Barcelona in the 1890s highlights the continuities between the organizational cultures present during the Restoration and the republic. In both cases, the government turned to a familiar playbook of suspending constitutional rights and appointing civil guards with reputations for toughness to confront the problem. The Civil Guard then implemented a largely unaltered investigative strategy of mass arrests and torture to extract information and confessions. Lastly, in both cases these harsh methods backfired insofar as they allowed the radical Left to find unity in their denunciations of these methods, following a pattern partially developed in the wave of Montjuïc of first accounts from prisons leaked abroad, then a sustained campaign of criticism in newspapers and pamphlets, and finally cooption of the rhetoric by politicians on the campaign trial.

The differences between Montjuïc and what went on in Las Adoratrices are, however, perhaps even more revealing. The death toll in the Barcelona bombings of the 1890s numbered in the dozens, whereas in the Asturias in 1934 eighty-six civil guards were themselves killed in the initial assaults. Afterward, guards sought to avenge their fallen comrades and the insult to their institution's honor that these attacks represented. Barcelona in the 1890s experienced nothing like the massacres at the Pelayo Barracks and Carbayín. The Civil Guard's formal response was also orders of magnitude larger: there is no comparison between Portas's three hundred arrests and Doval's ten thousand or more. The reason for the difference in scale lies in what these officers were trying to achieve. Portas's goal was investigative; even if he did not really know who threw the bomb in the Corpus Christi procession, he had to deliver suspects to the military tribunal. In contrast, although Doval's mission was also investigative insofar as he was supposed to find the leaders of the revolt and the stolen weapons and money, his mandate clearly exceeded bringing the ringleaders to trial. Rather, he was to punish the entire community of mine workers in Asturias. Unlike the climatic trial and execution of Ascheri and company at Montjuïc, the trials that took place following the Asturias revolt were not the focus of the press coverage of the repression, and there were few executions. The difference in emphasis was a consequence of the intentions of these two officers' actions. Portas's controversial goal was to prove to Spain's elites that the Civil Guard was capable delivering investigative results in an urban setting. There was still hope that the anarchist threat could be stamped out and that the Restoration could continue to deliver on its mandate of bringing political stability to Spain. After Asturias, when thousands had risen up against the government and its representatives at the local level, the civil guards, that hope of eliminating the revolutionary threat through prosecuting a few leaders was gone. Only through instilling fear in working-class society could the government and the Civil Guard hope to maintain their hold on power.

TEN

ANDALUSIA
Violence Unleashed

The massacres perpetrated by the rebels in the Spanish Civil War were by far the deadliest in interwar Western Europe.[1] They formed the beginning of a culture of violent political repression that would continue, to a lessening extent, until the end of the Franco dictatorship. Understanding the origins of this culture of violence has long been of interest to historians. While many have identified the *africanistas* as the principal instigators of this violence, launching the coup that sparked it and giving the orders to carry it out, they could not have done so by themselves.[2] An entire apparatus of military, police, and judicial forces had to be mobilized to find and eliminate those deemed politically dangerous. This chapter begins by tracing how a series of perceived threats to their honor and their very existence led most civil guards eventually to join the rebel side in the Civil War. It then argues that the Civil Guard was a crucial element of the rebels' apparatus as a militarized force with experience in local policing and repression that could easily be made to serve the rebels' goal of eliminating the political left in Spain. It does so by concentrating on the western Andalusia region (the provinces of Cádiz, Córdoba, Huelva, and Seville, with some mention also made of neighboring Jaén and Badajoz), which witnessed some of the bloodiest repression in the entire country, as rebels occupied it early in the war and it was home to some of Spain's most bitter preexisting social conflicts. Western Andalusia is therefore an extreme example, and that extremity means that patterns of repressive practice can be seen with enhanced clarity there.

The Civil Guard was the most important force that the rebellion's leaders had for carrying out their cleansing of Spain. Unlike the ill-disciplined conscript army, which was concentrated in military bases, the Civil Guard was a professional force with men in almost every town in the country who had local knowledge and experience acting as a force of political repression. Civil guards had the discipline and knowledge to lead small units of Falangist and (to a lesser extent) Carlist militiamen that would carry out much of the repression in the rebellion's initial months. Later, as the nascent Francoist state took more firm control of the repression, the Civil Guard also played a key role in this second phase, becoming the leading force for finding and investigating victims for summary military trials. This culture of repression, enabled by the Civil Guard, would become a lasting feature of the Franco regime.

THE CIVIL GUARD IN THE SPRING OF 1936

While estimates of the percentage of civil guards who joined the July 1936 uprising run as low as 41 percent, around 70 percent is probably closer to the truth when defections and initially reluctant units are taken into account.[3] It may seem surprising that so many in an institution that emphasized political neutrality and that acquiesced to the coming of the Second Republic in 1931 turned against it five years later. But the civil guards' sense of honor demanded the respect of the public and public figures in return for their sacrifices. Guards did not take kindly to·the reduction in their institution's prestige from the republic's administrative reforms nor to the criticism leveled at them by politicians and protesters. Meanwhile, rebel army officers could speak the Civil Guard's language of honor, respect, and order. In a speech General Franco made over the Civil Guard's radio transmitter in Tetuán, Morocco, a few days after the rebellion began, he appealed directly to guards to join the uprising in precisely this language: "Self-sacrificing civil guard! Veteran soldiers who voluntarily embraced the teachings of the Duque de Ahumada! How much you must have suffered to see how justice has been dishonored, how disorder and violence reigned in the countryside and in the towns, led by those criminals who yesterday you had arrested!"[4]

The most important factor, however, in predisposing guards to join the uprising was the October 1934 revolution in Asturias. Indeed, within the

Civil Guard, October 1934 had marked a dramatic shift in its vision of itself. Whereas previously its more progressive elements had pushed a transition from military to less lethal policing equipment, such as pistols, batons, and tear gas, these arguments suddenly disappeared from the pages of the *RTGC* after October 1934. From that point on, the magazine was filled with articles advocating more militarization; they called for machine guns, grenades, and fortified *casas-cuarteles* so that the Civil Guard could better fend off the next revolt.[5] One writer thought that each post should have fifteen to twenty guards and that each section should have one or two rapid-response forces that could be dispatched in trucks from fortified buildings.[6] Another envisioned four "vanguard groups" situated in Madrid, Barcelona, Sevilla, and Mieres in Asturias. Each group would have four hundred men equipped with machine guns, grenades, and motor vehicles and would be ready for prolonged assignments with field kitchens, radios, and medical stations.[7] None of these plans came to fruition because of a lack of funding, but the shift in thinking they represented was important in and of itself. These articles saw the Civil Guard not as a force for maintaining public order with discretion but rather as a military unit that provided the state's first line of defense against a rebellious, revolutionary citizenry.

Meanwhile, on the national political stage, when the Popular Front government took power in February 1936, it sought to restart the stalled reforms of the republic's early years, such as land redistribution, regional autonomy, and military reorganization, and accelerate their pace. The Popular Front victory also meant that working-class groups, such as the Socialists and communists, were again able to operate in the open, and they pushed for rapid change by staging even more strikes than at the beginning of the republic. Some rank-and-file members took it upon themselves to carry out reforms, such as by seizing land extralegally. On the other side of the political spectrum, after October 1934, many conservatives were no longer willing to acquiesce to a left-wing government that they felt was ushering in a period of disorder that would spark another revolution. Therefore, they left the CEDA, which had been willing to work within the republican system, for more radical groups, such as the monarchist Renovación Española and the fascist Falange, which sought the violent overthrow of the republic. The Falange, in particular, while its membership was still small, took the political mobilization of the Right in a new direction by sending its youthful members out to fight working-class groups for control of the streets, especially in urban areas. Workers, meanwhile, were also aggressive in fighting back against the Falange, which, they feared, threatened to bring fascism to Spain.[8]

In other words, by 1936 the mass political mobilization that had been one of the defining features of the Second Republic had reached new heights, but its character had also been profoundly altered. Polarization was the word of the day as the political center lost adherents to radical groups on both sides of the political spectrum. These groups saw violence as a political tool and toleration of the other side as impossible. In this atmosphere of political tension and violence, the two phenomena that civil guards hated most came rushing back after the lull of 1935: public disorder and criticism of their institution. In fact, in the first seven-and-a-half months of 1936, there were more deaths from political violence than in any other entire year of the republic, if October 1934 is excluded. The numbers do not suggest that the Civil Guard was more violent once the Popular Front government took power in February 1936 (although it still held its place as the most violent group that could be identified among professions and political persuasions), but rather that other groups, especially the Falange, became more violent.[9] In other words, the high level of political violence during the Popular Front period can be explained by the combination of the forces of public order's continued frequent recourse to violence and the increasing use of violent street confrontations as a principal strategy of political contestation by radical groups on both sides of the political spectrum.

Given the Civil Guard's desire for order, it is ironic that its harsh repression of the October 1934 rebellion was one of the factors that drove this polarization in the first place. Right-wing opposition groups, like the CEDA and the monarchist Renovación Española, made every effort to create the perception that the Popular Front was allowing public order to slip out of control. This perception was one of the primary reasons why many civil guards became open to abandoning their commitment to political neutrality in favor of rebellion against the government in power, even though the Civil Guard itself was in fact one of the main perpetrators of the violence.[10] Meanwhile, emboldened socialists and communists resumed their calls for the dissolution of the force in the press and in letters of complaint with an even more biting tone.[11] For guards, the temptation to take extralegal action to silence these voices was strong. Many drew close to far-right groups like the Carlists and the Falange, whose increasingly militarized rhetoric called for a counterrevolutionary uprising of their own. These groups made intense efforts to develop contacts and coordination plans with the Civil Guard, with some success.[12] As the loyalty of more and more officers to the Popular Front diminished, the government felt the need to make frequent transfers and dismissals to keep disloyal commanders out of key posts, which made guards feel that the government was politicizing their institution.[13]

In April 1936, the willingness of more guards to disobey the Popular Front government, coupled with the violence of radical youth groups in particular on both sides of the political spectrum, initiated a new spiral of revenge killings that would augment support for a military rebellion that was supposed to restore public order. On April 14, a Civil Guard second lieutenant was killed during the Republic Day parade in Madrid. The Civil Guard had become such a divisive symbol that the government prohibited a public funeral, but a command chief disobeyed this order, and, sure enough, Assault Guard Lieutenant José Castillo, who was linked to the Socialist Youth, and his men killed six as the procession became a street battle between different radical groups.[14] On July 12, Falangists retaliated by killing Castillo. That very night, a group of assault guards and Socialists led by Civil Guard Captain Fernando Condés Romero, who also had ties to the Socialist Youth, then murdered a prominent monarchist leader in return.[15] Conspirators who had been plotting a military coup felt that the assassination would shatter enough people's confidence in the ability of the Popular Front to maintain order that they could set the date of their rising on mainland Spain for July 18. As for Condés, his commitment to revolutionary socialism was certainly unusual for a civil guard, even though left-leaning civil and assault guards were not uncommon in elite urban units in Madrid, Barcelona, and Valencia, where rented housing in working-class neighborhoods put them in more contact with the civilian population than was usually the case.[16] Ultimately, the Civil War, the conditions for which Condés inadvertently helped create, would reveal that many guards shared his willingness to break the law in the name of vengeance by the summer of 1936.

THE CIVIL GUARD IN THE REBELLION OF JULY 1936

Historians have documented the stance that each Civil Guard command adopted at the beginning of the July 1936 rising, but the question of what patterns these decisions took deserves further study.[17] Suffice it to say here that, since the Civil Guard was highly disciplined, the decision of each province's commanders about whether or not to join when the military uprising began on July 18, 1936, usually determined the attitude of all of that province's civil guards. The Popular Front government had ensured that most of the Civil Guard's commanding officers were loyal to the republic. Despite the institution's commitment to political neutrality, however, some low-ranking officers were involved in the planning, and not only through their contacts with the army but also through close cooperation with local right-wing leaders and the Falange. Often, rightists assumed that the Civil Guard was on their side and took refuge in Civil Guard posts. For example, in Jaén, Civil Guard Captain José Rodríguez de Cueto worked with landowner organizations and the Falange to plot the uprising there, and the whole plan hinged on the support of the corps since there was no military garrison there.[18] While the Civil Guard's provincial commanders wound up holding off on declaring support for the rebellion in the face of rapid worker mobilization, many rightists still took shelter in Civil Guard posts. The trust that property owners had in the Civil Guard is not surprising, since one of the corps's primary missions had always been to defend private property and civil guards had long had a close relationship with landowners. But the connections to the growing Falange, a clear violation of the Civil Guard's commitment to political neutrality, suggest that more civil guards became willing to violate that neutrality after the victory of the Popular Front in the February 1936 elections made them increasingly concerned about their own safety.

Following the general pattern in civil wars—most people collaborate with the side that is in control of their geographical location—safety was the primary consideration for most guards in determining which side they would choose during the initial rebellion.[19] If it seemed safe to rebel in a particular province, its guards usually did, but if the working classes' strength in that province seemed overwhelming, then its guards maintained their loyalty. What is revealing is that in several provinces civil guards declared for the rebellion despite working-class strength (leading to prolonged sieges), and in several others the guards' professed loyalty turned out to be only a temporary survival tactic; in no province where the rebels were strong did guards declare for the government. These patterns indicate that sympathy for the rebellion among the Civil Guard was very widespread, although not universal. When they could, almost all guards, except those in the largest cities, sided with the rebellion.

Western Andalusia followed the typical pattern. In provinces where there were military garrisons, Cádiz, Córdoba, and Seville, the army took the lead in rebelling and the Civil Guard units in the province followed suit. The rebels took control of the capitals of these provinces fairly easily, with the Civil Guard taking part in securing important buildings and in street fighting. For example, in Seville, where civil guards had been sympathetic to the Falange since 1934, they participated alongside soldiers and militiamen in the fighting to take the civil government building in the downtown area and the working-class neighborhoods of Triana and La Macarena.[20] Jaén and Huelva, however, did not have military garrisons, so the commanders in both these provinces held off on joining rebellion. Yet some junior officers still devised plans of their own to rebel. In Huelva, Major Gregorio Haro Lumbreras led a column of civil guards that was ordered to link up with miners and then retake Seville for the republic. Instead, he killed some of the miners and arrested the rest and brought them to Seville, where he joined the forces of General Gonzalo Queipo de Llano, who had taken charge of the rebellion there. The remaining miners were then executed.[21] The rebel press dubbed Haro the Hero of La Pañoleta, the place where the confrontation with the miners took place.

The case of Badajoz Province, just north of western Andalusia, provides further evidence of where the sympathies of most civil guards lay. In contrast to western Andalusia, there the provincial army and Civil Guard commanders reminded loyal to the republic, but the columns that Civil Guard Major José Vega Cornejo sent to Madrid defected to the rebels, as did the guards in several towns in the province. In August, as rebel forces from Seville advanced through Badajoz Province, more guards joined the rebels until finally Vega Cornejo's own men in the city of Badajoz rose up on their own initiative; however, they did so too soon and had to surrender to republican militiamen.[22]

In all of these cases, the civil guards' time-honored tactic of concentrating their forces in the provincial capitals in times of severe unrest, since they would be hopelessly outnumbered in the towns, served them well. The problem was that this left the towns entirely out of their control, and the rightists they had been protecting were easily arrested and sometimes killed.[23] Indeed, in each province in western Andalusia, the rebels initially held the capitals, but the workers held the rural areas. Detachments from the capitals went town-by-town over the next few months to secure these outlying areas for the rebellion. The Civil Guard had proved essential to the rebels in the initial rebellion, but in the next phase it would further prove its usefulness in a political repression that would make Major Doval's work in Asturias seem diminutive by comparison.

THE CLEANSING OF THE REARGUARD 1: THE HOT PHASE

The rearguard repression perpetrated by the rebels in the Spanish Civil War can be divided into two phases, and these have been best delineated by Peter Anderson. He describes an initial "hot" phase of the violence from the outbreak of the war through the end of 1936. In this phase, much of the violence was either perpetrated in a wholly spontaneous manner by militias or organized by officers placed in charge of public order who acted with little oversight. The second phase, what Anderson terms "selective violence," began in early 1937 and lasted through the end of the war. In it, the emerging Francoist state took full control of the violence, instituting an investigative and summary judicial apparatus that was installed throughout the country and tasked with weeding out perceived threats to the new order that had escaped the purges of the first phase.[24] Javier Rodrigo notes that the violence in both stages, even though less directly controlled by the state in the first, was always rational and planned insofar as the leaders of the rebellion envisioned a violent homogenization of Spanish society from the beginning, first through the behind-the-lines executions they allowed to take place or directly ordered and then through the state apparatus that they developed as they advanced.[25] After all, even before the rebellion began, General Emilio Mola, who led its planning, made statements like "this war has to end with the extermination of the enemies of Spain."[26]

The Civil Guard was essential to the implementation of both phases of the repression. The initial phase was the deadliest, with an estimated thirty to thirty-five thousand killed in the summer of 1936 alone.[27] The rebellion had a body of manpower already indoctrinated in a violent ideology available to it in the form of the Falangist militias, and the Civil Guard had the local presence and organizational skills needed to organize these militias into effective execution squads. At the very beginning of the war, the Falange in rural areas was primarily composed of young aristocrats who had a history of working with the Civil Guard and a long list of grievances against working-class elements who had challenged their property rights.[28] Civil guards' knowledge of local politics and the prewar monitoring of political activities that they had carried out proved essential for determining who was to be purged. Beginning on the very day of the coup attempt, the rebels simply went through the Civil Guard's police files to determine whom to arrest.[29] These targets were primarily leftist and republican members of town councils and the local leaders of workers' councils and unions. The goal of the repression was the complete elimination of the leadership of local worker and republican organizations, thereby rendering them unable to organize any resistance to the new regime. The fear created by this elimination of prominent members of local communities had a powerful deterrent effect on any potential opposition as well, of course.[30] And so even in this initial "hot" phase of the repression, the violence of the Civil Guard was selective rather than completely indiscriminate; it targeted those who were perceived as potential political threats to the new order, even if that "threat" was as minor as association with a republican or workers' political party or union.[31]

It was in carrying out this extremely crude selection process that civil guards played a large role. As rebel forces took each of the provincial capitals in western Andalusia in turn, civil guards formed part of many of the groups that arrested republican leaders. In Córdoba, for example, the rebels detained fifteen hundred people in the first week of the uprising alone. While a hastily assembled "civic guard" composed of Falangists made many of these arrests, the Civil Guard also detained prominent republicans, including the mayor and a communist member of parliament.[32]

The rebellion had been initiated by provincial military commanders declaring martial law. After the initial rounds of purges to secure their control over the provincial capitals, these leaders then used their self-declared authority to appoint public-order delegates who would coordinate the repression. The rebel officers recognized the expertise of the Civil Guard in this area by often appointing guards to these positions, and in a few cases army officers serving as delegates were replaced by guards when their performance was not satisfactory.[33] Queipo de Llano in Seville appointed an army officer and fellow *afri-canista*, Captain Manuel Díaz Criado, public-order delegate for all of Andalusia and Extremadura just a week after the rebellion began. Díaz Criado chose as his second-in-command a civil guard, Sargeant José Rebollo Montiel, who led the torture and interrogation of prisoners. However, Díaz Criado proved to be more wantonly cruel than thorough, sparing some prisoners who bribed him with money or sex.[34] In November, Franco forced Queipo to replace Díaz Criado with Santiago Garrigós Barnabéu, a Civil Guard major who conducted a more systematic repression that included executing the prisoners whom Díaz Criado had previously spared.[35]

Meanwhile, Queipo de Llano rewarded Major Haro, the Hero of La Pañoleta, by declaring him the civil and military governor of Huelva Province. In this capacity, he oversaw the executions of 1,918 people in the months of August and September alone.[36] Having obtained a list of the Freemasons in the province, his campaign against them was particularly relentless. But Haro went a step too far when he targeted a masonic friend of the army's inspector general, Miguel Cabanellas, who promptly relieved Haro of his post in February 1937 and charged him with using money and precious metals donated to the rebel cause to hire prostitutes. Fortunately for Haro, Cabanellas died the next year, and the charges were dropped.[37]

Perhaps the case of Córdoba is the best example of Civil Guard officers carrying out the repression with the level of thoroughness that the rebel generals wanted. Although mass arrests were made at the beginning of the rebellion, Queipo de Llano was disappointed that the garrison commander here, Colonel Ciriaco Cascajo Ruiz, was not killing more people.[38] Therefore, from August 16, Civil Guard Major Luis Zurdo took over control of public order and increased the number of executions to around one hundred per day.[39] Civil guards carried out some of these executions themselves. The words of a priest present at one such execution no doubt captured the attitude of many of them: "We have to kill them, because, if not, they will do the same to us."[40] Zurdo himself echoed similar sentiments upon taking his post, mixing the Civil Guard's traditional concern for honor with the rebels' developing troupes for demonizing the republicans: "Death for mother country constituents the greatest glory for all honorable Spaniards, so we seek, if it is necessary, to die in her defense rather than see her bleed out under the emblem of communism."[41]

On September 22, Zurdo was replaced by another civil guard, Lieutenant Colonel Bruno Ibáñez Gález, known as Don Bruno, who also linked his profession as a civil guard with his perceived duty to serve the new regime in his first public message upon assuming the post. He described his mission as "based solely on the doing of one's duty, which as a civil guard I have always consecrated with blind obedience to my commanders, putting all my energy and good will at the service of my *Patria*." Don Bruno took the repression in

Córdoba to new extremes and made no secret about his intentions; in the same message, he wrote: "Those that do not feel the love that good sons should have for the idolized Mother Country are not worthy of living in her and should leave or disappear forever from Spanish territory."[42] His method of finding his victims was typical of the Civil Guard: he relied on denunciations from priests and employers.[43] In fact, after he was thanked for "having cleansed Córdoba of Marxists," Don Bruno admitted that "when I came to Córdoba, I didn't know anyone. I have limited myself to signing the lists you put in front of me."[44] The traditional power holders told Don Bruno whom to kill, and their targets were for the most part members of the working classes and republicans who had been attempting to change the social order, including many railroad workers and teachers. An average of fifty people per day were shot every morning in the cemeteries of Córdoba through the fall of 1936.[45] One resident recalled the psychological effect of Don Bruno's reign of terror when he appeared at a bull-fight: "As he came out of the ring people cringed. He had blue eyes, I'll always remember. To get out of his way the people would have incrusted themselves in the walls if they could. Everyone was electrified with terror and fear. Don Bruno could have shot all Córdoba, he was sent here with carte blanche."[46]

With this power came corruption. Don Bruno became increasingly autocratic and maniacal as he occupied himself with a "labor of moral cleaning," burning thousands of "pornographic" and "leftist" books and magazines and launching a campaign against blasphemy.[47] He accumulated large amounts of money by charging middle-class liberals huge fines and by forcing donations to the rebel cause, going after first gold and then silver and threatening those who did not comply with "fatal consequences."[48] These schemes became even more egregious when he became civil governor in January 1937. Word of the corruption reached Franco and he transferred Don Bruno to Logroño, where he directed another repression.[49]

After the western Andalusian capitals had been secured by the rebels, they dispatched a column largely composed of colonial units from Seville to take Madrid by way of Badajoz. In the wake of this column's sweep toward Badajoz, a similar pattern repeated itself of Civil Guard officers directing a violent cleansing in the rear guard. For example, when Civil Guard Captain Ernesto Navarrete Alcal's mixed column of civil guards and volunteers took the town of Fuente de Cantos (Badajoz), it executed an estimated 330 people as a reprisal for the deaths of twelve in a church burning there in July.[50] In Mérida (Badajoz),

Civil Guard Major Manuel Gómez Cantos held nightly executions in the city's casino. He had a creative strategy for finding his victims. He would have a republican doctor walk around town and would later arrest anyone who greeted him.[51] Queipo de Llano was impressed with Gómez Cantos, and in 1937 he had the major receive Spain's second-highest medal for valor and gave him a mobile division to sweep Andalusia for any leftist leaders who might have been overlooked. Gómez Cantos went on to head repressive operations in parts of the Córdoba, Badajoz, Seville, Huelva, Málaga, Pontevedra, and Cáceres provinces, even though he had a long record of violating the Civil Guard's prohibition on contracting debts and many officers considered him to be insane.[52]

The most infamous episode of the Extremaduran campaign was the rebels' widespread looting and the massacre of some four thousand people after rebel forces had entered the city of Badajoz. Close to half of the executions occurred in the Badajoz bullring, where dozens of bodies were also mutilated. Colonial forces were the primary perpetrators of these atrocities, but the fact that many of those executed were militiamen and Carabineros loyal to the republic suggests that this was a political purge more than an uncontrolled sacking of the city.[53] A report by Gómez Cantos, who replaced Civil Guard Major Manuel Pereita Vela as public-order delegate, criticized his predecessor for not bringing the chaos under control and for keeping some of the loot for himself.[54] Such criticisms may seem strange coming from Gómez Cantos, one of the most notorious leaders of the repression in southern Spain, but they highlight the distinction that the rebel leaders made, as they had in Asturias, between their colonial and paramilitary forces: the former sowed fear on the frontlines while the latter established a new order in the rear guard.

The Extremaduran campaign was no exception to this pattern of civil guards using their local knowledge to find victims to be killed behind the lines. In the city of Badajoz, a Portuguese journalist observed that "hundreds of Marxists came tied up with ropes, one after the other in successive waves. The Civil Guard identified them, and those that had been arrested by mistake returned to their homes. The others wound up being turned over to the Foreign Legion."[55] Once again, the Civil Guard was also in charge of the more systematic repression after the initial wave of violence by the colonial forces. Guards also took over the massacre in the bullring and led some small groups of civilian supporters to round up and execute leftists who had remained in smaller towns as the rebel column had driven rapidly toward Badajoz.[56]

By the end of July, the rebels were in control of all of the provincial capitals in western Andalusia, but, as mentioned above, outlying areas were still largely in republican hands, in no small part thanks to the fact that civil guards had concentrated in the capitals. In each province, they were heavily involved as participants and leaders in the sallies from the capitals that established rebel control over these towns.[57] Civil guards had the discipline and military experience to lead these expeditions, which were composed of mixed groups of Falangists, Carlists, civil guards, soldiers in the regular army, and colonial forces. As the main column advanced toward Badajoz, for instance, Captain Navarrete led smaller detachments from Fuente de Cantos to secure the main column's flanks by capturing towns in southern Badajoz.[58] In such mopping-up operations throughout southwestern Spain, civil guards reintroduced their nineteenth-century *ley de fugas* technique, in which they executed guerrilla fighters with the excuse that the prisoners had been trying to escape.[59]

Civil guards played an integral part in every aspect of the initial phase of repressive violence on the part of the rebels in southwestern Spain. Their records and local knowledge proved crucial in determining whom to arrest, their widespread distribution meant that they provided some of the manpower needed to carry out the repression, and their experience allowed them often to be the leaders of repressive efforts at the local and provincial levels. Therefore, the case of the Civil Guard's involvement is an example of how the outbreak of the Civil War had elements of both continuity and rupture with the preceding republic period.[60] Previous chapters have already explored how civil guards had maintained order before and during the republic with little civilian oversight—sometimes using violence with few repercussions—what Eduardo González Calleja calls a *carte gris*. But with the rebels' declaration of war placing all power fully in the hands of the military (including the Civil Guard), *carte gris* became *carte blanche*.[61] Rebel officers like Queipo de Llano had simply to appoint a particularly bloodthirsty officer to become a public-order delegate and then give that person free rein. He usually named civil guards to these posts, not because their institution as a whole was particularly bloodthirsty but because it was the one most experienced in repression. The Civil Guard provided the preexisting means for carrying out a thorough repression, using techniques that dated back to the nineteenth century and that had been applied with heightened animosity after the October 1934 rebellion, which had led guards to conclude that the honor and integrity of their institution were incompatible with working-class demands. Ultimately, however, it was army officers like Queipo during the Civil War who directed guards to apply their methods on a scale and level of brutality that was previously inconceivable.

THE CLEANSING OF THE REAR GUARD 2:
THE SELECTIVE PHASE

The problem with these sadistic public order delegates was that they were ruthless but sloppy. Díaz Criado in Seville, Haro Lumbreras in Seville, Don Bruno in Córdoba, and Pereita Vela in Badajoz were all accused of corruption—their personal gains had upset the property owners whose support was also crucial for the rebellion. Therefore, as the year 1937 began, Franco sought to continue the repression in a more controlled manner, now that the most obvious targets had been eliminated, by channeling it through an extensive system of military courts. The attributes of the Civil Guard that made it so useful in the first phase of the repression—widespread distribution, local knowledge, and investigative experience—now made it the primary instrument used by the courts in this second phase to identify and capture perceived threats beyond those marked by the institution's prewar monitoring. The existence of the Civil Guard meant that it was unnecessary for the Francoists to build a new policing and surveillance structure from scratch. Its techniques for carrying out a political repression, monitoring local politics, relying on denunciations to identify suspects, and bringing these suspects before military courts for summary trial, were simply scaled up to encompass the entire country.

Anderson has documented the extent to which the Franco regime deliberately designed an apparatus to monitor and classify Spaniards in this second phase of the repression.[62] As the war went on, civil guards returned to their rural posts and resumed their normal policing activities, but these now included being the Francoist state's most important agents of this monitoring and classification at the local level, maintaining files on suspects, verifying letters of good conduct, and even compiling reports assessing the conduct of each town during the war.[63] Denunciations from collaborators were crucial for allowing the Francoist state to identify its supposed enemies.[64] The civil guards not only received these denunciations from the public but also made denunciations of their own before the courts.[65]

The transition to more selective repressive violence occurred around the same time as the unification of the Falange and the Carlists as part of a broader consolidation of a new National-Catholic state led by Franco. In the new state, the close collaboration between the Falange and the Civil Guard, already in evidence before and at the beginning of the rebellion, became official. For example, a Civil Guard captain in Seville served as both chief of police and provincial delegate of information there for the FET y de las JONS, as the Falange was known once it was merged with the Carlists.[66] The fact that professionals like civil guards already often led militia units made the incorporation of these units into the regular army all the easier.[67] Such measures were also part of the state's effort to streamline the narratives of its coalition's disparate elements. Prior to unification, the Falange's ranks in Seville Province had swelled with working-class members and its newspaper had adapted an antibourgeois and even revolutionary tone.[68]

The other advantage of the Civil Guard's military structure for the rebellion was that deployments in frontline combat and for military policing were already considered part of civil guards' duties. They frequently joined in, and sometimes even led, combat operations, participating in all the major battles of the war.[69] They also played an important role as military policemen in forging Franco's conscript army through serving draft notices and tracking down deserters. In addition, the Civil Guard had an intimate relationship with the various manifestations of the Francoist state's secret police during the war; together they monitored the loyalty to the new regime of both conscript troops at the front and civilians behind the lines.[70]

Surprisingly, given the level of support for the rebellion within the Civil Guard, Franco contemplated disbanding the institution after the war since it had not joined the uprising in its entirety. However, it quickly proved its usefulness to the postwar Francoist state through maintaining the system of control and surveillance established in the second phase of the war, playing important roles in the rounding up of so-called reds who remained at large, in the management of the extensive postwar concentration camp system, and in the fight against the guerrilla fighters known as maquis, who continued to resist Francoism after the end of the war.[71] While the campaigns against the maquis are beyond the scope of this book, it is worth noting that many of the same patterns of repression observed during the war were carried on afterward, with the Civil Guard's experience, rural distribution, and local knowledge making it the ideal force to lead the counterinsurgency effort, while the army and colonial units provided additional manpower.[72] Therefore, the Francoist state's efforts against the maquis and the Civil Guard's role in them are best understood as a third phase of the wartime repression.[73]

The incorporation of the Civil Guard into the Francoist policing apparatus can be seen as part of the larger process of uniting the disparate elements of the rebel coalition into what would become the Francoist state. One must always keep in mind that the rebellion was at its core a military coup and the Franco regime a military dictatorship. Therefore, the regime's National-Catholic ideology was built around the army's principal values of discipline and sacrifice for the *patria* and to that base were added significant elements from Catholicism, fascism, and traditionalism. The Civil Guard shared the army's values, but its focus was slightly different, with more emphasis on honor, loyalty, and service. The multiple ways in which these values can be understood allowed the Civil Guard to be open to the republic in 1931 and made some feel obliged to maintain their loyalty to it in 1936. Yet under Francoism, while guards were still allowed to speak of honor and to venerate the founder of their institution, the uniqueness of their organizational culture was diminished as their rhetoric repeated the usual National-Catholic tropes. The institution's organizational structure also changed profoundly as Franco merged it with the Carabineros and increased the army's control over it.[74] The Civil Guard's own contributions to the Francoist war effort in the Civil War were downplayed in favor of the dominate narrative of Franco's victory. For example, Francoist propaganda made much of the relief of the besieged Alcázar of Toledo by Franco's forces in September 1936, but made little mention of the fact that more than half of the fighters inside the complex were civil guards.[75] Also receiving less attention was the siege of the civil guards at the Santuario de la Virgen de la Cabeza, which lasted even longer and whose defenders were never rescued.[76]

Civil guards took their commitment to discipline and loyalty seriously, and these values did persuade some to maintain their loyalty to the republic, but more often the promise that the rebellion held of ensuring that guards received the respect they felt they deserved proved to be more persuasive. A more openly confrontational attitude toward the working classes after October 1934 and the perceived increase in political violence and social disorder under the Popular Front also explain why so many guards joined the July 1936 rebellion. The importance of the Civil Guard in this initial rebellion is well known, but it was equally important in consolidating these initial gains and in securing a long-lasting societal transformation through a political repression of sweeping scope and thoroughness. Even in the "hot" violence of the first days of the uprising, Civil Guard police files became arrest lists and guards participated in execution squads. Frequent close coordination between civil guards, Falangists, and other conspirators before and during the rebellion indicates that many guards were also willing to violate their commitment to political neutrality if it meant supporting a cause that they believed to be righteous. As the rebel generals secured their control over western Andalusia, they implemented the same pattern of repression that they had pioneered in Asturias, but now on a much wider, and ultimately national, scale. In both 1934 and 1936, civil guards led most of the political repression, taking their preexisting practices of mass arrests, torture, and extrajudicial executions to new extremes and introducing them to mixed groups of militiamen and colonial soldiers whose prewar practices, while also sometimes brutal, tended to be defined by street fights and murders in the case of the former and violent looting in the case of the latter. The guards' experience, discipline, and professionalism also proved useful to the generals in street fighting, mopping-up operations, and on the front lines, especially at the beginning of the war when the motley regular army was of little use. When Franco moved to consolidate his position and make the rearguard violence more selective, starting in 1937, the Civil Guard was again critical for conducting investigations and making arrests for the military court system. By the end of the war, the organization had been integrated into the Francoist state as the primary enforcer of the new order in the countryside, while its repressive practices had become those of the regime as a whole. Its previous experiences combatting anarchist and socialist resistance offered the rebel army officers the tools that they needed to carry out a thorough political repression, but it was the decisions of these officers to launch the rebellion and to empower their most bloodthirsty subordinates that led those tools to be applied to the Spanish populace with unprecedented scale and violence.

CONCLUSION

This book has sought to explain why civil guards were the perpetrators of so much of the Second Republic's violence. The sheer number of protests that guards had to respond to during the republic and the reality that rifles were often their only weapons are facts that partially explain their violence. This book has demonstrated that a structural factor, the Civil Guard's organizational culture, including both its military structure and policing mission, is also key to explaining its violence, and this book has looked all the way back to the founding of the institution to examine how this culture came to have such deadly implications.

The decisions made at the Civil Guard's foundational moment had profound implications for the subsequent history of the institution. Principal among these decisions was the one to endow the force with a military structure, which gave it the discipline necessary to avoid corruption and weather the nineteenth century's political storms but also produced an insularity and rigidity that would make it difficult to adapt to changing sociopolitical conditions as that century came to an end. The other defining feature of the corps's organizational culture was the outsized influence of its founding father, the Duque de Ahumada, who adapted his aristocratic idea of honor to the liberal purpose of enforcing the dictates of the Spanish state. On the one hand, the longevity of the Civil Guard has proven Ahumada right that a culture of honor would build institutional solidarity and further shield it from corruption. On the other hand, from the beginning, his hope that a desire for the respect of the public would guide guards in responding to resistance in a measured fashion was tempered by the instructions in his *Cartilla* that seemed to authorize guards to resort to violence quickly should they not receive that respect.

As guards fanned out across the country to perform their policing duties, their organizational culture developed many of the classic characteristics of a police culture: autonomy, isolation, solidarity, and an "us vs. them" mentality. When guards faced perceived disorder, their regulations gave them few options to respond aside from employing warnings and opening fire to assert that their honor must be respected. While they responded with violence to those who resisted their imposition of state authority, their desire for public affirmation created the opportunity for de facto alliances with local elites, who knew how to flatter them with material support, letters of praise, and homages. During the Restoration period, as Spain's liberal elites prevented true democratic political participation through the *turno* system, the anarchist movement emerged as a challenge to government authority in general. When anarchists turned to violence as the only means of resistance, the state and alarmed conservatives encouraged guards to respond harshly. The case study of the "crimes of Montjuïc" in 1890s Barcelona illustrates how guards had brought the same investigative techniques, principally mass arrests and the beating of prisoners, that they had developed combatting banditry in rural areas to the difficult task of pursuing anarchist terrorists. Applying these same methods on a wider scale in an urban setting generated an outcry in the mass press and among populist politicians that the Civil Guard was unable to counter effectively. Civil guards were now firmly in the business of policing political dissent, but opposition groups had also now learned how much political value could be gained from denouncing the excesses of the forces of public order.

Since military culture is determined by not only a unit's regulations but also by its unwritten habits, examining the social origins, training, and daily life of its members was also essential to understanding its behavior. In the case of the Civil Guard, which lacked any schools or formal training programs of its own (except the Colegio de Guardias Jóvenes), army experiences and apprenticeships formed the core of the Civil Guard's acculturation process, transforming rural laborers into militarized policemen who were members of the town elite. In the army of early-twentieth-century Spain, many future guards experienced the brutalities of war in Morocco, and officers, from the time of their training at the Infantry Academy, were exposed to the army's increasingly interventionist view of honor as fighting for the *patria* on the battlefield. The apprenticeship period, then, was key to teaching Civil Guard aspirants how to be policemen, including how to seek honor from the maintenance of order rather than from valor in battle. While this form of training allowed for a high degree of continuity and discretion as guards passed down the habits that they had learned on the job, it gave the state no ability to shape the culture of these guards.

With the advent of the Second Republic, mass political participation and contestation meant that the positions on the Civil Guard of some of the re-public's most important political players became critical in determining how the institution would relate to the new democratic regime. Meanwhile, guards responded to the mass mobilization of the time with the same tactics that they had used for decades, resulting in an increase in violence and polarization. While republicans were initially wary of the Civil Guard, they came to see its utility for maintaining public order in a politically unstable time. Distracted by their effort to form a new urban quick-response force, republicans failed to hear the calls for practical reforms emanating from the Civil Guard itself that might have reduced the violence in rural areas where much of it was taking place. The culture of the guards serving under the Second Republic may have been similar to that of their predecessors, but the mass political mobilization of the time called for adaptation rather than entrenchment. Unprecedented levels of strike and protest activity accompanied the republic, and these events often involved insulting guards in some fashion. They frequently responded as they always had, with violence, becoming a major contributor to the surge in political violence that also accompanied the republic. Socialists like Mar-garita Nelken, taking advantage of newfound freedoms of expression, discov-ered denouncing such actions by the Civil Guard to be an effective rallying cry for uniting their fractious party. The Civil Guard's sense of political neutrality blocked it from launching a public relations campaign of its own in response, and so the conservative sectors of society, rapidly developing a mass politics as well, were the ones to sing the institution's praises, deepening the perception that guards were the servants of reaction.

Castilblanco, Arnedo, and Asturias were some of the most extraordinary outbreaks of violence during the Second Republic; in this work they each illus-trated in their own way how the sociopolitical dynamics at work during that period resulted in clashes with the Civil Guard. These newsworthy incidents had political implications that began an escalating cycle of violence that culminated in the Civil War. Castilblanco and Arnedo were virtual opposites in that civil guards were the primary victims at Castilblanco while protesters were the victims at Arnedo. Both incidents, however, resulted from the combination of the Civil Guard's unaltered crowd-control techniques and culture of rigidly enforcing the letter of the law. The lack of imagination in the face of rapidly changing circumstances was not limited to the local level, however. After these incidents, the Socialists did little to alter their crowd-pleasing criticisms of the force, while guards, represented by Director General Sanjurjo, showed little tact when responding to these perceived insults in the national media spotlight. The steps that the government did take to reform the Civil Guard alienated guards from the republic without addressing the core factors contributing to the violence, namely equipment, training, and tactics.

The responses of civil guards to attack during the republic's largest outbreak of violence prior to the Civil War, the October 1934 rebellion in Asturias, served as test of their own self-conceptions—whether they viewed defending their posts in combat as a military duty or as a task that far exceeded their obligations as policemen. The answer was found to be somewhere in the middle, with most guards willing to surrender after putting up a substantial resistance, while some did fight to the death in military fashion and others surrendered or evacuated relatively quickly. Courts-martial in the aftermath of the rebellion, however, made clear that civil guards were expected by judges to combat civilian resistance with as much violence as an army fighting a foreign enemy. The growing impossibility of the Civil Guard earning the respect of all classes of society meant that this more militarist version of honor gained ground within the force.

The repression of the Asturias revolt proved the climatic example of the increased political tensions caused by the Civil Guard's culture confronting the political mobilization of the republic. Civil guards had used mass arrests and torture as tools of political repression since the nineteenth century, but in Asturias, the fact that seemingly the entire region had risen up against them meant that for the first time they carried out a systematic program of instilling fear. Yet the guards' efforts to avenge the physical attacks against them backfired when the mass political parties and media of the Popular Front made scathing criticism of the repression the focal point of the 1936 election campaign. The Civil Guard that the new Popular Front government took control of in February 1936 was more antagonistic toward Spain's working classes and less committed to political neutrality than ever before.

While I have emphasized the continuities in the Civil Guard's culture throughout this book, its culture had changed over the course of the republic too, although not in a way that made its policing less violent. During the Civil War, the Civil Guard was vital to the rebels' political cleansing of captured territory. It provided local intelligence, led execution squads, and enforced discipline. Despite guards' initial rhetoric against becoming a force of repression, their professionalism, widespread dispersion, and local knowledge made them the ideal tools for such work, and they had gradually transformed into such a force, starting in the nineteenth century at the local level, then at the regional level in 1934, and finally at the national level in 1936. While guards had demonstrated differing interpretations of what their relationship to the communities that they policed should be up until 1934, after the Asturias revolt, most gravitated toward the vision that the rebels of 1936 held of a violent, uncompromising military confrontation, in which the population would be forced to show obedience and respect.

Taken as a whole, this book has examined how the key components of the Civil Guard's organizational culture, its values rooted in a nineteenth-century aristocratic notion of honor, its tense relations with the rural pueblos it policed, and the military focus of its training, made it difficult for guards to police peacefully the political mobilization that accompanied the Second Republic. Looking across the different instances of political violence involving the Civil Guard in this book, a pattern can be identified of these incidents emerging from the interactions among the corps's organizational culture, the mass mobilizations of the Second Republic, the policies of the different republican governments, and the choices of individual actors. The Civil Guard had developed a culture that could survive regime changes, but it lacked the flexibility to adapt to the mass political participation of the Second Republic, where ordinary citizens, mobilized by political groups such as the Socialists, felt able to criticize government institutions and take to the streets to demand reform. While republican governments believed that forces like the Civil Guard were necessary for maintaining the order that they needed to stabilize the new regime, they took almost no steps to adapt these forces to the new situations that they faced under the republic. Instead, successive republican governments kept in place, appointed, or failed to punish Civil Guard officers who enabled the worst practices within the institution's culture. Under such leadership, guards' desire for revenge and lack of training in investigative techniques meant that they turned to mass arrests and torture to punish populations that did not respect them. In a governmental system with a free press and legal opposition parties, such practices would not go uncriticized, but this criticism further antagonized an institution so sensitive to insult, creating a cycle of violence that the republic was never able to break. In other words, when the cultural continuity ensured by the Civil Guard's strong organizational culture clashed with the rupture of the Second Republic's new political culture, the resulting violence created an environment that was unfavorable to democratic stabilization and ultimately contributed to the fall of the republic. Although the rebellion of July 1936 was ostensibly meant to restore order, it instead unleashed violence on a scale Spain had not seen for over a hundred years.

NOTES

Works and archives frequently cited have been identified by the following abbreviations:

AAA   Archivo del Ayuntamiento de Arnedo
ACD   Archivo del Congreso de los Diputados
AGMM   Archivo General Militar de Madrid
AGMS   Archivo General Militar de Segovia
AHN   Archivo Histórico Nacional
AHPLR   Archivo Histórico Provincial de La Rioja
BOGC   *Boletín Oficial de la Guardia Civil*
CDMH   Centro Documental de la Memoria Histórica, Salamanca
DSCD   *Diario de Sesiones del Congreso de Diputados*
FC   Fondos contemporáneos
GC   Gobierno Civil
HGC   *El Heraldo de la Guardia Civil*
leg   legajo
Mº   Ministerio
PS   Político-social
REHGC   *Revista de Estudios Históricos de la Guardia Civil*
RTGC   *Revista Técnica de la Guardia Civil*
SEHGC   Servicio de Estudios Históricos de la Guardia Civil
sig   signatura
SGC   Sección Guardia Civil del Archivo General del Ministerio del Interior

Introduction

1. Eduardo González Calleja counts 2,629 deaths from political violence during the Second Republic period and reaches these comparative conclusions. I will follow his lead in concentrating on deaths since they can be counted much more reliably than other types of violence. I will also follow his definition of an incident of sociopolitical violence as "an individual or collective confrontation over power." See his *Cifras cruentas: Las víctimas mortales de la violencia sociopolítica en la Segunda República (1931–1936)* (Granada: Editorial Comares, 2015), 2, 6–7, 57, 64, 75.

2. For general histories of the Second Republic, see Julián Casanova, *República y Guerra Civil*, dir. Josep Fontana and Ramón Villares, Historia de España, vol. 8 (Madrid: Crítica/Marcial Pons, 2007); Stanley G. Payne, *Spain's First Democracy: The Second Republic, 1931–1936* (Madison: University

of Wisconsin Press, 1993); and Paul Preston, *The Coming of the Spanish Civil War: Reform, Reaction and Revolution in the Second Republic, 1931–1936*, 2nd ed. (London: Routledge, 1994).

3. Excluding the Asturias rebellion of October 1934, González Calleja finds that the Civil Guard (and the Carabineros customs police) killed 413 people, or over 25 percent of the above total. *Cifras cruentas*, 114.

4. For a portrait of civil guards as simply obedient to their orders, see Fernando del Rey, "Reflexiones sobre la violencia política en la II República española," in *Conflicto político, democracia y dictadura: Portugal y España en la década de 1930*, ed. Mercedes Gutiérrez Sánchez and Diego Palacios Cerezales (Madrid: Centro de Estudios Políticos, 2007), 39–40.

5. Randall Collins, *Violence: A Micro-sociological Theory* (Princeton, NJ: Princeton University Press, 2008), 21.

6. For examples of this perspective, see Gerald Brenan, *The Spanish Labyrinth: The Social and Political Background of the Spanish Civil War* (New York: Cambridge University Press, 1990 [1943]), 157, and Chris Ealham, *Class, Culture, and Conflict in Barcelona, 1898–1937* (Oxon: Routledge, 2005), 17–18.

7. See, for examples, Joaquín Arrarás, "Frente Popular," chap. 9 in vol. 2 of *Historia de la Cruzada Española* (Madrid: Ediciones españolas, 1940); Eduardo Comín Colomer, *La mayoría de edad (16 de febrero de julio de 1936): periodo de bolchevización*, in *Historia del Partido Comunista de España* (Madrid: Editora Nacional, 1967), vol. 3; and Fernando Rivas Gómez, *El Frente Popular: antecedentes de un alzamiento* (Madrid: Librería San Martín, 1976).

8. This figure includes those killed in battle and in the rear guard, but not those who died in the war's aftermath. Paul Preston, *The Spanish Holocaust: Inquisition and Extermination in Twentieth-Century Spain* (New York: Norton, 2012), xi.

9. Juan J. Linz, "From Great Hopes to Civil War: The Breakdown of Democracy in Spain," chap. 5 in *The Breakdown of Democratic Regimes: Europe*, ed. Juan J. Linz and Alfred Stepan (Baltimore: Johns Hopkins University Press, 1978).

10. For the former, see, for example, Payne, *Spain's First Democracy*. For the latter, see Pamela Beth Radcliff, *From Mobilization to Civil War: The Politics of Polarization in the Spanish City of Gijón, 1900–1937* (Cambridge: Cambridge University Press, 1996), and Julián Casanova, *De la calle al frente: El anarcosindicalismo en España (1931–1939)* (Barcelona: Crítica, 1997).

11. Manuel Ballbé, *Orden público y militarismo en la España constitucional (1812–1983)* (Madrid: Alianza Editorial, 1985); Diego López Garrido, *La Guardia Civil y los orígenes del Estado centralista* (Barcelona: Editorial Crítica, 1982); and Diego López Garrido, *El aparato policial en España: historia, sociología e ideología* (Barcelona: Ariel, 1987).

12. Eduardo González Calleja, *En nombre de la autoridad: La defensa del orden público durante la Segunda República Española (1931–1936)* (Granada: Editorial Comares, 2014), 90–93; Rey Reguillo, "Reflexiones sobre la violencia política"; Fernando del Rey, *Paisanos en lucha: Exclusión política y violencia en la Segunda República española* (Madrid: Biblioteca Nueva, 2008); Fernando del Rey, ed., *Palabras como puños: la intransigencia política en la Segunda República española* (Madrid: Editorial Tecnos, 2011); Sergio Vaquero Martínez, "La democratización del orden público en la Segunda República española: cultura, política y policía, 1931–1936," *Bulletin d'Histoire Contemporaine de l'Espagne* 54 (2020): 2; and Sergio Vaquero Martínez, "Reformar la policía: Los debates sobre el orden público en las cortes constituyentes de la Segunda República Española, 1931–1933," chap. 9 in Joana Dias Pereira, Ana Sofia Ferreira, and Manuel Loff, coordinators, *Construção do Estado, Movimentos Sociais e Economia Política* (Lisbon: Instituto de História Contemporânea, 2020).

13. Gerald Blaney Jr., "The Civil Guard and the Spanish Second Republic 1931–1936" (PhD diss., University of London, 2007), 3. Blaney's full critique of Ballbé and López Garrido's argument can

be found in his article "La historiografía sobre la Guardia Civil. Crítica y propuesta de investigación," *Política y sociedad* 42, no. 3 (2005): 34.

14. Gerald Blaney Jr., "Between Order and Loyalty: The Civil Guard and the Spanish Second Republic, 1931-1936," in *Conflict and Legality: Policing Mid-Twentieth Century Europe*, ed. Gerald Oram (London: Francis Boutle, 2003), 42-43.

15. Clifford Geertz, "Thick Description: Toward an Interpretive Theory of Culture," in *The Interpretation of Cultures* (New York: Basic Books, 1973): 3-30.

16. Edgar Schein, "How Culture Forms, Develops, and Changes," in *Gaining Control of the Corporate Culture*, ed. Ralph H. Kilmann, Mary J. Saxton and Roy Serpa (San Francisco: Jossey-Bass Publishers, 1986), 19-20, and Edgar H. Schein, *Organizational Culture and Leadership*, 3rd ed. (San Francisco: Jossey-Bass, 2004), 17.

17. Don M. Snider, "An Uninformed Debate on Military Culture," *Orbis*, no. 1 (1999): 11-26.

18. Isabel V. Hull, *Absolute Destruction: Military Culture and the Practices of War in Imperial Germany* (Ithaca, NY: Cornell University Press, 2005), 2, 93.

19. Peter H. Wilson, "Defining Military Culture," *Journal of Military History* 72, no. 1 (2008): 20.

20. Ibid., 16, and S. I. Hayakawa, *Language in Thought and Action* (New York: Harcourt, Brace & World, 1964), 299-300.

21. This argument, in varying forms, is found in Barry R. Posen, "Explaining Military Doctrine," chap. 2 in *The Sources of Military Doctrine: France, Britain, and Germany between the World Wars* (Ithaca, NY: Cornell University Press, 1984); Stephen Peter Rosen, *Winning the Next War: Innovation and the Modern Military* (Ithaca, NY: Cornell University Press, 1991), 20-21; and Williamson Murray and Allen R. Millet, eds., *Military Innovation in the Interwar Period* (Cambridge: Cambridge University Press, 1996).

22. John A. Nagl, "How Armies Learn," chap. 1 in *Learning to Eat Soup with a Knife: Counterinsurgency Lessons from Malaya and Vietnam* (Chicago: University of Chicago Press, 2005).

23. Tom Cockcroft, *Police Culture: Themes and Concepts* (Oxford: Routledge, 2013), 18-25.

24. Ibid., 46-50; Jerome H. Skolnick, "Operational Environment and Police Discretion,'" chap. 4 in *Justice without Trial: Law Enforcement in Democratic Society*, 4th ed. (New Orleans: Quid Pro Books, 2011 [1966]); James Q. Wilson, "Police Discretion," chap. 4 in *Varieties of Police Behavior: The Management of Law and Order in Eight Communities* (Cambridge, MA: Harvard University Press, 1978 [1968]); Carl B. Klockars, "Selective Enforcement," chap. 5 in *The Idea of Police* (Beverly Hills: SAGE Publications, 1985); and Peter K. Manning, *Police Work: The Social Organization of Policing* (Cambridge, MA: MIT Press, 1977), 300-304.

25. Skolnick, "A Sketch of the Police Officer's 'Working Personality,'" chap. 3 in *Justice without Trial*.

26. Cockcroft, *Police Culture*, 56-60; William A. Westley, "The Public as Enemy," chap. 3 in *Violence and the Police: A Sociological Study of Law, Custom, and Morality* (Cambridge, MA: MIT Press, 1970); and Jonathan Rubinstein, "Suspicions," chap. 6 in *City Police* (New York: Farrar, Straus, and Giroux, 1973).

27. Westley, "The Morality of Secrecy and Violence," chap. 4 in *Violence and the Police*.

28. Benjamin Bowling, Robert Reiner, and James Sheptychi, *The Politics of the Police* (Oxford: Oxford University Press, 2019), 165; Janet Chan, "Changing Police Culture," *British Journal of Criminology* 36, no. 1 (Winter 1996): 109-34; and P. A. J. Waddington, "Police (Canteen) Sub-Culture: An Appreciation," *British Journal of Criminology* 39, no. 2 (Spring 1999): 287-309.

29. Bowling, Reiner, and Sheptychi, *Politics of the Police*, 34; Peter K. Manning, "Occupational Culture," in *The Encyclopedia of Police Science*, ed. Jack R. Greene (New York: Routledge, 2007), 867;

and Megan O'Neill and Anne-Marie Singh, introduction to *Police Occupational Culture: New Debates and Directions*, ed. Megan O'Neill, Monique Marks, and Anne-Marie Singh (Oxford: Elsevier, 2007), 2.

30. Bertram Wyatt-Brown, *Southern Honor: Ethics and Behavior in the Old South* (New York: Oxford University Press, 1986), 14.

31. Javier Guillamón Álvarez, *Honor y honra en la España del siglo XVIII* (Madrid: Departamento de Historia Moderna, Facultad de Geografía e Historia, Universidad Complutense, 1981), 6–7, and *Diccionario de la lengua española*, 23rd ed. (2014), s.v. "honor."

32. Lorien Foote, *The Gentlemen and the Roughs: Manhood, Honor and Violence in the Union Army* (New York: NYU Press, 2010), 6.

33. Julian Pitt-Rivers, "Honor," in *International Encyclopedia of the Social Sciences*, ed. David L. Sills (New York: Macmillan, 1968), 6:506, 509.

1. Foundation

1. Fernando Rivas, "Los documentos de la época fundacional (II) Los servicios," *REHGC* 12, no. 23 (1979), 135.

2. Cockcroft, *Police Culture*, 47–50.

3. Mary Vincent, *Spain, 1833–2002: People and State* (Oxford: Oxford University Press, 2007), 1.

4. Magdalena de Pazzis Pi Corrales, "La seguridad pública en España (1833–1844)," in *VI Seminario Duque de Ahumada: La Fundación de la Guardia Civil (9, 10 y 11 de mayo de 1994)* (Madrid: Ministerio de Justicia e Interior, 1995), 28.

5. Eduardo González Calleja, *La razón de la fuerza. Orden público, subversión y violencia política en la España de la Restauración (1874–1917)* (Madrid: Consejo Superior de Investigaciones Científicas, 1998), 144–45, 148.

6. Pazzis Pi Corrales, "Seguridad pública," 19–20.

7. Raymond Carr, *Spain, 1808–1975*, 2nd ed. (Oxford: Clarendon Press, 1982 [1966]), 159, and Vincent, *Spain*, 30.

8. Fernando Rivas, "Los documentos de la época fundacional (I)," *REHGC* 12, no. 23 (1979), 11–12, and Diego López Garrido, "La naturaleza de la Guardia Civil en su primer medio siglo de existencia," *REHGC* 14, no. 26 (1981), 9–10.

9. Ballbé, *Orden público y militarismo*, 33, and López Garrido, *Aparato policial*, 31–32.

10. López Garrido, *Guardia Civil*, 19.

11. For more on the Maréchaussée, see Clive Emsley, "The Most Useful Corps for the Nation . . . The Maréchaussé," chap. 2 in *Gendarmes and the State in Nineteenth Century Europe* (New York: Oxford University Press, 1999).

12. Miguel Martínez García, "La Guardia Civil e instituciones de seguridad extranjeras," in *Fundación de la Guardia Civil*, 86. For more information, see Emsley, *Gendarmes and the State*, 37–77.

13. Pazzis Pi Corrales, "Seguridad pública," 20–21, 23. See Ballbé, *Orden público y militarismo*, 99–102, for more information on the founding of the Carabineros.

14. Ballbé, *Orden público y militarismo*, 127.

15. Blaney, "Civil Guard," 31, and Emilio de Diego García, "Los artífices de la fundación de la Guardia Civil," in *Fundación de la Guardia Civil*, 105.

16. Martínez García, "Guardia Civil e instituciones de seguridad," 87–88.

17. López Garrido, *Aparato policial*, 44, and López Garrido, "Naturaleza de la Guardia Civil," 10.

18. López Garrido, *Guardia Civil*, 81–82, 87.

19. Real decreto organizando el ramo de protección y seguridad pública, *Gaceta de Madrid*, January 27, 1844.

20. Real decreto creando un cuerpo especial de fuerza armada de infantería y caballería bajo la dependencia del ministerio de la Gobernación de la Península, y con la denominación de Guardias civiles, *Gaceta de Madrid*, March 31, 1844.

21. Eduardo Martínez Viqueira, *Hombres de honor. El duque de Ahumada y la fundación de la Guardia Civil* (Madrid: La Esfera de los Libros, 2019), 15, 30–33, and AGMS, Expedientes de Personas Célebres, caja 67, exp. 13.

22. AGMS, Expedientes de Personas Célebres, caja 67, exp. 13.

23. López Garrido, *Guardia Civil*, 97.

24. Blaney, "Civil Guard," 28, and Diego García, "Artífices de la fundación," 108.

25. Enrique Martínez Ruiz, *Creación de la Guardia Civil* (Madrid: Editora Nacional, 1976), 34–35, and Rivas, "Documentos de la época fundacional (I)," 21.

26. López Garrido, *Guardia Civil*, 95.

27. Art. 25, Real decreto declarando que la guardia civil depende del ministerio de la Guerra en lo concerniente á su organización, personal, disciplina, material y percibo de sus haberes, y del ministerio de la Gobernación por lo relativo á su servicio peculiar y movimientos, *Gaceta de Madrid*, May 14, 1844, and Rivas, "Documentos de la época fundacional (I)," 28. Narváez was able to act unilaterally because the Cortes had been suspended during a state of emergency. Miguel López Corral, *La Guardia Civil: Nacimiento y consolidación, 1844–1874* (Madrid: Editorial Actas, Ministerio de Justicia e Interior, Secretaría General Técnica, 1995), 38–39, and Joaquín de Azcarraga Servert, "Decretos y reglamentos fundacionales de la Guardia Civil," in *Fundación de la Guardia Civil*, 42–43.

28. Art. 2; López Garrido, *Guardia Civil*, 100; and Martínez Ruiz, *Creación de la Guardia Civil*, 374–75.

29. López Garrido, *Guardia Civil*, 101, 106, 180.

30. Miguel Martínez García, "La Gendarmería Nacional francesa y la fundación de la Guardia Civil," *Cuadernos de la Guardia Civil*, no. 16 (1996): 202.

31. Art. 1, Real decreto aprobando el reglamento para el servicio de la Guardia civil, *Gaceta de Madrid*, October 10, 1844; Martínez García, "Guardia Civil e instituciones de seguridad," 81–82, 91–92; and López Garrido, *Guardia Civil*, 103.

32. Art. 1, and Martínez Ruiz, *Creación de la Guardia Civil*, 123.

33. Art. 56.

34. The document was refined in 1852 and updated in 1923. *Contestaciones completas del "Instituto Reus" para el ingreso en el Cuerpo de la Guardia Civil* (Madrid: "Instituto Reus" Centro de enseñanza y publicaciones, 1935), 115. All quotes in this section are from the 1844 original.

35. Francisco Aguado Sánchez, *Historia de la Guardia Civil* (Madrid: Cupsa editorial, Editorial Planta, 1984), 1:226.

36. Real decreto aprobado el reglamento militar para la Guardia civil, *Gaceta de Madrid*, October 16, 1844; Martínez García, "Guardia Civil e instituciones de seguridad," 90–91; López Garrido, *Guardia Civil*, 102–3; Blaney, "Civil Guard," 29; and Aguado Sánchez, *Historia de la Guardia Civil*, 1:223.

37. Schein, *Organizational Culture and Leadership*, 226.

38. Francisco Aguado Sánchez, *El duque de Ahumada. Fundador de la Guardia Civil* (Madrid: Dirección General de la Guardia Civil, Servicio Histórico, 1969), 313, 400, and Maximiliano Lasen Paz, "La acción social en el Cuerpo," in *Fundación de la Guardia Civil*, 199.

39. Martínez García, "Gendarmería Nacional francesa," 204; López Garrido, *Guardia Civil*, 106; and Aguado Sánchez, *Historia de la Guardia Civil*, 1:221.

40. Circular expedida por el Excmo. Sr. Inspector general del Cuerpo N.° 1024, 24 April 1857, *Recopilación de reales órdenes y circulares de interés general para la Guardia Civil* 12 (1857): 156, and Rivas, "Documentos de la época fundacional (II)," 38.

41. José Díaz Valderrama, *Historia, servicios notables, socorros, comentarios de la Cartilla, y reflexiones sobre el Cuerpo de la Guardia Civil* (Madrid: J. M. Ducazcal, 1858), 44.

42. Martínez García, "Guardia Civil e instituciones de seguridad," 90.

43. *Cartilla del Guardia Civil* (Madrid: Imprenta del Boletin oficial de la Guardia Civil, n.d.), 7.

44. Robert A. Nye, *Masculinity and Male Codes of Honor in Modern France* (New York: Oxford University Press, 1993), 15.

45. Scott K. Taylor, *Honor and Violence in Golden Age Spain* (New Haven: Yale University Press, 2008).

46. Pieter Spierenburg, "Masculinity, Violence, and Honor: An Introduction," in *Men and Violence: Gender, and Rituals in Modern Europe and America*, ed. Pieter Spierenburg (Columbus: Ohio State University Press, 1998), 6.

47. Guillamón Álvarez, *Honor y honra*, and Real Cedula de S.M. y señores de Consejo por la cual se declara que no solo el oficio de curtidor . . . (Madrid: En la Imprenta de Don Antonio Marin, 1783), 1.

48. Nye, *Masculinity and Male Codes*, 8.

49. Julio Ponce Alberca and Diego Lagares García, *Honor de oficiales. Los tribunales de honor en el ejército de la España contemporánea (siglos XIX–XX)* (Barcelona: Ediciones Carena, n.d.), 29, 54.

50. *Cartilla del Guardia Civil*, 7.

51. Martínez Ruiz, *Creación de la Guardia Civil*, 371–72.

52. The fact that honor was so important to the Civil Guard may remind readers of stereotypes about honor's outsized role in Spanish society. However, this book only concerns honor as a guide to the Civil Guard's actions. Whether or not Ahumada's choice to emphasize honor in the *Cartilla* was also a result of a particular obsession within the Spanish nobility is outside the scope of this study. For more on the idea of honor in Spain, see José Luis Pitarch, "El honor," in *El honor y el honor militar* (Barcelona: Ediciones Grijalbo, 1984), 27–54.

53. *Cartilla del Guardia Civil*, 7–8.

54. Ibid., Art. 32, 13.

55. Chap. 6, Reglamento militar para la Guardia Civil.

56. Martínez Ruiz, *Creación de la Guardia Civil*, 66, 373–75.

57. Rivas, "Documentos de la época fundacional (I)," 29–30, 72–74, 108; Miguel López Corral, *La Guardia Civil. Claves históricas para entender a la Benemérita y a sus hombres (1844–1975)* (Madrid: La Esfera de los Libros, 2011), 36; and Gonzalo Jar Couselo, "El Oficial de la Guardia Civil en el momento fundacional," in *Fundación de la Guardia Civil*, 118.

2. On Patrol

1. Martínez Ruiz, *Creación de la Guardia Civil*, 36–44.

2. Miguel López Corral, "Proyección inicial de la Institución," in *Fundación de la Guardia Civil*, 46.

3. Pueblo means both "town" and refers to a community of people, whether the people of a town or even the people of a nation as a whole.

4. Juan Carlos Rodríguez Burdalo, "La casa-cuartel," in *Fundación de la Guardia Civil*, 144.

5. Rivas, "Documentos de la época fundacional (II)," 100.

6. Martínez Ruiz, *Creación de la Guardia Civil*, 103, and López Garrido, *Aparato policial*, 51.

7. Julian Pitt-Rivers, *The People of the Sierra* (Chicago: University of Chicago Press, 1961), 138. In this chapter, I draw on this anthropological study of a small Andalusian town in the 1940s, although it describes a slightly later period, because it is still one of the most highly regarded analyses of small-town society in Spain, and most of the characteristics of rural life Pitt-Rivers describes were not new in the 1940s. Pitt-Rivers has been criticized for reading the stereotype of Mediterranean "backwardness" onto rural Spain, but his work still offers an anthropological window into rural life at a time close to that under study here. Taylor, *Honor and Violence*, 4–5.

8. López Garrido, *Guardia Civil*, 147.

9. Rivas, "Documentos de la época fundacional (I)," 83.

10. Lasen Paz, "Acción social en el Cuerpo," 185.

11. Fernando Rivas, "Rebeldía y represión en Casas Viejas," *REHGC* 16, no. 29 (1983): 136.

12. Martínez Ruiz, *Creación de la Guardia Civil*, 75, and Circular expedida por el Excmo. Sr. Director general del Cuerpo, no. 87, 1 September 1865, *Recopilación de reales órdenes* 20 (1865): 259–60.

13. Personnel service records from the Restoration and Second Republic periods confirm that these practices were common.

14. Martínez Ruiz, *Creación de la Guardia Civil*, 77.

15. Taylor, *Honor and Violence*, 111.

16. Lasen Paz, "Acción social en el Cuerpo," 184, and Martínez Ruiz, *Creación de la Guardia Civil*, 81–82.

17. Martínez Ruiz, *Creación de la Guardia Civil*, 72–73, 376. The requirements mentioned were later altered to three years of military service and a minimum age of twenty-three for officers. *Escalafón General de los Generales, Jefes y Oficiales de la Guardia Civil en 1.° de enero de 1932* (Madrid: Taller-Escuela de Artes Gráficos de la Gua. Civil, [1932]), 92, and "Matrimonio," *RTGC* 22, no. 261 (November 1931): 536.

18. "Revistas de inspección," in Aguado Sánchez, *Historia de la Guardia Civil*, 4:352.

19. Lara, "Notas del mes," *RTGC* 26, no. 307 (September 1935): 365–66.

20. Martínez Ruiz, *Creación de la Guardia Civil*, 376–77, and López Corral, *Guardia Civil en la Restauración*, 263.

21. Chap. 5, art. 1, Reglamento militar para la Guardia Civil.

22. Chap. 6, art. 1, ibid.

23. López Corral, *Guardia Civil en la Restauración*, 272.

24. Circular expedida por el Excmo. Sr. Inspector general del Cuerpo, no. 1025, 26 April 1857, *Recopilación de reales órdenes* 12 (1857): 157–58; López Corral, *Guardia Civil: Claves históricas*, 30; and Martínez Ruiz, *Creación de la Guardia Civil*, 104, 115.

25. "Revistas de inspección," Aguado Sánchez, *Historia de la Guardia Civil*, 4:352.

26. In *Contestaciones completas del "Instituto Reus,"* 113.

27. González Calleja, *Nombre de la autoridad*, 249–50.

28. *Cartilla del Guardia Civil*, 10–11, and *Contestaciones completas del "Instituto Reus,"* 124, 126.

29. Cockcroft, *Police Culture*, 57, and Bowling, Reiner, and Sheptychi, *Politics of the Police*, 173–74.

30. Chan, "Changing Police Culture," 112.

31. Blaney, "Civil Guard," 45–46, 168.

32. Óscar Bascuñán Añover, "Justicia popular: el castigo de la comunidad en Spain, 1895–1923," *Hispania* 79, no. 263 (2019): 705. The Civil Guard continued to prevent lynching during the Second Republic. See Blaney, "Civil Guard," 168–69.

33. Javier Moreno Luzón, "Teoría del clientelismo y estudio de la política caciquil," *Revista de Estudios Políticos* (Nueva Epoca), no. 89 (July–September 1995): 194–96, 215.

34. Pitt-Rivers, *People of the Sierra*, 131, 140, 156, 206.

35. For an example of this way of thinking, see "Servicios," *RTGC* 24, no. 284 (October 1933): 369–70.

36. Chap. 1, art. 18, *Cartilla del Guardia Civil*, 9.

37. Art. 9 of the *Cartilla* prohibits civil guards from accepting any compensation for services rendered beyond thanks, and there is surprisingly little evidence of civil guards ever accepting bribes. *Cartilla del Guardia Civil*, 8. Not even left-wing critics, who denounced the Civil Guard in every way they could, accused it of being corrupt. For example, Brenan, *Spanish Labyrinth*, 157.

38. Reglamento para el servicio, arts. 581–92, in *Contestaciones completas del "Instituto Reus,"* 133–35.

39. Gobernador civil a Ministro de la Gobernación, 16 June 1931 and 20 June 1931, AHN, FC-Mº del Interior, Serie A, legajo 39, exp. 16, Jaén, nos. 1048, 1084 and A Ministro Gobernación and Ministro Gobernación a Gobernador civil, AHN, FC-Mº del Interior, Serie A, legajo 39, exp. 14, Badajoz.

40. Chap. 11, arts. 18–22, *Cartilla del Guardia Civil*, 37–38.

41. Martínez Ruiz, *Creación de la Guardia Civil*, 139. See, for example, Real orden espedida por el Ministerio de la Guerra, no. 235, 22 April 1847, *Recopilación de reales órdenes* 2 (1847): 21.

42. Helen Graham, *The Spanish Republic at War: 1936–1939* (Cambridge: Cambridge University Press, 2002), 6.

43. For example, in 1911 the director general of the Civil Guard praised a captain for arresting a priest who was wanted for "dishonest abuses." AHN, FC-Tribunal Supremo Reservado, Exp. 22, f. 127.

44. Cockcroft, *Police Culture*, 58.

45. Chap. 11, art. 16, *Cartilla del Guardia Civil*, 37.

46. José Sanjurjo, "The Spanish Civil Guard," *Police Journal* 4, no. 33 (1931): 532.

47. Chap. 2, arts. 8, 13, *Cartilla del Guardia Civil*, 14–15.

48. Gabriel Ferreras Estrada, *Memorias del sargento Ferreras* (León: Imprenta Provincial, 2002), 59–60.

49. Chap. 2, art. 2, *Cartilla del Guardia Civil*, 13.

50. Sanjurjo, "Spanish Civil Guard," 532.

51. Chap. 11, art. 21, *Cartilla del Guardia Civil*, 38, and Sanjurjo, "Spanish Civil Guard," 535.

52. However, civil guards were prohibited from spying directly. Chap. 1, art. 27, *Cartilla del Guardia Civil*, 12.

53. López Garrido, *Guardia Civil*, 164, 182.

54. During the Second Republic, more of the *RTGC*'s pages were concerned with fighting ordinary crime than any other subject.

55. Joseph Goldstein, "Police Discretion Not to Invoke the Criminal Process: Low-Visibility Decisions in the Administration of Justice," *Yale Law Journal* 69, no. 4 (March 1960): 543–94.

56. Skolnick, "Democratic Order and the Rule of Law," chap. 1 in *Justice without Trial*.

57. Michael Banton, *The Policeman in the Community* (London: Tavistock Publications, 1964), 127.

58. Egon Bittner, "The Police on Skid-Row: A Study of Peace Keeping," *American Sociological Review* 32, no. 5 (October 1967): 699–715, and William Foote Whyte, *Street Corner Society: The Social Structure of an Italian Slum*, 4th ed. (Chicago: University of Chicago Press, 1993 [1943]), 136.

59. Wilson, *Varieties of Police Behavior*, 140–41, 172.

60. López Corral, *Guardia Civil en la Restauración*, 389.

61. Eric J. Hobsbawm, "The Social Bandit," chap. 2 in *Primitive Rebels: Studies in Archaic Forms of Social Movement in the 19th and 20th Centuries* (New York: Norton, 1965), and Eric J. Hobsbawm, *Bandits* (New York: New Press, 2000 [1969]).

62. Julio Caro Baroja, "Honour and Shame: A Historical Account of Several Conflicts," in *Honour and Shame*, 116–17.

63. Radcliff, *Mobilization to Civil War*, 275–77.

64. "Un cabo de la guardia civil mata de un tiro á un muchacho," *El Noroeste*, October 24, 1919.

65. For more on the Investigation and Vigilance Corps, see Diego Palacios Cerezales, "Ansias de normalidad. La policía y la República," in *Palabras como puños*, 596–646, and González Calleja, *Nombre de la autoridad*, 159–70.

66. Reglamento para el servicio, art. 36, in *Contestaciones completas del "Instituto Reus,"* 120.

67. Quoted in Rivas, "Documentos de la época fundacional (I)," 107.

68. For an example of this pattern, see "Servicios," 369.

69. José Osuna Pineda, "Educación Moral: Sanas doctrinas," *RTGC* 22, no. 260 (October 1931): 443 and Al Sr Ministro Gobernación, 1 July 1931, AHN, FC-Mº del Interior, Serie A, legajo 39, exp. 14, Almería, no. 58.

70. Chap. 2, arts. 10, 17, *Cartilla del Guardia Civil*, 15–16 and Real orden espedida por el Ministerio de la Gobernacion, no. 98, 22 August 1847, *Recopilación de reales órdenes* 1 (1846): 12.

71. John P. Crank, "Danger Through the Lens of Culture," chap. 10 in *Understanding Police Culture*, 2nd ed. (Oxon: Routledge, 2015).

3. Barcelona

1. "Une lettre du fusillé Ascheri," *L'Intransigeant*, May 16, 1897.

2. "Lettre de Sebastian Sunye," *Les Temps Nouveaux*, April 10, 1897.

3. "Autre document," *Les Temps Nouveaux*, April 10, 1897. While it is difficult to confirm the veracity of these letters, their sheer number and similarity have led to a consensus among historians that prisoners were tortured at Montjuïc. José Álvarez Junco, *El emperador del paralelo. Lerroux y la demagogia populista* (Madrid: Alianza Editorial, 1990), 159n63.

4. For a description of how the inequality of fin-de-siècle Paris made it a breeding ground for anarchism in the 1890s, see John Merriman, *The Dynamite Club: How a Bombing in Fin-de-Siècle Paris Ignited the Age of Modern Terror* (New Haven, CT: Yale University Press, 2016).

5. The historian who most forcefully makes this argument that the original intent of the Civil Guard was not suppressing political protest is López Corral in *Guardia Civil. Claves históricas*.

6. Rivas, "Documentos de la época fundacional (II)," 22.

7. Martínez Ruiz, *Creación de la Guardia Civil*, 129–30, 198.

8. Ibid., 372; López Corral, "Proyección inicial de la Institución," 74; and López Corral, *Guardia Civil. Claves históricas*, 118.

9. Aguado Sánchez, *Duque de Ahumada*, 339.

10. See Aguado Sánchez, "Se impone el relevo," chap. 30 in ibid., for more on the duke's role in the events of 1854.

11. Martínez Ruiz, *Creación de la Guardia Civil*, 230–31.

12. López Corral, *Guardia Civil: nacimiento y consolidación*, 101.

13. See López Corral, *Guardia Civil. Claves históricas*, 99–106, for more on the Civil Guard's role in Pavía's coup.

14. López Corral, *Guardia Civil en la Restauración*, 58–59.

15. González Calleja, *Razón de la fuerza*, 53, and Aguado Sánchez, *Historia de la Guardia Civil*, 4:68.

16. López Corral, *Guardia Civil en la Restauración*, 65–66. *HGC* complained constantly about this.

17. González Calleja, *Razón de la fuerza*, 23, 50, and Ballbé, *Orden público y militarismo*, 236–37. This is also one of the main arguments in López Corral, *Guardia Civil en la Restauración*.

18. "Carne á las fieras," *HGC*, September 16, 1893.

19. This is one of the main arguments in López Corral, *Guardia Civil en la Restauración*.

20. George Richard Esenwein, *Anarchist Ideology and the Working-Class Movement in Spain, 1868–1898* (Berkeley: University of California Press, 1989), 59–61, 70–71.

21. López Corral, *Guardia Civil en la Restauración*, 556–67, 562–63, and Temma Kaplan, *The Anarchists of Andalusia, 1868–1903* (Princeton, NJ: Princeton University Press, 1977), 179–80.

22. Fernando Tarrida del Mármol, *Les inquisiteurs d'Espagne. Montjuich, Cuba, Philippines* (Paris: P.-V. Stock, 1897), 1–10, and Rafael Núñez Florencio, *El terrorismo anarquista, 1880–1909* (Madrid: Siglo XXI de España, 1983), 49–50.

23. Temma Kaplan, *Red City, Blue Period: Social Movements in Picasso's Barcelona* (Berkeley: University of California Press, 1992), 31.

24. Kaplan, *Red City, Blue Period*, 29.

25. "Barcelona," *Diario de Barcelona*, September 25, 1893, and AGMM, sig. 5846.10.

26. López Corral, *Guardia Civil en la Restauración*, 574.

27. Juan Montseny, *Consideraciones sobre el hecho y muerte de Pallás* (La Coruña: Tipografía la Gutenberg, 1893), 31.

28. "La dinamita en Barcelona," *El Imparcial*, November 10, 1893; Alfredo Opisso, *La Guardia Civil y su tiempo* (Barcelona: Molinas y Maza, n.d.), 121; Esenwein, *Anarchist Ideology*, 186; López Corral, *Guardia Civil en la Restauración*, 573–74; and González Calleja, *Razón de la fuerza*, 272.

29. "La dinamita en Barcelona," *El Imparcial*, November 9, 1893.

30. "La Guardia civil en Barcelona," *HGC*, September 24, 1894. See also "La Guardia civil en Barcelona," *HGC*, October 8, 1894.

31. López Corral, *Guardia Civil en la Restauración*, 576; González Calleja, *Razón de la fuerza*, 272–74; and Ley estableciendo las penas que sufrirán los que atentaren contra las persona ó causaren daño en las cosas empleando para ello sustancias ó aparatos explosivos, *Gaceta de Madrid*, July 11, 1894.

32. AGMM, sig. 5846.10, and López Corral, *Guardia Civil en la Restauración*, 575.

33. AGMS, Expedientes Personales, sect. 1, legajo 584.

34. Angel Smith, "Barcelona through the European Mirror: From Red and Black to Claret and Blue," in *Red Barcelona: Social Protest and Labour Mobilization in the Twentieth Century*, ed. Angel Smith (London: Routledge, 2002), 7; Álvarez Junco, *Emperador del paralelo*, 133–34; and I. Bo y Singla, *Montjuich: Notas y Recuerdos históricos* (Barcelona: Maucci, [1917]).

35. "El atentado de Barcelona," *El País*, December 20, 1893; "Los anarquistas en Barcelona," *El País*, December 23, 1893; "El anarquismo," *El País*, December 24, 1893; and "Los anarquistas," *El Imparcial*, December 24, 1893.

36. These letters in Juan Montseny, *El proceso de un gran crímen* (La Coruña: Tipografía la Gutenberg, 1895).

37. Puente, "Los anarquistas," *El Imparcial*, January 2, 1894; Gimeno, "Los anarquistas," *El Imparcial*, January 3, 1894; and Vela, "Fusilamiento de los anarquistas de Barcelona," *El País*, May 22, 1894.

38. Álvarez Junco, *Emperador del paralelo*, 148–50, and Bo y Singla, *Montjuich*, 102.

39. AGMS, Expedientes Personales, sect. 1, legajo 584.

40. Núñez Florencio, *Terrorismo anarquista*, 99–100.

41. Amadeu Hurtado, *Quaranta anys d'advocat. Història del meu temps, 1894–1920*, 2nd ed. (Barcelona: Ediciones Ariel, 1969), 28–29; AHN FC-Mº del Interior, Serie A, legajo 63, Exp. 17; González Calleja, *Razón de la fuerza*, 279–81; and López Corral, *Guardia Civil en la Restauración*, 571–72.

42. Conferencia telegráfica entre el Sr. Ministro de la Guerra y el Comandante en Jefe del 4º Cuerpo de Ejército, 8 June 1896, AGMM, sig. 5846.13.

43. Real decreto suspendiendo las garantías constitucionales en Barcelona y su provincia, *Gaceta de Madrid*, June 9, 1896.

44. Ley estableciendo la penalidad para los que atentaren contra las personas ó las cosas empleando sustancias ó aparatos explosivos, *Gaceta de Madrid*, September 4, 1896.

45. Hurtado, *Quaranta anys d'advocat*, 30.

46. Federico Urales, *El castillo maldito* (Toulouse: Presses Universitaires de Mirail, 1992), 190–92. Although this play, written under a pseudonym by Juan Montseny, is a work of fiction, it provides a more complete picture of how the events unfolded beyond the information in the official documentation.

47. Núñez Florencio, *Terrorismo anarquista*, 58, and González Calleja, *Razón de la fuerza*, 278, 284.

48. In "Lettre du fusillé Ascheri."

49. Urales, *Castillo maldito*, 193.

50. "L'atentat del Carrer de Cambis Nous," *La Campana de Gracia*, September 12, 1896.

51. Ministro Guerra a Comandante en Jefe, 19 September 1896, AGMM, sig. 5916.3; Real orden dictando reglas relativas para la formación del nuevo Cuerpo de Policía Judicial, *Gaceta de Madrid*, September 20, 1896; and Opisso, *Guardia Civil*, 187.

52. José Morah, "La policía judicial," *HGC*, November 24, 1896.

53. "El tentiente Portas," *HGC*, September 16, 1896, and "En honor del teniente Portas," *HGC*, November 24, 1896.

54. Causa instruida, AGMM, sig. 5846.13.

55. Datos del Consejo de Guerra celebrado en Montjuich los días 11, 12, 13, 14 y 15 de diciembre de 1896, in [Ricardo Mella and José Prats], *La barbarie gubernamental de España* (New York: Imp. de *El Despertar*, 1897), 22, 24.

56. "El proceso de los anarquistas," *El País*, December 20, 1896, and Datos del Consejo de Guerra, in *Barbarie gubernamental de España*, 28–30.

57. Datos del Consejo de Guerra, in *Barbarie gubernamental de España*, 25, 27–28.

58. Núñez Florencio, *Terrorismo anarquista*, 94.

59. Sentencia de pena de muerte impuesta á Tomás Ascheri Fossetti, José Molás Duran, Antonio Nogués Figueras, Juan Alsina Vicente y Luis Más Gacio, por delito de atentado contra las personas por medio de aparatos explosivos, 29 April 1897, AGMM, sig. 5846.13. For a description of the execution, see Figuerola, "Los anarquistas de Barcelona," *La Correspondencia de España*, May 5, 1897.

60. "Anarquistas extrañados," *Heraldo de Madrid*, May 28, 1897.

61. Hurtado, *Quaranta anys d'advocat*, 30.

62. Pere Coromines, *Les presons imaginaries* (Barcelona: Tipografia «L'Avenç», 1899), and Pere Coromines, *Diaris i records de Pere Coromines*, vol. 1, *El anys de joventut I. El procés de Montjuïc* (Barcelona: Curial Edicions Catalans, 1974).

63. Coromines, *Anys de joventut*, 100, 160, and Coromines, "La marx del batalló," in *Presons imaginaries*, 97–115. The original December 21, 1896, petition is in AGMM, sig. 5846.13.

64. Fernando Tarrida de Mármol, "Un mois dans les prisons d'Espagne," *La Revue blanche* 9 (July–December 1896): 337–41.

65. Álvarez Junco, *Emperador del paralelo*, 156–57; Tarrida de Mármol, *Inquisiteurs d'Espagne*, 93–94, 118–20; and Hurtado, *Quaranta anys d'advocat*, 26.

66. A thorough review of the French coverage is in Tarrida de Mármol, *Inquisiteurs d'Espagne*.

67. "2e lettre de J. Molas," *Les Temps Nouveaux*, April 3, 1897.

68. Álvarez Junco, *Emperador del paralelo*, 158–59, and "Carta de Juan Montseny," *El Progreso*, May 17, 1898. The work in question is Montseny, *Proceso de un gran crímen*.

69. Álvarez Junco, *Emperador del paralelo*, 160.

70. An early example is "El proceso de los anarquistas," *El País*, November 11, 1896.

71. Álvarez Junco, *Emperador del paralelo*, 139, 162.

72. See the articles entitled "Revisión de proceso: Las infamias de Montjuich," in *El Progreso* from January 13, 1898.

73. A review of the press is in "Las infamias de Montjuich," *El Progreso*, January 22, 1898.

74. Emili Salut, *Vivers de revolucionaris. Apunts històrics del districte cinquè* (Barcelona: Llibreria Catalònia, 1938), 48.

75. "Lo de Montjuich: Mitin en Barcelona," *El Socialista*, July 7, 1899.

76. "Las infamias de Montjuich," *El Progreso*, February 14, 1898, and Álvarez Junco, *Emperador del paralelo*, 165–68.

77. Datos del Consejo de Guerra, in *Barbarie gubernamental en España*, 30.

78. See a popular song mentioning Portas in Salut, *Vivers de revolucionaris*, 48, and Urales, *Castillo maldito*, 177.

79. "Atentado anarquista contra el teniente Portas," *HGC*, September 5, 1897.

80. López Corral, *Guardia Civil en la Restauración*, 600–601; Esenwein, *Anarchist Ideology*, 199; "El proceso de Sempau," *La Publicidad*, September 7, 1897, evening edition; and "Sempau y Portas," *El Progreso*, December 12, 1898.

81. "Las infamias de Montjuich," *El Progreso*, January 16, 1898.

82. Álvarez Junco, *Emperador del paralelo*, 79; Rafael Abella, *Lances de honor* (Barcelona: Planeta, 1995), 127–28; and "Un incidente," *El Imparcial*, August 22, 1902.

83. "Capitán Portas," *La Publicidad*, August 22, 1902, morning edition.

84. Un teniente, "Llamamiento á la Benemérita," *El Progreso*, February 27, 1898.

85. "Atentado anarquista."

86. Despujol a Ministro Guerra, 26 July 1897, AGMS, 2ª Sección, 12ª División, legajo (leg.) 151.

87. Letter to Enrique Marzo, AGMS, 2ª Sección, 12ª División, leg. 151.

88. Junta Consultiva de Guerra, 20 December 1897, AGMS, 2ª Sección, 12ª División, leg. 151.

89. Real decreto conmutando por las de extrañamiento perpetuo ó temporal las penas que están sufriendo las autores de los atentados de la Gran Vía y calle de Cambios Nuevos de Barcelona, y otorgando otros indultos, *Gaceta de Madrid*, January 26, 1900.

90. Capitán General de Cataluña Eulogio Despujol a Presidente del Consejo Supremo de la Guerra, 30 November 1899, AGMM, sig. 5846.13 and Capitán General a Ministro Guerra, 15 December 1896, AGMM, sig. 5846.13.

91. Dictámen del Señor Fiscal Togado, AGMM, sig. 5846.13.

92. AGMS, Expedientes Personales, sect. 1, legajo 584.

93. Lucienne Domergue, "Le procès de Montjuich (1896–1897). L'événement et son contexte," in Urales, *Castillo maldito*, 19.

94. Real decreto relativo á las prescripciones de ley sobre facultades gubernativas para supresión de periódicos y centros anarquistas, August 14, 1897, *Gaceta de Madrid*.

95. For more on this shift, see Angel Smith, "Workers against the State: Anarchism, Republicanism, Popular and Working-Class Protest, 1898 to 1909," chap. 5 in *Anarchism, Revolution and Reaction: Catalan Labour and the Crisis of the Spanish State, 1898–1923* (New York: Berghahn Books, 2007); López Corral, "Las agitaciones de masas," in *Guardia Civil en la Restauración*, 469–536; and Pamela Radcliff, "The emerging challenge of mass politics," chap. 9 in *Spain since 1808*, ed. José Álvarez Junco and Adrian Shubert (New York: Oxford University Press, 2000).

96. The idea that the Civil Guard's prestige declined as it became a force for suppressing political protest during the Restoration is another central argument of López Corral in *Guardia Civil en la Restauración*.

97. AGMS, 2ª Sección, 10ª División, leg. 145–46.

98. Dirección General de la Guardia Civil a Ministro de la Guerra, 4 May 1903, AGMS, 2ª Sección, 10ª División, leg. 145.

99. AGMS, 2ª Sección, 10ª División, leg. 146–47.

100. Kaplan, *Red City, Blue Period*, 61, 81.

101. For a detailed account and analysis of the Tragic Week, see Joan Connelly Ullman, *The Tragic Week: A Study of Anticlericalism in Spain, 1875–1912* (Cambridge, MA: Harvard University Press, 1968).

102. Smith, *Anarchism, Revolution and Reaction*, 182.

103. For more on this period, see Eduardo González Calleja, *El máuser y el sufragio. Orden público, subversión y violencia política en la crisis de la Restauración (1917–1931)* (Madrid: Consejo superior de investigaciones científicas, 1999).

104. Bowling, Reiner, and Sheptychi, *Politics of Policing*, 24.

105. Westley, *Violence and the Police*, 111–18.

4. Training

1. Ferreras, *Memorias del sargento Ferreras*, 31–32, 41, 43, 53–55, 57.

2. Schein, *Organizational Culture and Leadership*, 18.

3. Such assertions are based on the personnel service records of forty-three enlisted civil guards housed in the SGC.

4. Blaney, "Civil Guard," 42, and Agustín M. Pulido Pérez, *La Guardia Civil ante el Bienio Azañista, 1931/33* (Madrid: Almena Ediciones, 2008), 27.

5. Sanjurjo, "Spanish Civil Guard," 375.

6. Sebastian Balfour, "Cultures, Conditions, and Corruption," chap. 8 in *Deadly Embrace: Morocco and the Road to the Spanish Civil War* (Oxford: Oxford University Press, 2002), and Daniel Macías Fernández, "Piojos, ratas y moscas: Marruecos y el soldado español," chap. 8 in *A cien años de Annual: La guerra de Marruecos*, ed. Daniel Macías Fernández (Madrid: Desperta Ferro Ediciones, 2021).

7. Bernando Rubio López, *Nuestros soldados* (Bolaños, 2004), 9. Before 1912 the term of service was four years.

8. Macías Fernández, "Piojos, ratas y moscas," 334, and Real decreto disponiendo se publiquen en este periódico oficial los artículos que forman la ley de Reclutamiento y Reemplazo del Ejército, *Gaceta de Madrid*, January 21, 1912.

9. Francisco Manfredicano, "La Compañía de Guardias Jóvenes de la Guardia Civil," *REHGC* 3, no. 6 (1970): 139–40.

10. Faustino Ramírez Barreto, *Listado de las vicisitudes de los alumnos del colegio de guardias jóvenes "Duque de Ahumada"* (1.853–2.003) (con motivo de la celebración de su 150° aniversario) (Valdemoro, 2002), XIII.

11. "Relación de las cantidades donadas a favor de los Colegios de Huérfanos Guardia Civil," *BOGC* 10, no. 34 (December 1, 1935): 1482.

12. López Corral, *Guardia Civil en la Restauración*, 219.

13. In Ramírez Barreto, *Listado de las vicisitudes*, LXXVII.

14. Pedro Calderón de la Barca, *Para vencer amor, querer vencerle*, in *Obras completas*, ed. Angel Valbuena Briones, 2nd ed. (Madrid: Aguilar, 1960), 2:529, 540.

15. Taylor, *Honor and Violence*, 6–7.

16. Manfredicano, "Compañía de Guardias Jóvenes," 142, 149.

17. Jesús Narciso Núñez Calvo, "XC Aniversario del patronazgo de la Virgen del Pilar en la Guardia Civil (1913–2003)," *Guardia Civil*, no. 706 (February 2003): 79.

18. Faustino Ramírez Barreto, *Semblanza histórica de la Asociación Pro-Huérfanos de la Guardia Civil* (Madrid: Asociación Pro-Huérfanos de la Guardia Civil, 2008), 132.

19. In ibid., 133.

20. Ibid., 64–65, and AGMS, Expedientes Personales, sect. 1, legajo P-501.

21. "Reglamento de 1916," quoted in Ramírez Barreto, *Listado de las vicisitudes*, LVI.

22. Ibid.

23. Fernando Rivas Gómez, "La enseñanza de la Guardia Civil," *REHGC* 7, no. 13 (1974): 152.

24. The literacy rate among Spanish males in 1910 was 46 percent. Narciso de Gabriel, "Alfabetización, semialfabetización y analfabetismo en España (1860–1991)," *Revista Complutense de Educación* 8, no. 1 (1997): 203.

25. Rivas Gómez, "Enseñanza de la Guardia Civil," 153.

26. Schein, *Organizational Culture and Leadership*, 262.

27. Westley, "On Becoming a Policeman," chap. 5 in *Violence and the Police*.

28. For a personal account of being an *aspirante*, see Ferreras, "Aspirante en activo. La incipiente agitación social," in *Memorias del sargento Ferreras*, 55–57.

29. SGC, Expediente Personal, Pedro Manzanares Ureta.

30. SGC, Expediente Personal, Miguel Abajo Ortega.

31. Cartilla del Guardia Civil, Art. 187, in Miguel Arlégui Bayones, *Doctrinal de Servicio para la Guardia Civil* (Valladolid: Imprenta Castellana, 1908), 135.

32. Antonio de Reparaz and Tresgallo de Souza, *Desde el Cuartel General de Miaja al Santuario de la Virgen de la Cabeza* (Valladolid: Artes Gráficas Afrodisio Aguado, 1937), 28–29.

33. Rivas Gómez, "Enseñanza de la Guardia Civil," 152–53, 157.

34. Assertions about Civil Guard officers in this section are based on a survey of eighty-seven personnel service records housed in the SGC and AGMS.

35. Balfour, *Deadly Embrace*, 181, and Paul Preston, *Franco: A Biography* (London: Harper Collins Publishers, 1993), 2.

36. "Oficialidad de la Guardia Civil," 11. Varying but always small numbers of officer vacancies were also filled by promotions from the ranks.

37. José Luis Isabel Sánchez, "La formación de los oficiales de Infantería entre 1909 y 1921," in *El Protectorado Español en Marruecos: La historia trascendida*, directed by Manuel Aragón Reyes (2013), 3:332.

38. Carolyn Boyd, *Historia Patria: Politics, History, and National Identity in Spain 1875–1975* (Princeton, NJ: Princeton University Press, 1997), xiv, 5, 13–14.

39. Of the eighty-seven officers examined by the author through their service records, sixty-six attended the second Infantry Academy. Morris Janowitz, *The Professional Soldier: A Social and Political Portrait* (London: Collier-Macmillan, 1960), 127.

40. At times, I will draw upon accounts of experiences at the Infantry Academy by officers who would not go on to join the Civil Guard since it can be assumed that all shared similar experiences in their years as cadets.

41. Isabel Sánchez, "Formación de los oficiales," 326–27.

42. Preston, *Franco*, 9.

43. SGC, Expediente Personal, Lisardo Doval Bravo.

44. Geoffrey Jensen, *Irrational Triumph: Cultural Despair, Military Nationalism, and the Ideological Origins of Franco's Spain* (Reno: University of Nevada Press, 2002), 26–27; Geoffrey Jensen, "Military Nationalism and the State: The Case of fin-de-siècle Spain," *Nations and Nationalism* 6, no. 2 (2000): 262–63; and Carlos Blanco Escolá, *La Academia General Militar de Zaragoza (1928–1931)* (Barcelona: Editorial Labor, 1989), 222.

45. For more on Regenerationism, see Sebastian Balfour, *The End of the Spanish Empire, 1898–1923* (Oxford: Oxford University Press, 1997).

46. Preston, *Franco*, 6.

47. José Ibáñez Marin and Luis Angulo Escobar, *Los cadetes* (Madrid: Establecimiento tipográfico «el trabajo», [1903]), 13.

48. Geoffrey Jensen, "Moral Strength through Material Defeat? The Consequences of 1898 for Spanish Military Culture," *War & Society* 17, no. 2 (October 1999): 28–31, and Azar Gat, *The Development of Military Thought: The Nineteenth Century* (Oxford: Clarendon Press, 1992), 67–68.

49. Enrique Ruiz Fornells, *La educación moral del soldado*, 6th ed. (Toledo: Imprenta Librería y Encuadernación de Rafael Gómez-Menor, 1909). For an extensive analysis of this book as representing the thinking of the liberal faction within the Spanish Army at that time, see Geoffrey Jensen, "Ilustrar a los soldados: Enrique Ruiz-Fornells y el liberalismo militar," chap. 6 in *Cultura militar española. Modernistas, tradicionalistas y liberales* (Madrid: Bilbioteca Nueva, 2014).

50. Hilario González, *Resumen histórico de la Academia de Infantería* (Toledo: Imprenta-Escuela Tipográfica del Colegio de M.ª Cristina para Huérfanos de la Infantería, 1925), 195.

51. Francisco Franco quoted in Vicente Pozuelo, *Los últimos 476 días de Franco* (Barcelona: Editorial Planeta, 1980), 92.

52. *Academia de Infantería: Memoria de los cursos de 1918–1919 y 1919–1920* (Escuela tipográfica y encuadernación del Colegio de María Cristina para Huérfanos de la Infantería, [1920]), 164.

53. Vicente Cacho Viu, "Francia 1870–España 1898," in *Repensar el 98* (Madrid: Biblioteca Nueva, 1997), 77–115, and Jensen, *Irrational Triumph*, 26, 62.

54. Michael Howard, "The Influence of Clausewitz," In *On War*, by Carl von Clausewitz, ed. and trans. Michael Howard and Peter Paret (Princeton, NJ: Princeton University Press, 1976), 34, 36–37, and Gat, "The Cult of the Offensive: The Sources of French Military Doctrine 1871–1914," in *Development of Military Thought*, 114–72.

55. [Antonio García Pérez], *Breve Bosquejo Histórico de la Academia de Infantería* ([1924]).

56. Carolyn Boyd, *Praetorian Politics in Liberal Spain* (Chapel Hill: University of North Carolina Press, 1979), 27, 32–34.

220 NOTES TO PAGES 72–78

57. Balfour, *Deadly Embrace*, 81, 213, and Preston, *Franco*, 13.

58. Fernando Puell de la Villa, *Historia del Ejército en España* (Madrid: Alianza Editorial, 2000), 105.

59. Balfour, *Deadly Embrace*, 213.

60. Stanley G. Payne, *Politics and the Military in Modern Spain* (Stanford: Stanford University Press, 1967), 123.

61. Eloy Martín Corrales, *La imagen del magrebí en España. Una perspectiva histórica, siglos XVI–XX* (Barcelona: Ediciones Bellaterra, 2002).

62. Martín Corrales, *Imagen del magrebí*, 23–24, 28, 78–79, 94, 102.

63. Geoffrey Jensen, "Military Consequences of Cultural Perceptions: The Spanish Army in Morocco, 1912–1927," *Journal of the Middle East and Africa* 8, no. 2 (2017): 136–46.

64. Martín Corrales, "El traidor enemigo (1909–1927)," chap. 5 in *Imagen del magrebí*, and Rocío Velasco de Castro, "La imagen del «moro» en la formulación e instrumentalización del africanismo franquista," *Hispania* 74, no. 246 (January–April 2014): 209–11.

65. Geoffrey Jensen, "Morocco and Spain in the Eyes of Antonio García Pérez," in Aragón Reyes, *Protectorado español en Marruecos*, 3:506–7; Mateo Dieste, *«Hermandad» hispano-marroquí*, 61–62; and Geoffrey Jensen, "Muslim Soldiers in a Spanish Crusade: Tomás García Figueras, Mulai Ahmed er Raisuni and the Ideological Context of Spain's Moroccan Soldiers," in *Colonial Soldiers in Europe, 1914–1945: "Aliens in Uniform" in Wartime Societies*, ed. Eric Storm and Ali Al Tuma (New York: Routledge, 2016), 187–89.

66. Balfour, *Deadly Embrace*, 202.

67. Jensen, "«Viva la muerte!» José Millán-Astray y las raíces intelectuales de la «cruzada nacional»," chap. 7 in *Cultura militar española*.

68. Balfour, *Deadly Embrace*, 172, 202.

69. Payne, *Politics and the Military*, 154.

70. *Enseñanzas de la campaña de Rif en 1909* (Madrid: Talleres del Depósito de la guerra, 1911), 11.

71. Payne, *Politics and the Military*, 155.

72. Balfour, *Deadly Embrace*, 82.

73. See especially Gustau Nerín, *La guerra que vino de África* (Barcelona: Crítica, 2005), and Balfour, *Deadly Embrace*.

74. "Oficialidad de la Guardia Civil," 16.

75. *Africanista* types would have been more attracted to the Spanish Legion, which enjoyed a privileged place within the army in exchange for frequent front-line deployments.

76. "Oficialidad de la Guardia Civil," 11, 17, and Balfour, *Deadly Embrace*, 181.

77. "Oficialidad de la Guardia Civil," 17. The entry process varied somewhat over the years.

78. Ibid., 13, 16.

79. Wilson, *Varieties of Police Behavior*, 152–53.

5. The Republic

1. Miguel Maura, *Así cayó Alfonso XIII* (Barcelona: Editorial Ariel, 1981 [1962]), 243–45, and González Calleja, *Cifras cruentas*, 310.

2. Maura, *Así cayó Alfonso XIII*, 246.

3. Ibid., 252–54, 257.

4. González Calleja, *Cifras cruentas*, 310–11.

5. For instance, the number of strikes in Spain almost doubled in 1931 compared with the previous year. Payne, *Spain's First Democracy*, 141.

6. González Calleja, *Máuser y el sufragio*, 278.

7. See, for example, "La Seguridad publica en el periodo constitucional," *REHGC* 15, no. 28 (1982): 112.

8. González Calleja, *Nombre de la autoridad*, 44.

9. Janowitz, *Professional Soldier*, 35–36.

10. Emilio Esteban-Infantes, *General Sanjurjo. (Un Laureado en el penal del dueso)*, 2nd ed. (Barcelona: Editorial AHR, 1958), 19; Enrique Sacanell Ruiz de Apodaca, *El general Sanjurjo, héroe y víctima* (Ediciones Altaya, 2008), 25; and A. Díaz Carmona, "El 10 de agosto de 1932. I.-Un General romántico y una Patria que se hunde," *REHGC* 1, no. 2 (1968): 62.

11. AGMS, caja 1161, exp. 14.

12. Quoted in Sacanell, *General Sanjurjo, héroe y víctima*, 28–29.

13. Díaz Carmona, "El 10 de agosto de 1932," 63, and Esteban-Infantes, *General Sanjurjo*, 26, 28–29.

14. Esteban-Infantes, *General Sanjurjo*, 37, 50; Gabriel Cardona, *El poder militar en la España contemporánea hasta la guerra civil* (Madrid: Siglo veintiuno editores, 1983), 33; and AGMS, caja 1161, exp. 14.

15. AGMS, caja 1161, exp. 14, and Esteban-Infantes, *General Sanjurjo*, 45.

16. AGMS, caja 1161, exp. 14.

17. Ibid.

18. Sacanell, *General Sanjurjo, héroe y víctima*, 59.

19. Esteban-Infantes, *General Sanjurjo*, 68–69, and Balfour, *Deadly Embrace*, 247.

20. López Corral, *Guardia Civil. Claves históricas*, 291, and Esteban-Infantes, *General Sanjurjo*, 94–99, 230.

21. Sacanell, *General Sanjurjo, héroe y víctima*, 73.

22. Díaz, "El 10 de agosto de 1932," 68, and Esteban-Infantes, *General Sanjurjo*, 107–8.

23. C. Gallego Pérez, *La lucha contra el crimen y el desorden (Memorias de un teniente de la Guardia Civil)* (Madrid: Rollán, 1957), 169. The *RTGC* was effusive in its praise of Sanjurjo. See, for example, "Lealtad de la Guardia Civil," *RTGC* 22, no. 255 (May 1931): 242–43, and especially "El general Sanjurjo," *RTGC* 22, no. 258 (August 1931): 347.

24. Quoted in Fernando Rivas Gómez, "La República en marcha. I.—Historia de tres meses inaugurales," *REHGC* 9, no. 17 (1976): 155.

25. "Guardia Civil: Cantos de sirena," *La Correspondencia Militar*, March 18, 1931, and Blaney, "Civil Guard," 75–76, 78–79.

26. Blaney, "Civil Guard," 75.

27. "Guardia Civil: Sinceridad electoral," *La Correspondencia Miliar*, January 24, 1931.

28. Blaney, "Civil Guard," 84, 90.

29. Esteban-Infantes, *General Sanjurjo*, 131–33. See Blaney, "Civil Guard," 94–100, for more on this debate.

30. Blaney, "Civil Guard," 100–103.

31. Manuel Azaña, *Diarios completos. Monarquía, República, Guerra Civil* (Barcelona: Crítica, 2000), 425.

32. "La República española," *RTGC* 22, no. 255 (May 1931): 241.

33. González Calleja, *Nombre de la autoridad*, 121.

34. For the versions in effect during the Second Republic, see *Contestaciones completas del "Instituto Reus."*

35. Maura, *Así cayó Alfonso XIII*, 206.

36. Miguel López Corral, "Los gobiernos izquierdas y la Guardia Civil," *Guardia Civil*, no. 521 (September 1987): 41.

37. Ladera, "Cuarenta y cinco minutos de charla, sobre la Guardia Civil, con el Excmo. Sr. D. Santiago Casares Quiroga, Ministro de la Gobernación," *RTGC* 24, no. 280 (August 1933): 283.

38. González Calleja makes this argument in *Nombre de la autoridad*.

39. Ley declarando actos de agresión a la República los que se mencionan, *Gaceta de Madrid*, October 22, 1931, and González Calleja, *Nombre de la autoridad*, 193.

40. Sergio Martínez Vaquero, "En defensa del orden: la cultura profesional de la policía en la Segunda República, 1931–1936," *Ayer* 135, no. 3 (2024): 79–80.

41. Maura, *Así se cayó Alfonso XIII*, 265, 274.

42. Blaney, "Civil Guard," 154.

43. Ibid., 157.

44. Palacios Cerezales, "Ansias de normalidad," 616, and González Calleja, *Nombre de la autoridad*, 143.

45. Palacios Cerezales, "Ansias de normalidad," 614; Vaquero Martínez, "Defensa del orden," 87; and Ballbé, *Orden público y militarismo*, 339.

46. Vaquero Martínez, "Defensa del orden"; Palacios Cerezales, "Ansias de normalidad," 609–10; Diego Palacios Cerezales, "«En la era del aeroplano». La policía y sus modernidades en el periodo de entreguerras," *Ayer* 135, no. 3 (2024): 34–38; "Lo que se impone," *RTGC* 22, no. 258 (August 1931): 376; and "La pistola asfixiante," *RTGC* 22, no. 258 (August 1931): 390.

47. "El artículo 7.° de la Cartilla," *RTGC* 23, no. 270 (August 1932): 322–23.

48. "Modernización," *RTGC* 24, no. 279 (May 1933): 175, and "Armamento," *RTGC* 24, no. 279 (May 1933): 176.

49. See Aguado Sánchez, *Historia de la Guardia Civil*, 5:49–54, for details on pay.

50. Adrian Shubert, *The Road to Revolution Spain: The Coal Miners of Asturias, 1860–1934* (Urbana: University of Illinois Press, 1987), 12, and Rivas, *Frente Popular*, 36.

51. See, for example, Gobernador a Ministro, 10 July 1931, AHN FC-M° del Interior, Serie A, legajo 39, Exp. 15, Gerona, no. 613, and the Cimas case discussed below.

52. Radcliff, *Mobilization to Civil War*, 2.

53. See Linz, "From Great Hopes to Civil War."

54. This paragraph is based on the court records found in AHN FC-Tribunal Supremo Recursos.

55. In Azaña, *Diarios completos*, 425.

56. Maura, *Así cayó Alfonso XIII*, 245, 249.

57. Gabriel Morón, *En el camino de la historia. El fracaso de una revolución* (Madrid: Gráfica socialista, 1935), 81.

58. Acta de la Circunscripción de Badajoz. Reclamación sobre la capacidad legal de Dª Margarita Nelken Mansbergen, Diputado electo por dicha circunscripción, 4 October 1931, ACD, Serie General, Legajo 481, n. 27.

59. Paul Preston, "Margarita Nelken: A Full Measure of Pain," in *Doves of War: Four Women of Spain* (Harper Collins, 2002), 300–301, 306–7, and Robert Kern, "Margarita Nelken: Women and the Crisis of Spanish Politics," in *European Women on the Left: Socialism, Feminism, and the Problems*

Faced by Political Women, 1880 to the Present, ed. Jane Slaughter and Robert Kern (Westport, CT: Greenwood Press, 1981), 148.

60. Autobiography quoted in Josebe Martínez Gutiérrez, *Margarita Nelken (1896–1968)* (Madrid: Ediciones del Orto, [1997]), 15–16.

61. Preston, "Margarita Nelken," 307.

62. Ibid., 304–5, 307–8, 312.

63. Sacanell, *General Sanjurjo, héroe y víctima,* 103.

64. Margarita Nelken, *La condición social de la mujer en España. Su estado actual: su posible desarrollo* (Barcelona: Editorial Minerva, [1919]), 29, 231.

65. Blaney, "Civil Guard," 113, and Esteban-Infantes, *General Sanjurjo,* 171.

66. Ramiro Trullén Floría, "Castilblanco como sinécdoque. El discurso contrarrevolucionario de la Segunda República," *Historia Social,* no. 83 (2015): 65.

67. Preston, "Margarita Nelken," 318.

68. Juan-Simeón Vidarte, *Las Cortes Constituyentes de 1931–1933. Testimonio del Primer Secretario del Congreso de Diputados* (Barcelona: Ediciones Grijalbo, 1976), 83.

69. Preston, "Margarita Nelken," 319.

70. Acta de la Circunscripción de Badajoz. Reclamación sobre la capacidad legal de Dª Margarita Nelken Mansbergen, Diputado electo por dicha circunscripción, 4 October 1931, ACD, Serie General, Legajo 481, n. 27.

71. Azaña, *Diarios completos,* 426.

72. Preston, "Margarita Nelken," 300.

73. Shirley Mangini, "Visible Women of the Second Spanish Republic," chap. 2 in *Memories of Resistance: Women's Voices from the Spanish Civil War* (New Haven, CT: Yale University Press, 1995), 31.

74. Preston, "Margarita Nelken," 321–22, 332.

75. Manuel García Mercadillo, *Guía del Instructor,* 2nd ed. (Zamora: Calamita, 1935), 58–59. See Blaney, "Civil Guard," 126–27, for a list of examples of such cases.

76. La comisión a Ministro Gobernación, 10 September 1931, AHN FC-Mº del Interior, Serie A, legajo 39, exp. 14, Badajoz; Propietarios y vecinos al Ministro de la Gobernación, 16 November 1931, AHN FC-Mº del Interior, Serie A, legajo 39, exp. 14, Badajoz; Ministro de la Gobernación a Director Guardia Civil, 10 December 1931, AHN FC-Mº del Interior, Serie A, legajo 39, exp. 17, Madrid, no. 246; and Ministro de la Gobernación a Director Guardia Civil, 19 December 1931, AHN FC-Mº del Interior, Serie A, legajo 39, exp. 17, Madrid, no. 501.

77. Vaquero Martínez, "Democratización del orden público" documents the homages to the Civil Guard that took place during the Second Republic.

78. "Homenaje a la Guardia Civil en Salamanca," *RTGC* 26, no. 306 (August 1935): 322, contains a transcription of such a speech.

79. José Manuel Macarro Vera, *La utopía revolucionaria. Sevilla en la Segunda República* (Monte de Piedad y Caja de Ahorros de Sevilla, 1985), 193–94.

80. See the eleven telegrams on the Cimas case in AHN, FC-Mº del Interior, Serie A, legajo 39, Exp. 15, Granada.

81. For example, AHN, FC-Mº del Interior, Serie A, legajo 39, exp. 14, Alicante.

82. Numerosos vecinos de Berlanga (Badajoz) a Ministro de la Gobernación, 14 October 1931, AHN, FC-Mº del Interior, Serie A, legajo 39, exp. 14, Badajoz.

83. Presidentes Sindicatos Agrícolas al Sr Mtro Gobernación, 29 September 1931, AHN, FC-Mº del Interior, Serie A, legajo 39, exp. 17, Málaga, no. 1301.

84. Presidente Gallardo a Ministro de la Gobernación, 27 August 1931, AHN, FC-M° del Interior, Serie A, legajo 7, exp. 12, Sevilla 1931, and Ruego del señor Marcos Escudero, *DSCD*, September 11, 1931.

85. Quoted in "Leyendo la prensa," *RTGC* 22, no. 261 (November 1931): 550.

86. Manuel Martín Rubio, "La conservación del orden público," *RTGC* 24, no. 280 (June 1933): 214.

87. Ley dando nueva redacción al apartado que señala del artículo 7.° del Código de Justicia Militar, 27 August 1932, in *BOGC* 7, no. 26 (September 10, 1932): 758.

88. See García Mercadillo, *Guía del Instructor*, 69–70, for a complete list of the actions and phrases that were considered insulting to the armed forces.

89. Julian Pitt-Rivers, "Honour and Social Status," in *Honour and Shame: The Values of Mediterranean Society*, ed. J. G. Peristiany (Chicago: University of Chicago Press, 1966), 29.

90. Penal Code, Article 252, quoted in "Ecos," *RTGC* 24, no. 279 (May 1933): 176.

91. Enrique Luque, "Sobre orden público," *RTGC* 26, no. 303 (May 1935): 190.

92. Arlégui Bayonés, *Doctrinal de Servicio*, 8.

93. Francisco Carmona, in "Ecos," *RTGC* 25, no. 288 (February 1934): 57.

94. This assertion is based on the fact that in every case of Civil Guard violence, the *RTGC* always mentioned a provocation and then deemed the violence justified.

95. "Ecos," *RTGC* 24, no. 279 (May 1933): 176.

96. "Servicios," *RTGC* 23, no. 273 (November 1932): 463, 465.

97. Obligaciones del soldado de infantería, Article 39, *Contestaciones completas del "Instituto Reus,"* 7.

98. Sanjurjo, "Spanish Civil Guard," 380.

99. "Sucesos y servicios recientes," *RTGC* 24, no. 275 (January 1933): 15–16.

100. Centro socialista a Ministros Gobernación, Guerra, Justicia, Tranajo [sic], y "El Socialista," 9 June 1931, AHN, FC-M° del Interior, Serie A, legajo 39, exp. 15, Córdoba, no. 665.

101. Eladio Urien, "Trabajadores del Orden," *RTGC* 24, no. 277 (March 1933): 110.

6. Castilblanco

1. Martin Baumeister, "Castilblanco or the Limits of Democracy: Rural Protest in Spain from Restoration Monarchy to the Early Second Republic," trans. Jane Rafferty, *Contemporary European History* 7, no. 1 (March 1998): 19, and Marie-Claude Chaput, "Castilblanco (Badajoz, 31 de diciembre de 1931): La marginación de la periferia," *Centros y periferias: prensa, impresos y territorios en el mundo hispánico contemporáneo: homenaje a Jacqueline Covo-Maurice* (PILAR, 2004), 204.

2. The influence of the Civil Guard's culture is also explored in González Calleja, "La sombra de Castilblanco: El papel represivo y la dudosa lealtad de la Guardia Civil," chap. 3 in *Nombre de la autoridad*.

3. For a summary of the land tenure system in early-twentieth-century Badajoz, see David Kenneth Henderson, "El Mar de Extremadura: Irrigation, Colonization and Francoism in Southwestern Spain, 1898–1978" (PhD diss., University of California, San Diego, 2017), 85–89.

4. Francisca Rosique Navarro, *La reforma agraria en Badajoz durante la II ª República (La respuesta patronal)* (Departamento de Publicaciones de la Excma. Diputación Provincial de Badajoz, 1988), 55–56.

5. Preston, "Margarita Nelken," 332, and Rosique Navarro, *Reforma agraria en Badajoz*, 83.

6. Martin Baumeister, "¿Del motín a la huelga? Protesta social y lucha contra obrera organizada

en Badajoz," chap. 4 in *Campesinos sin tierra: supervivencia y resistencia en Extremadura, 1880–1923,* trans. Joaquín Abellán (Madrid: Ministerio de Agricultura, Pesca y Alimentación, Secretaría General Técnica, 1997).

7. See "Delincuencia, estado y sociedad rural en Badajoz," chap. 3 in Baumeister, *Campesinos sin tierra,* for background on the history of petty crime as a social phenomenon in Badajoz.

8. Juan García Pérez, "La II República: nueva ocasión perdida para la transformación del campo extremeño," in *Historia de Extremadura,* ed. Ángel Rodríguez Sánchez, vol. 4, *Los tiempos actuales* (Badajoz: Universitas Editorial, Consejería de Educación y Cultura, [1985]), 1001.

9. N. de Pablo, "Paro general: Se anuncia para los días 30 y 31 en todos los pueblos de la provincia," *La Verdad Social,* December 25, 1931.

10. "Fuerzas madrileñas de Intendencia, en Badajoz," *ABC,* January 2, 1932. This paragraph is based on telegrams from November and December 1931 in AHN, FC-Mº del Interior, Serie A, legajo 39, exp. 14, Badajoz.

11. Copies of all of these articles in *La Verdad Social* can be found in AHN, FC-Tribunal Supremo Recursos, legajo 86, exp. 6. Margarita Nelken, "Carta abierta al señor ministro de la Gobernación," *El Socialista,* December 26, 1931.

12. Pablo, "Paro general."

13. Francisco Largo Caballero, quoted in "Información telefónica de la mañana," *Diario de Cádiz,* January 6, 1932.

14. Instituto Nacional de Estadística (INE), Alternaciones de los municipios en los Censos de Población desde 1842, Badajoz, Castilblanco.

15. Esteban-Infantes, *General Sanjurjo,* 172.

16. Glicerio Sánchez Recio, introduction to *Castilblanco,* by Jiménez de Asúa, Vidarte, Rodríguez Sastre, and Trejo (Publicaciones de la Universidad de Alicante, [2011]), 28–29.

17. González Calleja, *Nombre de la autoridad,* 98; "Informe del letrado Sr. Rodríguez Sastre al consejo de guerra," in *Castilblanco,* 233; and Francisco Espinosa Maestre, *La primavera del Frente Popular. Los campesinos de Badajoz y el origen de la guerra civil (marzo–julio de 1936)* (Barcelona: Crítica, 2007), 34.

18. All of the personal information above is from SGC, Expedientes Personales, Francisco González Borrego, José Matos González, and Agripino Simón Martín.

19. "La Guardia Civil de Castilblanco," *Faro de Vigo,* January 3, 1932. The letter was published in the *RTGC* after his death. "Por los mártires de Castilblanco," *RTGC* 23, no. 264 (February 1932): 62.

20. "Por los mártires." It is possible that this letter was fabricated; if so, it is an interesting window into what civil guards *thought* an ideal station commandant should be like.

21. Sánchez Recio, introduction to *Castilblanco,* 14.

22. Baumeister, "Castilblanco or the Limits of Democracy," 18–19.

23. Preston, *Coming of the Spanish Civil War,* 94.

24. "Después del asesinato de los cuatro guardias civiles en Castilblanco," *ABC,* January 3, 1932.

25. Sánchez Recio, introduction to *Castilblanco,* 15; "Informe del letrado Sr. Jiménez de Asúa al consejo de guerra," in *Castilblanco,* 260–65; and AHN, FC-Tribunal Supremo Reservado, exp. 23, n. 10..

26. Collins, *Violence,* 85.

27. Pedro de Pereda Sanz, quoted in Aguado Sánchez, *Historia de la Guardia Civil,* 4:271–72.

28. Whyte, *Street Corner Society,* 136.

29. Trullén Floría, "Castilblanco como sinécdoque," 56.

30. Eduardo Comín Colomer, *De Castilblanco a Casas Viejas* (Madrid: Temas españoles, 1959), 11.

31. Statement of Deputy Sediles, *DSCD*, January 12, 1932.

32. Vicente Santiago Hodsson, "Visita a Castilblanco," *RTGC* 23, no. 264 (February 1932): 57.

33. "Entierro de las víctimas de Castilblanco," *El Debate*, January 5, 1932.

34. Esteban-Infantes, *General Sanjurjo*, 175–76, and Santiago Hodsson, "Visita a Castilblanco," 57.

35. In "De los graves sucesos de Badajoz," *Diario de Barcelona*, January 5, 1932.

36. In Santiago Hodsson, "Visita a Castilblanco," 57.

37. In "El director general de la Guardia Civil en Badajoz: 'Lo absurdo es que se haya creado una Oficina de información contra la Guardia civil y que esté dirigida por Margarita Nelken,'" *La Libertad*, January 5, 1932.

38. In ibid.

39. In "Habla Sanjurjo," *El Debate*, January 5, 1932.

40. These rumors are mentioned frequently in the January 5 edition of *El Sol*.

41. Gallego Pérez, *Lucha contra el crimen*, 176–78.

42. Esteban-Infantes, *General Sanjurjo*, 177.

43. Fernando Rivas Gómez, "El entierro del Alférez de los Reyes y su trascendencia histórica," *REHGC* 20, no. 37 (1987): 152.

44. "Palabras del general Sanjurjo," *Las Provincias*, January 6, 1932.

45. From January 5 to 8 *ABC* dedicated a full page every day to documenting funerals, homages, donations, and other demonstrations of support from around the country.

46. Discurso del Sr. Fatrás, *DSCD*, January 20, 1932.

47. "Antecedentes oficiales de distribución de los donativos hechos a las familias de las víctimas de tropa de la Guardia Civil, a partir del advenimiento de la República," *BOGC* 7, no. 335 (December 10, 1932): 1030–37.

48. "Repercusiones de los sucesos palpitantes en la situación política y parlamentaria," *ABC*, January 6, 1932.

49. Chaput, "Castilblanco: marginación de la periferia," 193–94.

50. "Después de la huelga de Badajoz: Lo que se debe comprender," *El Socialista*, January 3, 1932.

51. The files for these cases can be found in AHN, FC-Tribunal Supremo Recursos, legajo 85, exp. 1906; AHN, FC-Tribunal Supremo Recursos, legajo 86, exp. 6; and AHN, FC-Tribunal Supremo Recursos, legajo 86, exp. 1905.

52. Azaña, *Diarios completes*, 426.

53. Preston, "Margarita Nelken," 324–25.

54. Baumeister, "Castilblanco or the Limits of Democracy," 6.

55. Pregunta del Sr. Hidalgo, *DSCD*, January 5, 1932.

56. Intervención del Sr. Beunza, ibid.

57. Azaña, *Diarios completos*, 427.

58. "Durante el debate. Protestas contra la señora Nelken," *ABC*, January 6, 1932.

59. Discurso para alusiones, del Sr. Saborit, *DSCD*, January 5, 1932.

60. Vidarte, *Cortes constituyentes*, 299.

61. Intervención del Sr. Ortega y Gasset (D. Eduardo), *DSCD*, January 5, 1932.

62. Discurso del Sr. Presidente del Consejo de Ministros, ibid.

63. Discurso del Sr. Presidente del Consejo de Ministros, ibid.

64. Azaña, *Diarios completos*, 427–28.

65. "Calificación definitiva del fiscal," in *Castilblanco*, 113.

66. "Informe del letrado Sr. Reodríguez Sastre al consejo de guerra," in *Castilblanco*, 224.

67. Sánchez Recio, introduction to *Castilblanco*, 29–30.

68. "Informe del letrado Sr. Rodríguez Sastre al consejo de guerra," in *Castilblanco*, 201–19.

69. "Rectificación de Jiménez de Asúa," in *Castilblanco*, 311, and "Informe del letrado Sr. Rodríguez Sastre al consejo de guerra," in *Castilblanco*, 227.

70. "Informe del letrado Sr. Trejo al consejo de guerra," in *Castilblanco*, 120–21.

71. "Informe del letrado Sr. Vidarte al consejo de guerra," in *Castilblanco*, 146, 167.

7. Arnedo

1. Quoted in "Con ocasión de la huelga general, se produjeron ayer en Arnedo lamentabilísimos sucesos, resultado herido un cabo de la Guardia civil y seis paisanos muertos y unos veinticinco heridos, algunos de ellos de mucha gravedad," *La Rioja*, January 6, 1932.

2. Azaña, *Diarios completos*, 427.

3. INE, Alternaciones de los municipios en los Censos de Población desde 1842, Rioja (La), Arnedo.

4. Carlos Gil Andrés, *La República en la plaza: los sucesos de Arnedo de 1932* (Logroño: Gobierno de la Rioja/Instituto de Estudios Riojanos, 2002), 170, 172.

5. Francisco Bermejo Martín, *100 Años de Socialismo en La Rioja (1882–1992)* (Logroño: Gráficas Isasa, 1994), 102, 122.

6. Gil Andrés, *República en la plaza*, 61–67.

7. Ibid., 70, 74.

8. Statement of Deputy Sabrás, *DSCD*, January 6, 1932.

9. AHPLR, GC/M-18/2-6, and Gil Andrés, *República en la plaza*, 74–80.

10. AAA, sig. 518/3.

11. Ibid., and Gil Andrés, *República en la plaza*, 89.

12. AAA, sig. 518/3.

13. Relación nominal de la fuerza del Cuerpo de la Guardia Civil que tomaron parte en los sucesos ocurridos en esta Ciudad el dia 5 de los corriente, in Gil Andrés, *República en la plaza*, 233.

14. AGMS, Expedientes Personales, sect. 1, legajo C-3307.

15. Quoted in Gil Andrés, *República en la plaza*, 236.

16. Ibid., 235.

17. "Ocasión de la huelga general," and Gil Andrés, *República en la plaza*, 95, 97.

18. AAA, sig. 518/3.

19. Julián Hernández al Gobernador Civil, 3 February 1932, AHPLR, GC/M 18-2/6.

20. Gil Andrés, *República en la plaza*, 99, 101–3.

21. "Ocasión de la huelga general."

22. Gil Andrés, *República en la plaza*, 101–8, 113, 142.

23. Ibid., 113.

24. "Los sucesos de Arnedo: El entierro de las víctimas constituyó un acto de profunda emoción," *El Liberal*, January 8, 1932.

25. Gil Andrés, *República en la plaza*, 32, 108–22, 143.

26. Collins, *Violence*, 83.

27. The Calviño report makes these assertions. Gil Andrés, *República en la plaza*, 142–44.

28. Rivas, "República en marcha," 126, and Aguado Sánchez, *Historia de la Guardia Civil*, 4:280.

29. For example, see Payne, *Spain's First Democracy*, 76.

30. Blaney, "Civil Guard," 149, and Casanova, *Calle al frente*, 46.

31. AAA, *Arnedo: Libro de actas de la Comisión Municipal permanente del Ayuntamiento*, 72.

32. "Al cerrar la edicion: Ultimos telegramas: España," *Diario de Barcelona*, January 8, 1932; "El entierro en Arnedo del cadáver del fallecido en el Hospital de Logroño, de ocasión a una nueva manifestación de sentimiento," *La Rioja*, January 9, 1932; and Roberto Pastor Martínez, "Una página del movimiento obrero riojano. Sucesos de Arnedo, 5 de enero de 1932," *Cuadernos de Investigación Histórica* 10 (1984): 168.

33. Gil Andrés, *República en la plaza*, 168–69.

34. See "Sucesos de Arnedo: El entierro"; "Después de los sucesos de Arnedo: Manifestaciones del Sr. Calviño al corresponsal de EL LIBERAL en Logroño," *El Liberal*, January 9, 1932; and "Si en Logroño se plantea una huelga general, la organización socialista de Guipúzcoa se solidarizará con el movimiento," *Heraldo de Aragón*, January 7, 1932, for examples.

35. Gil Andrés, *República en la plaza*, 219.

36. "En el mítin celebrado ayer en el Frontón Beti-Jai, se atacó duramente a la Guardia civil y a los socialistas," *Diario de la Rioja*, January 8, 1932.

37. "El entierro de las víctimas de Arnedo, y un mitin de la U. G. T. y de la C. N. T.," *Heraldo de Aragón*, January 8, 1932.

38. "Después de los luctuosos sucesos de Arnedo, se declaró el paro general por veinticuatro horas en casi toda la provincia," *Diario de la Rioja*, January 8, 1932.

39. Quoted in "Sucesos de Arnedo: El entierro."

40. "Sucesos de Arnedo: El entierro."

41. Azaña, *Diario completos*, 427.

42. "Los sucesos de Arnedo," *El Liberal*, January 7, 1932.

43. Vidarte, *Corte Constituyentes*, 301.

44. Pregunta del Sr. Sabrás, *DSCD*, January 6, 1932.

45. Contestación del Sr. Ministro de la Gobernación, ibid.

46. Intervención del Sr. Balbotín, ibid.

47. Discurso del Sr. Presidente del Consejo de Ministros, ibid.

48. Azaña, *Diarios completos*, 428.

49. See, for example, Baumeister, "Castilblanco or the Limits of Democracy," 6.

50. Gil Andrés, *República en la plaza*, 130–31.

51. Ibid., 143–44.

52. Ibid., 146, 149, and AGMS, Expedientes Personales, sect. 1, legajo C-3307.

53. Gil Andrés, *República en la plaza*, 147–48.

54. Ibid., 155–57, and AGMS, Expedientes Personales, sect. 1, legajo C-3307.

55. Azaña, *Diarios completos*, 430.

56. "Orden general del Cuerpo del día 7 de Enero de 1932," *BOGC* 7, no. 2 (January 10, 1932): 33.

57. "El proyecto de reforma agraria será modificado antes de llevarlo a las Cortes," *El Liberal*, January 7, 1932.

58. Azaña, *Diarios completos*, 430–31.

59. Decreto nombrando Director general de Carabineros al Teniente general D. José Sanjurjo Sacanell, y disponiendo cese en el cargo de Director general de la Guardia civil, *Gaceta de Madrid*, February 5, 1932.

60. "Orden general de la Dirección General de la Guardia Civil del día 4 de Febrero de 1932," *BOGC* 7, no. 5 (February 10, 1932): 129.

61. Archivo Sanjurjo, notas autobiográficas, quoted in Sacanell, *General Sanjurjo, héroe y víctima*, 98.

62. Payne describes the conspiracy in *Politics and the Military*, 283–87, and *Spain's First Democracy*, 96–99.

63. Díaz Carmona, "El 10 de agosto de 1932," 126.

64. Eduardo de Guzmán, *La Segunda República fue así* (Barcelona: Editorial Planeta, 1977), 156.

65. In Esteban-Infantes, *General Sanjurjo*, 316.

66. Ibid., 204.

67. Esteban-Infantes, *General Sanjurjo*, 208–12, and Eduardo González Calleja, *Contrarrevolucionarios. Radicalización violenta de las derechas durante la Segunda República, 1931–1936* (Madrid: Alianza Editorial, 2011), 102.

68. Esteban-Infantes, *General Sanjurjo*, 212–17.

69. General Miguel García de la Herrán quoted in El Caballero Audaz, *General Sanjurjo (su vida y su gloria)* (Madrid: Caballero Audaz, 1940), 105–6. Esteban-Infantes, *General Sanjurjo*, 222.

70. Court documents in AGMS, caja 1161, exp. 14.

71. Decreto conmutando la pena de muerte impuesta a don José Sanjurjo y Sacanell por la de reclusión perpetua con todas las accesorias determinadas en el fallo del Tribunal sentenciador, *Gaceta de Madrid*, August 26, 1932.

72. Azaña, *Diarios completos*, 608.

73. AGMS, caja 1161, exp. 14.

74. Esteban-Infantes, *General Sanjurjo*, 227–32.

75. Decreto suprimiendo en el Ministerio de la Guerra la Dirección general de la Guardia civil; transfiriendo al Ministerio de la Gobernación todos los organismos y servicios del Instituto de la Guardia civil que no resulten suprimidos en virtud de este Decreto, y creando en el Ministerio de la Gobernación la Inspección general de la Guardia civil, *Gaceta de Madrid*, August 17, 1932.

76. Decreto declarando disuelto el 4º Tercio de la Guardia civil, *Gaceta de Madrid*, August 14, 1932. All of these reforms are summarized in Aguado Sánchez, *Historia de la Guardia Civil*, 4:319–21.

77. Vaquero Martínez, "Democratización del orden público," 221.

8. Asturias 1

1. Paco Ignacio Taibo II, *Asturias, Octubre 1934* (Barcelona: Crítica, 2013), 181–83.

2. AHN, FC-Tribunal Supremo Reservado, Exp. 22, fs. 4–6.

3. SEHGC, Carpeta no. 15, armario no. 3, Guerra Civil; Aguado Sánchez, *Revolución de octubre*, 507; J. A. Sánchez G.-Saúco, *La revolución de 1934 en Asturias* (Madrid: Editora Nacional, 1974), 144; and González Calleja, *Cifras cruentas*, 175. The number of dead in parentheses are according to the official statistics and are almost certainly an underestimate.

4. Shubert, *Road to Revolution*, 8.

5. González Calleja, *Cifras cruenta*, 175, and Pablo Gil Vico, *Verdugos de Asturias. La violencia y sus relatos en la revolución de Asturias de 1934* (Gijón: Ediciones Trea, 2019), 435.

6. González Calleja, *Cifras cruentas*, 75.

7. The most complete account of the incident is Jerome Mintz, "The Uprising at Casas Viejas," chap. 13 in *The Anarchists of Casas Viejas* (Chicago: University of Chicago Press, 1982).

8. González Calleja, *Nombre de la autoridad*, 146.

9. Mintz, *Anarchists of Casas Viejas*, 213–15.

10. AHN, FC-Tribunal Supremo Reservado, Exp. 22, and Payne, *Spain's First Democracy*, 132.

11. Vaquero Martínez, "Defensa del orden," and González Calleja, *Nombre de la autoridad*, 148–49, 152.

12. Preston, *Coming of the Spanish Civil War*, 108–19.

13. A. Ramos Oliveira, "Prólogo," in *La Revolución Española de Octubre: Documentos sensacionales inéditos* (Santiago: Editorial Occidente, 1935), 5–6, and Luis Araquistáin, "La Revolución Española de Octubre," in ibid., 14.

14. Preston, *Coming of the Spanish Civil War*, 186.

15. Payne, *Spain's First Democracy*, 183–84.

16. Preston, *Coming of the Spanish Civil War*, 165–66.

17. Payne, *Spain's First Democracy*, 212–23.

18. Shubert, *Road to Revolution*, 14–15, and Matthew Kerry, "Radical Politics in the Spanish Second Republic: Asturias, 1931–1936" (PhD diss., University of Sheffield, 2015), 207.

19. Payne, *Spain's First Democracy*, 214–16.

20. This paragraph is based on some of the main arguments made in Shubert, *Road to Revolution;* Gil Vico, *Verdugos de Asturias;* and Matthew Kerry, *Unite Proletarian Brothers! Radicalism and Revolution in the Spanish Second Republic* (London: University of London Press, 2020).

21. Gil Vico, *Verdugos de Asturias*, 38.

22. For examples, see Shubert, *Road to Revolution*, 86, and Kerry, *Unite Proletarian Brothers*, 26, 65.

23. Shubert, *Road to Revolution*, 106–7.

24. Rodolfo Llopis, "Etapas del proletariado español," in *Revolución Española de Octubre*, 50, 52, and González Calleja, *Razón de la fuerza*, 529.

25. Maximiano García Venero, *Melquíades Álvarez, Historia de un liberal*, 2nd ed. (Madrid: Ediciones Tebas, n.d.), 365.

26. David Ruiz, *Octubre de 1934. Revolución en la República española* (Madrid: Editorial Síntesis, n.d.), 157.

27. Angeles Barrio Alonso, *Anarquismo y anarcosindicalismo en Asturias (1890–1936)* (Madrid: Siglo veintiuno editores, 1988), 178.

28. Manuel Llaneza, "La huelga de Agosto en Asturias," *España* 3, no. 134 (November 1, 1917): 7.

29. Shubert, *Road to Revolution*, 150.

30. Kerry, *Unite Proletarian Brothers*, 53, 58, 65, 67–68, 110.

31. Taibo, *Asturias, octubre 1934*, 173.

32. Ibid., 134, and "Un violento tiroteo entre la fuerza pública y los manifestantes, resultando un muerto y seis heridos," *El Noroeste*, September 2, 1934.

33. "La fuerza pública disuelve a tiros una pacífica manifestación de mujeres, mata a un joven socialista y hiere a dos manifestantes, a tres transeúntes y a dos guardias," *Avance*, September 2, 1934.

34. Aguado Sánchez, *Revolución de octubre de 1934*, 122, 506.

35. Gil Vico, *Verdugos de Asturias*, 47–75.

36. For details, see Matthew Kerry, "Painted Tonsures and Potato-sellers: Priests, Passing and Survival in the Asturian Revolution," *Cultural and Social History* (2017): 1–19.

37. Some guards from La Felguera managed to hide out in the mountains, and two even reached Oviedo in disguise. Aguado Sánchez, *Revolución de Asturias de 1934*, 159.

38. Only one post in the Fourth Company surrendered without a fight (Pola de Lena), although a few did abandon their *casas-cuarteles* (see table 2). Taibo, *Asturias, octubre 1934*, 227.

39. Gil Vico, *Verdugos de Asturias*, 58–59, 73, 117.

40. Aguado Sánchez, *Revolución de octubre de 1934*, 159.

41. See, for example, Jenaro G. Geijo, *Episodios de la revolución* (Santander, 1935), 159–65.

42. Brian Bunk, *Ghosts of Passion: Martyrdom, Gender, and the Origins of the Spanish Civil War* (Durham: Duke University Press, 2007), 128.

43. Amongst the Fourth Company posts, ceasefires to release guards' families occurred at Sama, Ciaño, El Entrego, and Sotrondio.

44. INE, "Alternaciones de los municipios en los Censos de Población desde 1842," Asturias, Langreo, and Aguado Sánchez, *Revolución de octubre de 1934*, 149.

45. Aguado Sánchez, *Revolución de octubre de 1934*, 150.

46. "Hallazgo de bombas," *La Voz de Asturias*, May 9, 1933, and "Se facilita una nueva lista de los obreros que reanudarán el trabajo hoy y el lunes en la Fábrica," *La Voz de Asturias*, August 26, 1933.

47. AGMS, Expedientes Personales, sect. 1, A-1461.

48. For example, "Capitulo de bodas," *La Voz de Asturias*, September 15, 1933, and "Notas de Sociedad," *La Voz de Asturias*, June 28, 1934.

49. "Gobierno Civil," *Boletín Oficial de la Provincia de Oviedo*, January 2, 1931.

50. Archivo Municipal de Langreo, *Actas municipales del 7 de oct de 1934 al 16 de junio de 1934*, May 19, 1934.

51. Aguado Sánchez, *Revolución de octubre de 1934*, 150–51, 155.

52. Tomás, quoted in "Ataque a los cuarteles"; "En Gijón se ha organizado un gran Hospital Militar," *La Prensa*, October 23, 1934; and Aguado Sánchez, *Revolución de octubre de 1934*, 159–62.

53. Taibo, *Asturias, octubre 1934*, 218–20.

54. Aguado Sánchez, *Revolución de octubre de 1934*, 506, and Gallego, *Lucha contra el crimen*, 53.

55. Aguado Sánchez, *Revolución de octubre de 1934*, 168.

56. Lara, "Notas del mes," *RTGC* 25, no. 298 (December 1934): 528, and Taibo, *Asturias, octubre 1934*, 228.

57. Quoted in Aguado Sánchez, *Revolución de octubre de 1934*, 163.

58. Aguado Sánchez, *Revolución de octubre de 1934*, 165–66.

59. SGC, Expedientes Personales, Fernando Halcón Lucas.

60. Aguado Sánchez, *Revolución de octubre de 1934*, 169.

61. Lara, "Notas del mes," 529–30.

62. Taibo, *Asturias, octubre 1934*, 230.

63. For details, see Manuel Luengo Muñoz, "Revolución de Asturias de 1934. El Combate de Campomanes," *REHGC* 1, no. 1 (1968): 33–48.

64. Aguado Sánchez, *Revolución de octubre de 1934*, 170.

65. Lara, "Notas del mes," 531.

66. Taibo, *Asturias, octubre 1934*, 561.

67. Alberto Fernández, "Octubre de 1934. Recuerdos de un insurrecto," *Tiempo de historia* 17 (April 1976): 13–14.

68. The posts were at Caborana, Boo, and Santa Cruz. Aguado Sánchez, *Revolución de octubre de 1934*, 140–42, 147.

69. This account and the quotes that follow are based on the record of Torrens's trial, which is housed in AHN, FC-Tribunal Supremo Reservado, Exp. 14.

70. This section and the quotations it contains are based on record of the trial of Civil Guard commanders at Oviedo in AHN, FC-Tribunal Supremo Reservado, Exp. 22, unless otherwise noted.

71. Taibo, *Asturias, octubre 1934*, 312.

72. CDMH, PS-Madrid, 2121, Exp. 1.

73. Eduardo López Ochoa, *Campaña militar de Asturias en octubre de 1934 (Narración táctico-episódica)* (Madrid: Ediciones Yunque, n.d.), 101–10.

74. Sarah Sanchez, *Fact and Fiction: Representations of the Asturian Revolution (1934–1938)* (Leeds: Maney Publishers, 2003), 137.

75. "¡Gloria a los heroes!," *RTGC* 25, no. 297 (November 1934): 426, and "La revolución de octubre: Loor a 'la Benemérita,'" *RTGC* 25, no. 297 (November 1934): 425.

9. Asturias 2

1. In Taibo, *Asturias, octubre 1934*, 498–99.

2. Aguado Sánchez, "López Ochoa cumple su palabra," chap. 27 in *Revolución de octubre de 1934*, and Ruiz, *Octubre de 1934*, 257.

3. Aguado Sánchez, "El frente de Campomanes," chap. 28 in *Revolución de octubre de 1934*.

4. For more on the military defeat of the insurrection, see López Ochoa, *Campaña militar de Asturias*.

5. Taibo, "La rendición," chap. 26 in *Asturias, octubre 1934*.

6. Balfour, *Deadly Embrace*, 252–54.

7. José E. Álvarez, "The Spanish Foreign Legion during the Asturian Uprising of October 1934," *War in History* 18, no. 2 (2011): 219.

8. For details, see Balfour, *Deadly Embrace*, 253–55, and Gil Vico, *Verdugos de Asturias*, 123, 145–70.

9. Gil Vico, *Verdugos de Asturias*, 122–23, 130, 134–36, 182, 401.

10. "Las denuncias de Félix Gordón Ordás al Presidente de la República," in Ignotus, *La represión de octubre. Documentos para la historia de nuestra civilización* (Barcelona: Tierra y Libertad, 1936), 222–30.

11. Gil Vico, *Verdugos de Asturias*, 172–76.

12. See, for example, *ABC*, October 19, 1934.

13. Aguado Sánchez, *Revolución de octubre de 1934*, 504, and Taibo, *Asturias, octubre 1934*, 583–84.

14. Decreto declarando el estado de guerra en todo el territorio de la República Española, *Gaceta de Madrid*, October 7, 1934; Ley estableciendo las penas que se indican para sancionar los delitos que se determinan, *Gaceta de Madrid*, October 17, 1934; and González Calleja, *Nombre de la autoridad*, 217–18.

15. Taibo, *Asturias, octubre 1934*, 539, and Aguado Sánchez, *Revolución de octubre de 1934*, 506.

16. SGC, Expedientes Personales, Lisardo Doval Bravo, and CDMH, PS-Documentación particular, 637, Exps. 1–2.

17. Ruiz, *Octubre de 1934*, 348–49; José Ruiz del Toro, *Octubre (Etapas de un period revolucionario en España)* (Buenos Aires: Editorial Araujo, 1935), 185; and Juan-Simeón Vidarte, *El bienio negro y la insurrección de Asturias. Testimonio del entonces Vicesecretario y Secretario del PSOE* (Barcelona: Ediciones Grijalbo, 1978), 342.

18. Taibo, *Asturias, octubre 1934*, 490.

19. Comité Republicano Socialista a Ministro Gobernación, AHN, FC-Mº del Interior, Serie A, legajo 39, exp. 18, Oviedo, no. 1219.

20. Lorenzo Silva, *Sereno en el peligro. La aventura histórica de la Guardia Civil* (Madrid: Editorial EDAF, 2010), 235.

21. Diego Hidalgo, *¿Por qué fui lanzado del Ministerio de la Guerra?: Diez meses de actuación ministerial* (Madrid: Espasa-Calpe, 1934), 92, and López Ochoa, *Campaña militar de Asturias*, 180–82.

22. Gil Vico, *Verdugos de Asturias*, 182–83, 191, 198; Aguado Sánchez, *Revolución de octubre de 1934*, 314; and "La admirable labor que realiza en Asturias la fuerza pública a las órdenes del comandante Doval," *ABC*, November 14, 1934.

23. CDMH, PS-Gijón J, C. 50, Exp. 1.

24. Gil Vico, *Verdugos de Asturias*, 182.

25. AGM, Expedientes Personales, sect. 1, T-310, and Taibo, *Asturias, octubre 1934*, 515.

26. Gil Vico, *Verdugos de Asturias*, 200–210.

27. See Taibo, *Asturias, octubre 1934*, 513, 515, for a complete list of detention centers.

28. Quoted in "Admirable labor."

29. "Escrito de los presos de Oviedo al Fiscal General de la República," in Ignotus, *La represión de octubre*, 129. Given the government's secrecy about its operations, determining what occurred inside the detention centers requires relying on the investigative reports and eyewitness accounts contained in the books and pamphlets that the workers' parties published about the repression. While doubtless some of these accounts are exaggerated, their quantity and the similarities between them allow for at least a basic reconstruction of what occurred.

30. Gil Vico, *Verdugos de Asturias*, 222–24. Various examples of this in CDMH, PS-Gijón J, C. 50, Exp. 1, Órdenes y notas.

31. Taibo, *Asturias, octubre 1934*, 503.

32. Gil Vico, *Verdugos de Asturias*, 234–35, 239.

33. These assertions are based on a variety of accounts, especially those collected in Ignotus, *Represión de octubre*.

34. See Taibo, *Asturias, octubre 1934*, 551–52, 562.

35. Several such accounts can be found in Alexandre Jaume, *La insurrección de octubre. Cataluña, Asturias, Baleares* (Santi Jordi: Res publica Ediciones, 1997 [1935]).

36. *La Revolución de Asturias (Documentos)* (Mexico: Ediciones Defensa Roja, 1935), 17.

37. In Taibo, *Asturias, octubre 1934*, 498.

38. For example, Fernando Solano Palacios, *La revolución de octubre. Quince días de comunismo libertario* (Fundación de Estudios Libertarios, Anselmo Lorenzo, 1994 [1936]), 184, 188, 192, and Ignotus, *Represión de octubre*, 6.

39. Vidarte, *Bienio negro*, 342.

40. B. Díaz Nosty, *La comuna asturiana. Revolución de octubre de 1934*, 2nd ed. (Bilbao: Zero, 1975), 364.

41. Taibo, *Asturias, octubre 1934*, 495, 503.

42. "Incautación de armas y explosivos en Tuilla (Langreo)," *Región*, November 10, 1934, and "Detención importante," *Región*, November 13, 1934.

43. "Los horrores de Asturias," *El Socialista*, March 13, 1936, and "La bárbara tragedia de Carbayín," *La Libertad*, March 18, 1936.

44. Kerry, *Unite Proletarian Brothers*, 153.

45. Francisco de Cossio, "El comunismo de Langreo," *El Noroeste*, November 15, 1934.

46. "Gobierno Civil," *Boletín Oficial de la Provincia de Oviedo*, December 5, 1934.

47. Kerry, *Unite Proletarian Brothers*, 159–60.

48. Blaney, "Civil Guard," 209.

49. Antonio María Calero, "Octubre visto por la derecha," in *Octubre 1934*, 168.

50. Sanchez, *Fact and Fiction*, 37.

51. See Blaney, "Civil Guard," 215–20, for details.

52. CDMH, PS-Gijón J, C. 50, Exp. 1.

53. Ruiz del Toro, *Octubre*, 187. In November 1934, as the CEDA pushed for more power in the government, it suggested Doval for the post of inspector general. Octavio Ruiz Manjón, *El Partido Republican Radical, 1908–1936* (Madrid: Tebas, [1976]), 465.

54. Quoted in Díaz Nosty, *Comuna asturiana*, 364.

55. "Admirable labor."

56. Taibo, *Asturias, octubre 1934*, 526.

57. CDMH, PS-Gijon J, C. 50, Exp. 2, and "Ayer de madrugada fue capturado en Ablaña el cabecilla socialista de la revolución, González Peña," *El Noroeste*, December 4, 1934.

58. "Denuncias de Félix Gordón," in Ignotus, *Represión de octubre*.

59. Reparaz and Souza, *Cuartel General de Miaja*, 18–20.

60. Ricardo de la Cierva, *Fracaso del octubre revolucionario. 1934–1935. La represión* (Madrid: ARC editores, 1997), 108; González Calleja, *Nombre de la autoridad*, 235–36; and SGC, Expedientes Personales, Lisardo Doval Bravo.

61. Taibo, *Asturias, octubre 1934*, 530, and Díaz Nosty, *Comuna asturiana*, 370.

62. Quoted in Ruiz del Toro, *Octubre*, 187. "El Gobierno cree que es más interesante desarticular los medios revolucionarios que demostrar dureza en la represión," *ABC*, November 1, 1934.

63. Geoffrey Jensen, "Rico Avello en Marruecos," in *El sueño republicano de Manuel Rico Avello (1886–1936)*, coordinated by Juan Pan-Montojo (Madrid: Biblioteca Nueva, 2011), 142.

64. "Escrito de los presos," in Ignotus, *Represión de octubre*.

65. Ruiz, *Octubre de 1934*, 350–51, and "Comisión de servicios en Marruecos," *El Día Gráfico*, January 8, 1935.

66. Reparaz and Souza, *Cuartel General de Miaja*, 20, 28.

67. For details on attempts to do so, see Gil Vico, *Verdugos de Asturias*, 279–83.

68. For example, see Ignotus, *Represión de octubre*, 8, and Jaume, *Insurrección de octubre*.

69. Bunk, "'Your Comrades will not Forget!': Revolutionary Martyrs and Political Unity," chap. 3 in *Ghosts of Passion*.

70. Margarita Nelken, *Por qué hicimos la revolución*, 2nd ed. (Madrid: Balaños y Aguilar, [1936]).

71. Preston, "Margarita Nelken," 340–43, 345–48.

72. Nelken, *Por qué hicimos la revolución*, 62–63, 81.

73. Bunk, "Grandsons of the Cid," chap. 4 in *Ghosts of Passion*.

10. Andalusia

1. Paul Preston, *Spanish Holocaust*, xi.

2. This point is made most forcefully in Nerín, *Guerra que vino de África*.

3. Ramón Salas Larrazábal's 41 percent forms the lower bound, but Juan Blázquez Miguel and Carlos Engel Masoliver's estimates are both 71 percent. Salas Larrazábal, *Los datos exactos de la guerra civil* (Madrid: Ediciones Rioduero, 1980), 270–71; Blázquez Miguel, *La Guardia Civil durante la Segunda República y el 18 de Julio* (Madrid: María Tomás Pérez, 2010), 359; and Engel Masoliver, *El Cuerpo de Oficiales en la Guerra de España* (Valladolid: AF Editores, [2008]), 34.

4. Quoted in Miguel López Corral, "La Guardia Civil en Madrid durante la guerra," chap. 6 in *Guerra Civil. Madrid*, coordinated by Fernando Martínez de Baños Carrillo (Zaragoza: Delsan Libros, 2006), 258.

5. For example, Rafael F. Hermosa, "Charlas sobre armamento," *RTGC* 26, no. 310 (December 1935): 521–22.

6. "Miscelánea," *RTGC* 25, no. 298 (December 1934): 537.

7. Comandante España, "Asturias," *RTGC* 26, no. 301 (March 1935): 104.

8. For more on the sociopolitical conflicts of the Popular Front period, see the first half of Rafael Cruz, *En el nombre del pueblo: República, rebelión y guerra en la España de 1936* (Madrid: Siglo XXI de España Editores, 2006); Eduardo González Calleja and Rocío Navarro Comas, eds., *La España del Frente Popular. Política, sociedad, conflicto y cultura en la España de 1936* (Granada: Editorial Comares, 2011); and the second half of Stanley G. Payne, *The Collapse of the Spanish Republic, 1933–1936: Origins of the Civil War* (New Haven, CT: Yale University Press, 2006).

9. These assertions are made from data found in González Calleja, *Cifras cruentas*, 75.

10. See the famous debates about political violence in the Cortes in *DSCD*, April 15–16, 1936, and June 16, 1936.

11. Blaney, "Civil Guard," 238–40, and González Calleja, *Nombre de la autoridad*, 127. For an example of a critical newspaper article, see Margarita Nelken, "El orden que hay que mantener," *Claridad*, June 18, 1936. For examples of letters of complaint, see the more than fifty denunciations of guards near Reinosa (Santander) in CDMH, PS-Santander L, C. 463, Exp. 22, from March to April 1936.

12. Eduardo González Calleja, *Contrarrevolucionarios*, 261–62, 279, 341, 391.

13. For more on these measures and the reasons why so many guards turned against the Popular Front more generally, see Rivas, *Frente Popular*, especially 142–51, and Blaney, "Civil Guard," 227–49.

14. For more on these incidents, see Rivas Gómez, "Entierro del Alférez."

15. For more on these murders, see Ian Gibson, *La noche en que mataron a Calvo Sotelo* (Barcelona: Editorial Argos Vergara, 1982).

16. Aguado Sánchez, *Historia de la Guardia Civil*, 5:173–74.

17. Including Blázquez Miguel, *Guardia Civil durante la República*, and Blaney, "Civil Guard," 250–307.

18. Francisco Cobo Romero, *La Guerra Civil y la represión franquista en la provincia de Jaén* (Jaén: Instituto de Estudios Giennenses, 1994), 19–22.

19. Stathis N. Kalyvas, *The Logic of Violence in Civil War* (Cambridge: Cambridge University Press, 2006), 111–13.

20. Juan Ortiz Villalba, *Sevilla 1936: del golpe militar a la guerra civil* (Córdoba: Imprenta Vistalegre, 1998), 60–61; Alfonso Braojos Garrido, "El 18 de julio en Sevilla. La versión de la prensa en su primer aniversario (1937)," in Alfonso Braojos Garrido, Leandro Álvarez Rey, and Francisco Espinosa Maestre, *Sevilla 36: Sublevación fascista y represión* (Sevilla: Muñoz Moya y Montraveta, 1990), 122, 135; and Francisco Espinosa Maestre, "Sevilla 36. Sublevación y represión," in ibid., 191, 214, 216.

21. Preston, *Spanish Holocaust*, 146, and Francisco Espinosa Maestre, *La Guerra Civil en Huelva* (Huelva: Diputación Provincial, 1996), 85–103, 137–54.

22. Blaney, "Civil Guard," 291–92; SEHGC, Memorias de Comandancias, Badajoz; and Francisco Espinosa, "La toma de Badajoz," chap. 2 in *La columna de muerte. El avance del ejército franquista de Sevilla a Badajoz*, EPUB ed. (Barcelona: Crítica, 2003).

23. Cobo Romero provides many examples of this phenomenon in Jaén Province. *Guerra Civil y la represión*, 72–89.

24. Peter Anderson, *Friend or Foe? Occupation, Collaboration and Selective Violence in the Spanish Civil War* (Brighton: Sussex Academic Press, 2016).

25. Javier Rodrigo, *Hasta la raíz. Violencia durante la Guerra Civil y la dictadura franquista* (Madrid: Alianza Editorial, 2008), 201.

26. Quoted in ibid., 52.

27. Rodrigo, *Hasta la raíz*, 63.

28. Alfonso Lazo and José Antonio Parejo, "La militancia falangista en el suroeste español. Sevilla," *Ayer*, no. 52 (2003): 244.

29. Francisco Espinosa Maestre, *La Justicia de Queipo*, EPUB ed. (Barcelona: Editorial Crítica, 2006), 247.

30. Francisco Moreno Gómez, *El genocidio franquista en Córdoba* (Barcelona: Crítica, 2008), 517, 810.

31. For the distinction between selective and indiscriminate violence, see Kalyvas, *Logic of Violence*, 142.

32. Moreno Gómez, *1936. Genocidio franquista*, 507, 511–12, 515.

33. Espinosa Maestre, *Justicia de Queipo*, 281.

34. Preston, *Spanish Holocaust*, 142–45.

35. Francisco Gonzálbez Ruíz, *Yo he creído en Franco. Proceso de una gran desilusión (Dos meses en la cárcel de Sevilla)* (Paris, n.d.), 51–52, and Preston, *Spanish Holocaust*, 145.

36. Espinosa Maestre, *Guerra Civil en Huelva*, 385–86, and "El héroe de la Pañoleta, Don Gregorio de Haro Lumbreras," *Diario de Huelva*, July 21, 1937, in ibid., 417.

37. Espinosa Maestre, *Justicia de Queipo*, 134–35.

38. Preston, *Spanish Holocaust*, 166.

39. El comandante Zurdo, "El nuevo jefe superior de Policía dirige una alocución a los cordobeses," *La Voz*, August 17, 1936, and Moreno Gómez, *1936. El genocidio franquista*, 530, 537.

40. Report of Juan Martínez Imbern, September 28, 1981, quoted in Moreno Gómez, *1936. El genocidio franquista*, 546–48.

41. Zurdo, "Nuevo jefe superior."

42. El Jefe de Orden público Bruno Ibáñez, "Al pueblo de Córdoba y su provincia," *El Defensor de Córdoba*, September 22, 1936.

43. Interview with Rafael Castejón, July 13, 1983, quoted in Moreno Gómez, *1936. El genocidio franquista*, 564–65, and Francisco Poyatos López, *Recuerdos de un hombre de toga* (Córdoba, 1979), 132, quoted in ibid., 569.

44. Quoted in Moreno Gómez, *1936. El genocidio franquista*, 568.

45. Moreno Gómez, *1936. El genocidio franquista*, 565–71.

46. Luis Merida, quoted in Ronald Fraser, *Blood of Spain: The Experience of Civil War, 1936–1939* (Middlesex: Penguin Books, 1981), 162–63.

47. Bruno Ibáñez, "Una nota de la Jefatura de Orden Público," *El Defensor de Córdoba*, October 5, 1936, and Bruno Ibáñez, "Jefatura de Orden Público," *El Defensor de Córdoba*, October 13, 1936.

48. Bruno Ibáñez, "Jefatura de Orden Público," *El Defensor de Córdoba*, October 28, 1936, and Bruno Ibáñez, "Unas notas de la Jefatura de Orden Público," *El Defensor de Córdoba*, November 18, 1936.

49. Moreno Gómez, *1936. El genocidio franquista*, 578–79.

50. Cayetano Ibarra Barroso, *La otra mitad de la historia que nos contaron: Fuente de Cantos, República y Guerra 1931–1939* (Badajoz: Diputación de Badajoz, Departamento de publicaciones, 2005), 245, 294–307, 322–38.

51. Preston, *Spanish Holocaust*, 312.

52. Francisco Javier García Carrero, "Manuel Gómez Cantos, un mando de la Guardia Civil entre el deshonor y la represión," *Pasado y Memoria. Revista de Historia Contemporánea*, no. 11 (2012): 255–76, and Espinosa Maestre, *Justicia de Queipo*, 141.

53. Jay Allen, "Slaughter of 4,000 at Badajoz, 'City of Horrors,' Is Told by Tribune Man," *Chicago Daily Tribune*, August 30, 1936, and "La guerre civile en Espagne," *Le Temps*, August 17, 1936.

54. Espinosa Maestre, *Justicia de Queipo*, 138–39, and García Carrero, "Manuel Gómez Cantos," 276.

55. J. Simoes, *Diário da Manha*, August 16, 1936, quoted in Alberto Pena Rodríguez, *El gran aliado de Franco. Portugal y la Guerra Civil española. Prensa, radio, cine y propaganda* (A Coruña: Edicios de Castro, 1998), 286.

56. Preston, *Spanish Holocaust*, 323–24.

57. Juan Blázquez Miguel, *La Guardia Civil en la guerra de España (1936–1939)* (Madrid: Ediciones Barbarroja, n.d.), 52.

58. Espinosa, "El golpe de Queipo y el plan de Franco," chap. 1 in *Columna de muerte*.

59. Arnau Fernández Pasalodos, "La 'ley de fugas' durante la lucha antiguerrillera en España (1936–1952)," *Historia Social*, no. 101 (2021): 126–29.

60. For more on the continuities, see Cruz, *Nombre del pueblo*.

61. Eduardo González Calleja, "Experiencia en combate. Continuidad y cambios en la violencia represiva (1931–1939)," *Ayer* 76, no. 4 (2009): 39, 43, 58.

62. Anderson, *Friend or Foe*, 16–17, 21.

63. Jesús Narciso Núñez Calvo, prologue to Blázquez Miguel, *Guardia Civil en la guerra*, 12, and Henderson, "Mar de Extremadura," 151–52.

64. Anderson, *Friend or Foe*, 21, and Francisco Cobo Romero and Teresa María Ortega López, *Franquismo y posguerra en Andalucía Oriental* (Granada: Universidad de Granada, 2005), 121.

65. Various examples of this can be found in Espinosa Maestre, "Historias de mujeres," chap. 9 in *Justicia de Queipo*.

66. Ibid., 176, 181.

67. González Calleja, "Experiencia en combate," 53.

68. Lazo and Parejo, "Militancia falangista," 248–50.

69. Blázquez Miguel, *Guardia Civil en la guerra*.

70. Francisco J. Leira Castiñeira, *Soldados de Franco. Reclutamiento forzoso, experiencia de guerra y desmovilización militar* (Madrid: Siglo XXI, 2020), 149, 162, 174, 183.

71. López Corral, *Guardia Civil. Claves históricas*, 391, 413. See Javier Rodrigo, *Los campos de concentración franquista. Entre la historia y la memoria* (Madrid: Siete Mares, 2003).

72. López Corral, *Guardia Civil. Claves históricas*, 423–50.

73. Rodrigo, *Hasta la raíz*, 20.

74. López Corral, *Guardia Civil. Claves históricas*, 398–401, 466.

75. Blázquez, *Guardia Civil en la guerra*, 102.

76. López Corral, *Guardia Civil. Claves históricas*, 385–90.

BIBLIOGRAPHY

Archival Sources

Archivo del Ayuntamiento de Arnedo

Archivo del Congreso de los Diputados
    Serie General

Archivo General Militar de Madrid

Archivo General Militar de Segovia
    Expedientes Personales
    Expedientes de Personas Célebres
    2ª Sección

Archivo Histórico Nacional
Fondos contemporáneos
    Ministerio del Interior
    Tribunal Supremo Recursos
    Tribunal Supremo Reservado

Archivo Histórico Provincial de La Rioja
    Gobierno Civil

Archivo Municipal de Langreo

Centro Documental de la Memoria Histórica, Salamanca
Político-social
    Documentación Particular
    Gijón J
    Madrid
    Santander L

Instituto Nacional de Estadística
    Alternaciones de los municipios en los Censos de Población desde 1842

Sección Guardia Civil del Archivo General del Ministerio del Interior
    Expedientes Personales

Servicio de Estudios Históricos de la Guardia Civil
    Carpetas
    Memorias de Comandancias

Newspapers and Periodicals

ABC (Madrid)
Avance (Oviedo)
Boletín Oficial de la Guardia Civil (Madrid)
Boletín Oficial de la Provincia de Oviedo
    (Oviedo)
La Campana de Gracia (Barcelona)
Chicago Daily Tribune (Chicago)
Claridad (Madrid)
La Correspondencia de España (Madrid)
La Correspondencia Militar (Madrid)
El Debate (Madrid)
El Defensor de Córdoba (Córdoba)
El Día Gráfico (Barcelona)
Diario de Barcelona (Barcelona)
Diario de Cádiz (Cádiz)
Diario de la Rioja (Logroño)
Diario de Sesiones del Congreso de
    Diputados (Madrid)
España (Madrid)
Faro de Vigo (Vigo)
Gaceta de Madrid (Madrid)
Heraldo de Aragón (Zaragoza)
El Heraldo de la Guardia Civil (Madrid)
Heraldo de Madrid (Madrid)
El Imparcial (Madrid)

L'Intransigeant (Paris)
El Liberal (Bilbao)
La Libertad (Badajoz)
El Noroeste (Gijón)
El País (Madrid)
La Prensa (Gijón)
El Progreso (Madrid)
Las Provincias (Valencia)
La Publicidad (Barcelona)
Recopilación de reales órdenes y circulares
    de interés general para la Guardia Civil
    (Madrid)
Región (Oviedo)
Revista Técnica de la Guardia Civil
    (Madrid)
La Revue blanche (Paris)
La Rioja (Logroño)
El Socialista (Madrid)
El Sol (Madrid)
Le Temps (Paris)
Les Temps Nouveaux (Paris)
La Verdad Social (Badajoz)
La Voz (Córdoba)
La Voz de Asturias (Oviedo)

Contemporary Published Sources

Academia de Infantería: Memoria de los cursos de 1918–1919 y 1919–1920. Escuela tipográfica
    y encuadernación del Colegio de María Cristina para Huérfanos de la Infantería,
    [1920].
Arlégui Bayones, Miguel. Doctrinal de Servicio para la Guardia Civil. Valladolid: Imprenta
    Castellana, 1908.

Azaña, Manuel. *Diarios completos. Monarquía, República, Guerra Civil*. Barcelona: Crítica, 2000.

Bo y Singla, I. *Montjuich. Notas y Recuerdos históricos*. Barcelona: Maucci, [1917].

Brenan, Gerald. *The Spanish Labyrinth: The Social and Political Background of the Spanish Civil War*. Canto edition. New York: Cambridge University Press, 1990 [1943].

El Caballero Audaz [José María Carretero]. *El General Sanjurjo (su vida y su gloria)*. Madrid: Caballero Audaz, 1940.

Calderón de la Barca, Pedro. *Para vencer amor, querer vencerle*. In *Obras completas*. Edited by Angel Valbuena Briones. Vol. 2, *Comedias*, 529–66. 2nd ed. Madrid: Aguilar, 1960.

Cartilla del Guardia Civil. Madrid: Imprenta del Boletin oficial de la Guardia Civil, n.d.

Contestaciones completas del "Instituto Reus" para el ingreso en el Cuerpo de la Guardia Civil. Madrid: "Instituto Reus" Centro de enseñanza y publicaciones, 1935.

Coromines, Pere. *Diaris i records de Pere Coromines*. Vol. 1, *El anys de joventut I. El procés de Montjuïc*. Barcelona: Curial Edicions Catalans, 1974.

———. *Les presons imaginaries*. Barcelona: Tipografia «L'Avenç», 1899.

Enseñanzas de la campaña de Rif en 1909. Madrid: Talleres del Depósito de la guerra, 1911.

Escalafón General de los Generales, Jefes y Oficiales de la Guardia Civil en 1.° de enero de 1932. Madrid: Taller-Escuela de Artes Gráficos de la Gua. Civil, [1932].

Esteban-Infantes, Emilio. *General Sanjurjo. (Un Laureado en el penal del dueso)*. 2nd ed. Barcelona: Editorial AHR, 1958.

Fernández, Alberto. "Octubre de 1934: Recuerdos de un insurrecto." *Tiempo de Historia* 17 (April 1976): 11–21.

Ferreras Estrada, Gabriel. *Memorias del sargento Ferreras*. León: Imprenta Provincial, 2002.

Gallego Pérez, C. [Juan Español Cándido]. *La lucha contra el crimen y el desorden (Memorias de un teniente de la Guardia Civil*. Madrid: Rollán, 1957.

García Mercadillo, Manuel. *Guía del Instructor*. 2nd ed. Zamora: Calamita, 1935.

[García Pérez, Antonio.] *Breve Bosquejo Histórico de la Academia de Infantería*. [1924].

Geijo, Jenaro G. *Episodios de la revolución*. Santander, 1935.

González, Hilario. *Resumen histórico de la Academia de Infantería*. Toledo: Imprenta-Escuela Tipográfica del Colegio de M.ª Cristina para Huérfanos de la Infantería, 1925.

Guzmán, Eduardo de. *La Segunda República fue así*. Barcelona: Editorial Planeta, 1977.

Hidalgo, Diego. *¿Por qué fuí lanzado del Ministerio de la Guerra?: Diez meses de actuación ministerial*. Madrid: Espasa-Calpe, 1934.

Hurtado, Amadeu. *Quaranta anys d'advocat. Història del meu temps, 1894–1920*. 2nd ed. Barcelona: Ediciones Ariel, 1969.

Ibáñez Marín, José, and Luis Angulo Escobar. *Los cadetes*. Madrid: Establecimiento tipográfico «el trabajo», [1903].

Ibarra Barroso, Cayetano. *La otra mitad de la historia que nos contaron: Fuente de Cantos, República y Guerra 1931–1939*. Badajoz: Diputación de Badajoz, Departamento de publicaciones, 2005.

Ignotus [Manuel Villar]. *La represión de octubre. Documentos para la historia de nuestra civilización.* Barcelona: Tierra y Libertad, 1936.

Jaume, Alexandre. *La insurrección de octubre. Cataluña, Asturias, Baleares.* Santi Jordi: Res publica Ediciones, 1997 [1935].

Jiménez de Asúa, Vidarte, Rodríguez Sastre, and Trejo. *Castilblanco.* Universidad de Alicante, [2011].

López Ochoa, Eduardo. *Campaña militar de Asturias en octubre de 1934 (Narración táctico-episódica).* Madrid: Ediciones Yunque, n.d.

Montseny, Juan. *Consideraciones sobre el hecho y muerte de Pallás.* La Coruña: Tipografía la Gutenberg, 1893.

Maura, Miguel. *Así cayó Alfonso XIII.* Barcelona: Editorial Ariel, 1981 [1962].

[Mella, Ricardo, and José Prats.] *La barbarie gubernamental de España.* New York: Imp. de *El Despertar,* 1897.

Morón, Gabriel. *En el camino de la historia. El fracaso de una revolución.* Madrid: Gráfica socialista, 1935.

Nelken, Margarita. *La condición social de la mujer en España. Su estado actual: su posible desarrollo.* Barcelona: Editorial Minerva, [1919].

———. *Por qué hicimos la revolución.* 2nd ed. Madrid: Balaños y Aguilar, [1936].

Reparaz, Antonio de, and Tresgallo de Souza. *Desde el Cuartel General de Miaja al Santuario de la Virgen de la Cabeza.* Valladolid: Artes Gráficas Afrodisio Aguado, 1937.

La Revolución de Asturias (Documentos). Mexico: Ediciones Defensa Roja, 1935.

La Revolución Española de Octubre: Documentos sensacionales inéditos. Santiago: Editorial Occidente, 1935.

Ruiz del Toro, José. *Octubre (Etapas de un periodo revolucionario en España).* Buenos Aires: Editorial Araujo, 1935.

Ruiz Fornells, Enrique. *La educación moral del soldado.* 6th ed. Toledo: Imprenta Librería y Encuadernación de Rafael Gómez-Menor, 1909.

Salut, Emili. *Vivers de revolucionaris. Apunts històrics del districte cinquè.* Barcelona: Llibreria Catalònia, 1938.

Sanjurjo, José. "The Spanish Civil Guard." *Police Journal* 4, no. 33 (1931).

Solano Palacios, Fernando. *La revolución de octubre. Quince días de comunismo libertario.* Fundación de Estudios Libertarios, Anselmo Lorenzo, 1994 [1936].

Tarrida del Mármol, Fernando. *Les inquisiteurs d'Espagne. Montjuich, Cuba, Philippines.* Paris: P.-V. Stock, 1897.

Urales, Federico. *El castillo maldito.* Toulouse: Presses Universitaires de Mirail, 1992.

Vidarte, Juan-Simeón. *El bienio negro y la insurrección de Asturias. Testimonio del entonces Vicesecretario y Secretario del PSOE.* Barcelona: Ediciones Grijalbo, 1978.

———. *Las Cortes Constituyentes de 1931–1933. Testimonio del Primer Secretario del Congreso de Diputados.* Barcelona: Ediciones Grijalbo, 1976.

Secondary Sources

Abella, Rafael. *Lances de honor*. Barcelona: Planeta, 1995.

Aguado Sánchez, Francisco. *El duque de Ahumada. Fundador de la Guardia Civil*. Madrid: Dirección General de la Guardia Civil, Servicio Histórico, 1969.

———. *Historia de la Guardia Civil*. 7 vols. Madrid: Ediciones Históricas, Cupsa Editorial, Planeta, 1983–85.

———. *La revolución de octubre de 1934*. Madrid: Librería San Martín, 1972.

Álvarez, José E. "The Spanish Foreign Legion during the Asturian Uprising of October 1934." *War in History* 18, no. 2 (2011): 200–224.

Álvarez Junco, José. *El emperador del paralelo. Lerroux y la demagogia populista*. Madrid: Alianza Editorial, 1990.

Anderson, Peter. *Friend or Foe? Occupation, Collaboration and Selective Violence in the Spanish Civil War*. Brighton: Sussex Academic Press, 2016.

Aragón Reyes, Manuel, director. *El Protectorado Español en Marruecos: La historia trascendida*. Vol. 3. [2013].

Arrarás, Joaquín. "Frente Popular." Chap. 9 in vol. 2, *Historia de la Cruzada Española*. Madrid: Ediciones españolas, 1940.

Balfour, Sebastian. *Deadly Embrace: Morocco and the Road to the Spanish Civil War*. Oxford: Oxford University Press, 2002.

———. *The End of the Spanish Empire, 1898–1923*. Oxford: Oxford University Press, 1997.

Ballbé, Manuel. *Orden público y militarismo en la España constitucional (1812–1983)*. Madrid: Alianza Editorial, 1985.

Banton, Michael. *The Policeman in the Community*. London: Tavistock Publications, 1964.

Barrio Alonso, Angeles. *Anarquismo y anarcosindicalismo en Asturias (1890–1936)*. Madrid: Siglo veintiuno editores, 1988.

Bascuñán Añover, Óscar. "Justicia popular: el castigo de la comunidad en Spain, 1895–1923." *Hispania* 79, no. 263 (2019): 699–725.

Baumeister, Martin. *Campesinos sin tierra: supervivencia y resistencia en Extremadura, 1880–1923*. Translated by Joaquín Abellán. Madrid: Ministerio de Agricultura, Pesca y Alimentación, Secretaría General Técnica, 1997.

———. "Castilblanco or the Limits of Democracy: Rural Protest in Spain from Restoration Monarchy to the Early Second Republic." Translated by Jane Rafferty. *Contemporary European History* 7, no. 1 (March 1998): 1–19.

Bermejo Martín, Francisco. *100 Años de Socialismo en La Rioja (1882–1992)*. Logroño: Gráficas Isasa, 1994.

Bittner, Egon. "The Police on Skid-Row: A Study of Peace Keeping." *American Sociological Review* 32, no. 5 (October 1967): 699–715.

Blanco Escolá, Carlos. *La Academia General Militar de Zaragoza (1928–1931)*. Barcelona: Editorial Labor, 1989.

Blaney Jr., Gerald. "The Civil Guard and the Spanish Second Republic 1931–1936." PhD diss., University of London, 2007.

———. "La historiografía sobre la Guardia Civil. Crítica y propuesta de investigación." *Política y sociedad* 42, no. 3 (2005): 31–44.

———. "Between Order and Loyalty: The Civil Guard and the Spanish Second Republic, 1931–1936." Chap. 2 in *Conflict and Legality: Policing Mid-Twentieth Century Europe.* Edited by Gerald Oram. London: Francis Boutle Publishers, 2003.

Blázquez Miguel, Juan. *La Guardia Civil en la guerra de España (1936–1939).* Madrid: Ediciones Barbarroja, n.d.

———. *La Guardia Civil durante la Segunda República y el 18 de Julio.* Madrid: María Tomás Pérez, 2010.

Bowling, Benjamin, Robert Reiner, and James Sheptychi. *The Politics of the Police.* Oxford: Oxford University Press, 2019.

Boyd, Carolyn. *Historia Patria: Politics, History, and National Identity in Spain 1875–1975.* Princeton, NJ: Princeton University Press, 1997.

———. *Praetorian Politics in Liberal Spain.* Chapel Hill: University of North Carolina Press, 1979.

Braojos Garrido, Alfonso, Leandro Álvarez Rey, and Francisco Espinosa Maestre. *Sevilla 36: Sublevación fascista y represión.* Sevilla: Muñoz Moya y Montraveta, 1990.

Bunk, Brian D. *Ghosts of Passion: Martyrdom, Gender, and the Origins of the Spanish Civil War.* Durham, NC: Duke University Press, 2007.

Cacho Viu, Vicente. *Repensar el 98.* Madrid: Biblioteca Nueva, 1997.

Cardona, Gabriel. *El poder militar en la España contemporánea hasta la guerra civil.* Madrid: Siglo veintiuno editores, 1983.

Carr, Raymond. *Spain, 1808–1975.* 2nd ed. Oxford: Clarendon Press, 1982 [1966].

Casanova, Julián. *De la calle al frente: El anarcosindicalismo en España (1931–1939).* Barcelona: Crítica, 1997.

———. *República y Guerra Civil.* Vol. 8 of *Historia de España*, directed by Josep Fontana and Ramón Villares. Madrid: Crítica/Marcial Pons, 2007.

Chamberlin, Foster. "Guardias del orden: La cultura militar de la Guardia Civil." *Ayer* 135, no. 3 (2024): 49–73.

———. "Policing Practices as a Vehicle for Brutalization: The Case of Spain's Civil Guard, 1934–1936." *European History Quarterly* 50, no. 4 (October 2020): 650–68.

———. "The Roots of the July 1936 Coup: The Rebirth of Military Interventionism in the Spanish Infantry Academy, 1893–1927." *War & Society* 40, no. 4 (October 2021): 279–95.

———. "The Roots of the Repression: The Rebel Civil Guards in the Spanish Civil War." Chap. 3 in *The Crucible of Francoism: Combat, Violence, and Ideology in the Spanish Civil War.* Edited by Ángel Alcalde, Foster Chamberlin, and Francisco J. Leira-Castiñeira (Brighton: Sussex Academic Press, 2021).

Chan, Janet. "Changing Police Culture." *British Journal of Criminology* 36, no. 1 (Winter 1996): 109–34.

Chaput, Marie-Claude. "Castilblanco (Badajoz, 31 de diciembre de 1931): La marginación de la periferia." *Centros y periferias: prensa, impresos y territorios en el mundo hispánico contemporáneo: homenaje a Jacqueline Covo-Maurice*, 191–205. PILAR, 2004.

Cierva, Ricardo de la. *Fracaso del octubre revolucionario. 1934–1935. La represión*. Madrid: ARC editores, 1997.

Cobo Romero, Francisco. *La Guerra Civil y la represión franquista en la provincia de Jaén*. Jaén: Instituto de Estudios Giennenses, 1994.

Cobo Romero, Francisco, and Teresa María Ortega López. *Franquismo y posguerra en Andalucía Oriental*. Granada: Universidad de Granada, 2005.

Cockcroft, Tom. *Police Culture: Themes and Concepts*. Oxford: Routledge, 2013.

Collins, Randall. *Violence: A Micro-sociological Theory*. Princeton, NJ: Princeton University Press, 2008.

Comín Colomer, Eduardo. *De Castilblanco a Casas Viejas*. Madrid: Temas españoles, 1959.

———. *Historia del Partido Comunista de España*. Vol. 3, *La mayoría de edad (16 de febrero de julio de 1936): periodo de bolchevización*. Madrid: Editora Nacional, 1967.

Crank, John P. *Understanding Police Culture*. 2nd ed. Oxon: Routledge, 2015.

Cruz, Rafael. *En el nombre del pueblo: República, rebelión y guerra en la España de 1936*. Madrid: Siglo XXI de España Editores, 2006.

Díaz Carmona, A. "El 10 de agosto de 1932." *REHGC* 1–2, no. 2, 4 (1968–69).

Díaz Nosty, B. *La comuna asturiana. Revolución de octubre de 1934*. 2nd ed. Bilbao: Zero, 1975.

Díaz Valderrama, José. *Historia, servicios notables, socorros, comentarios de la Cartilla, y reflexiones sobre el Cuerpo de la Guardia Civil*. Madrid: J. M. Ducazcal, 1858.

Dirección General de la Guardia Civil, Universidad Nacional de Educación a Distancia. *VI Seminario Duque de Ahumada: La Fundación de la Guardia Civil (9, 10 y 11 de mayo de 1994)*. Madrid: Ministerio de Justicia e Interior, 1995.

Ealham, Chris. *Class, Culture, and Conflict in Barcelona, 1898–1937*. Oxon: Routledge, 2005.

Emsley, Clive. *Gendarmes and the State in Nineteenth Century Europe*. New York: Oxford University Press, 1999.

Engel Masoliver, Carlos. *El Cuerpo de Oficiales en la Guerra de España*. Valladolid: AF Editores, [2008].

Esenwein, George Richard. *Anarchist Ideology and the Working-Class Movement in Spain, 1868–1898*. Berkeley: University of California Press, 1989.

Espinosa Maestre, Francisco. *La columna de muerte. El avance del ejército franquista de Sevilla a Badajoz*. EPUB ed. Barcelona: Crítica, 2003.

———. *La Guerra Civil en Huelva*. Huelva: Diputación Provincial, 1996.

———. *La Justicia de Queipo*. EPUB ed. Barcelona: Editorial Crítica, 2006.

———. *La primavera del Frente Popular. Los campesinos de Badajoz y el origen de la guerra civil (marzo–julio de 1936)*. Barcelona: Crítica, 2007.

Fernández, Alberto. "Octubre de 1934. Recuerdos de un insurrecto." *Tiempo de historia* 17 (April 1976): 11–21.

Fernández Pasalodos, Arnau. "La 'ley de fugas' durante la lucha antiguerrillera en España (1936–1952)." *Historia Social*, no. 101 (2021): 125–44.

Foote, Lorien. *The Gentlemen and the Roughs: Manhood, Honor and Violence in the Union Army*. New York: NYU Press, 2010.

Fraser, Ronald. *Blood of Spain: The Experience of Civil War, 1936–1939*. Middlesex: Penguin Books, 1981.

Gabriel, Narciso de. "Alfabetización, semialfabetización y analfabetismo en España (1860–1991." *Revista Complutense de Educación* 8, no. 1 (1997): 199–231.

García Carrero, Francisco Javier. "Manuel Gómez Cantos, un mando de la Guardia Civil entre el deshonor y la represión." *Pasado y Memoria. Revista de Historia Contemporánea*, no. 11 (2012): 255–76.

García Pérez, Juan. "La II República: nueva ocasión perdida para la transformación del campo extremeño." In *Historia de Extremadura*. Edited by Ángel Rodríguez Sánchez. Vol. 4, *Los tiempos actuales*. Badajoz: Universitas Editorial, Consejería de Educación y Cultura, [1985].

García Venero, Maximiano. *Melquíades Álvarez, Historia de un liberal*. 2nd ed. Madrid: Ediciones Tebas, n.d.

Gat, Azar. "The Cult of the Offensive: The Sources of French Military Doctrine 1871–1914." Chap. 3 in *The Development of Military Thought: The Nineteenth Century*. Oxford: Clarendon Press, 1992.

Geertz, Clifford. "Thick Description: Toward an Interpretive Theory of Culture." In *The Interpretation of Cultures*, 3–30. New York: Basic Books, 1973.

Gibson, Ian. *La noche en que mataron a Calvo Sotelo*. Barcelona: Editorial Argos Vergara, 1982.

Gil Andrés, Carlos. *La República en la plaza: los sucesos de Arnedo de 1932*. Logroño: Gobierno de la Rioja/Instituto de Estudios Riojanos, 2002.

Gil Vico, Pablo. *Verdugos de Asturias. La violencia y sus relatos en la revolución de Asturias de 1934*. Gijón: Ediciones Trea, 2019.

Goldstein, Joseph. "Police Discretion Not to Invoke the Criminal Process: Low-Visibility Decisions in the Administration of Justice." *Yale Law Journal* 69, no. 4 (March 1960): 543–94.

Gonzálbez Ruíz, Francisco. *Yo he creído en Franco. Proceso de una gran desilusión (Dos meses en la cárcel de Sevilla)*. Paris, n.d.

González Calleja, Eduardo. *Cifras cruentas: Las víctimas mortales de la violencia sociopolítica en la Segunda República (1931–1936)*. Granada: Editorial Comares, 2015.

———. *Contrarrevolucionario. Radicalización violenta de las derechas durante la Segunda República, 1931–1936*. Madrid: Alianza Editorial, 2011.

———. *El máuser y el sufragio. Orden público, subversión y violencia política en la crisis de la Restauración (1917–1931)*. Madrid: Consejo superior de investigaciones científicas, 1999.

———. *En nombre de la autoridad. La defensa del orden público durante la Segunda República Española (1931–1936)*. Granada: Editorial Comares, 2014.

————. "Experiencia en combate: Continuidad y cambios en la violencia represiva (1931–1939)." *Ayer* 76, no. 4 (2009): 37–64.

————. *La razón de la fuerza. Orden público, subversión y violencia política en la España de la Restauración (1874–1917)*. Madrid: Consejo Superior de Investigaciones Científicas, 1998.

González Calleja, Eduardo, and Rocío Navarro Comas, eds. *La España del Frente Popular. Política, sociedad, conflicto y cultura en la España de 1936*. Granada: Editorial Comares, 2011.

Graham, Helen. *The Spanish Republic at War: 1936–1939*. Cambridge: Cambridge University Press, 2002.

Guillamón Álvarez, Javier. *Honor y honra en la España del siglo XVIII*. Madrid: Departamento de Historia Moderna, Facultad de Geografía e Historia, Universidad Complutense, 1981.

Hayakawa, S. I. *Language in Thought and Action*. New York: Harcourt, Brace & World, 1964.

Henderson, David Kenneth. "El Mar de Extremadura: Irrigation, Colonization and Francoism in Southwestern Spain, 1898–1978." PhD diss., University of California, San Diego, 2017.

Hobsbawm, Eric J. *Bandits*. New York: New Press, 2000 [1969].

————. *Primitive Rebels: Studies in Archaic Forms of Social Movement in the 19th and 20th Centuries*. New York: Norton, 1965.

Howard, Michael. "The Influence of Clausewitz." In *On War*, by Carl von Clausewitz, 27–44. Translated and edited by Michael Howard and Peter Paret, Princeton, NJ: Princeton University Press, 1976.

Hull, Isabel V. *Absolute Destruction: Military Culture and the Practices of War in Imperial Germany*. Ithaca: Cornell University Press, 2005.

Janowitz, Morris. *The Professional Soldier: A Social and Political Portrait*. London: Collier-Macmillan, 1960.

Jensen, Geoffrey. *Cultura militar española. Modernistas, tradicionalistas y liberales*. Madrid: Bilbioteca Nueva, 2014.

————. *Irrational Triumph: Cultural Despair, Military Nationalism, and the Ideological Origins of Franco's Spain*. Reno: University of Nevada Press, 2002.

————. "Military Consequences of Cultural Perceptions: The Spanish Army in Morocco, 1912–1927." *Journal of the Middle East and Africa* 8, no. 2 (2017): 135–50.

————. "Military Nationalism and the State: The Case of fin-de-siècle Spain." *Nations and Nationalism* 6, no. 2 (2000): 257–74.

————. "Moral Strength through Material Defeat? The Consequences of 1898 for Spanish Military Culture." *War & Society* 17, no. 2 (October 1999): 25–39.

————. "Muslim Soldiers in a Spanish Crusade: Tomás García Figueras, Mulai Ahmed er Raisuni and the Ideological Context of Spain's Moroccan Soldiers." Chap. 9 in *Colonial Soldiers in Europe, 1914–1945: "Aliens in Uniform" in Wartime Societies*. Edited by Eric Storm and Ali Al Tuma. New York: Routledge, 2016.

———. "Rico Avello en Marruecos." Chap. 3 in *El sueño republicano de Manuel Rico Avello (1886–1936)*. Coordinated by Juan Pan-Montojo. Madrid: Biblioteca Nueva, 2011.

Kalyvas, Stathis N. *The Logic of Violence in Civil War*. Cambridge: Cambridge University Press, 2006.

Kaplan, Temma. *The Anarchists of Andalusia, 1868–1903*. Princeton, NJ: Princeton University Press, 1977.

———. *Red City, Blue Period: Social Movements in Picasso's Barcelona*. Berkeley: University of California Press, 1992.

Kern, Robert. "Margarita Nelken: Women and the Crisis of Spanish Politics." In *European Women on the Left: Socialism, Feminism, and the Problems Faced by Political Women, 1880 to the Present*, 147–62. Edited by Jane Slaughter and Robert Kern. Westport: Greenwood Press, 1981.

Kerry, Matthew. "Painted Tonsures and Potato-sellers: Priests, Passing and Survival in the Asturian Revolution." *Cultural and Social History* (2017): 1–19.

———. "Radical Politics in the Spanish Second Republic: Asturias, 1931–1936." PhD diss., University of Sheffield, 2015.

———. *Unite Proletarian Brothers! Radicalism and Revolution in the Spanish Second Republic*. London: University of London Press, 2020.

Klockars, Carl B. *The Idea of Police*. Beverly Hills, CA: SAGE Publications, 1985.

Lazo, Alfonso, and José Antonio Parejo. "La militancia falangista en el suroeste español. Sevilla." *Ayer*, no. 52 (2003).

Leira-Castiñeira, Francisco J. *Soldados de Franco. Reclutamiento forzoso, experiencia de guerra y desmovilización militar*. Madrid: Siglo XXI, 2020.

Linz, Juan J. "From Great Hopes to Civil War: The Breakdown of Democracy in Spain." Chap. 5 in *The Breakdown of Democratic Regimes: Europe*. Edited by Juan J. Linz and Alfred Stepan. Baltimore: Johns Hopkins University Press, 1978.

López Corral, Miguel. "Los gobiernos izquierdas y la Guardia Civil." *Guardia Civil*, no. 521 (September 1987): 41–52.

———. *La Guardia Civil. Claves históricas para entender a la Benemérita y a sus hombres (1844–1975)*. Madrid: La Esfera de los Libros, 2011.

———. "La Guardia Civil en Madrid durante la guerra." Chap. 6 in *Guerra Civil. Madrid*. Coordinated by Fernando Martínez de Baños Carrillo. Zaragoza: Delsan Libros, 2006.

———. *La Guardia Civil: Nacimiento y consolidación, 1844–1874*. Madrid: Editorial Actas, Ministerio de Justicia e Interior, Secretaría General Técnica, 1995.

———. *La Guardia Civil en la Restauración (1875–1905). Militarismo contra Subversión y Terrorismo anarquista*. Madrid: Editorial ACTAS, 2004.

López Garrido, Diego. *El aparato policial en España: historia, sociología e ideología*. Barcelona: Ariel, 1987.

———. *La Guardia Civil y los orígenes del Estado centralista*. Barcelona: Editorial Crítica, 1982.

————. "La naturaleza de la Guardia Civil en su primer medio siglo de existencia." *REHGC* 14, no. 26 (1981): 9–31.

Luengo Muñoz, Manuel. "Revolución de Asturias de 1934. El Combate de Campomanes." *REHGC* 1, no. 1 (1968): 33–48.

Macarro Vera, José Manuel. *La utopía revolucionaria. Sevilla en la Segunda República.* Monte de Piedad y Caja de Ahorros de Sevilla, 1985.

Macías Fernández, Daniel. "Piojos, ratas y moscas: Marruecos y el soldado español." Chap. 8 in *A cien años de Annual: La guerra de Marruecos.* Edited by Daniel Macías Fernández. Madrid: Desperta Ferro Ediciones, 2021.

Manfredicano, Francisco. "La Compañía de Guardias Jóvenes de la Guardia Civil." *REHGC* 3, no. 6 (1970): 139–52.

Mangini, Shirley. "Visible Women of the Second Spanish Republic." Chap. 2 in *Memories of Resistance: Women's Voices from the Spanish Civil War.* New Haven, CT: Yale University Press, 1995.

Manning, Peter K. "Occupational Culture." In *The Encyclopedia of Police Science.* Edited by Jack R. Greene. New York: Routledge, 2007.

————. *Police Work: The Social Organization of Policing.* Cambridge, MA: MIT Press, 1977.

Martín Corrales, Eloy. *La imagen del magrebí en España. Una perspectiva histórica, siglos XVI–XX.* Barcelona: Ediciones Bellaterra, 2002.

Martínez García, Miguel. "La Gendarmería Nacional francesa y la fundación de la Guardia Civil." *Cuadernos de la Guardia Civil,* no. 16 (1996): 187–205.

Martínez Gutiérrez, Josebe. *Margarita Nelken (1896–1968).* Madrid: Ediciones del Orto, [1997].

Martínez Ruiz, Enrique. *Creación de la Guardia Civil.* Madrid: Editora Nacional, 1976.

Martínez Vaquero, Sergio. "En defensa del orden: la cultura profesional de la policía en la Segunda República, 1931–1936." *Ayer* 135, no. 3 (2024): 75–101.

————. "La democratización del orden público en la Segunda República española: cultura, política y policía, 1931–1936." *Bulletin d'Histoire Contemporaine de l'Espagne* 54 (2020).

Martínez Viqueira, Eduardo. *Hombres de honor. El duque de Ahumada y la fundación de la Guardia Civil.* Madrid: La Esfera de los Libros, 2019.

Mateo Dieste, Josep Lluís. *La «hermandad» hispano-marroquí. Política y religión bajo el Protectorado español en Marruecos (1912–1956).* Barcelona: Ediciones Bellaterra, 2003.

Merriman, John. *The Dynamite Club: How a Bombing in Fin-de-Siècle Paris Ignited the Age of Modern Terror.* New Haven, CT: Yale University Press, 2016.

Mintz, Jerome. *The Anarchists of Casas Viejas.* Chicago: University of Chicago Press, 1982.

Moreno Gómez, Francisco. *1936. El genocidio franquista en Córdoba.* Barcelona: Crítica, 2008.

Moreno Luzón, Javier. "Teoría del clientelismo y estudio de la política caciquil." *Revista de Estudios Políticos* (Nueva Epoca), no. 89 (July–September 1995): 191–224.

Murray, Williamson, and Allen R. Millet, eds. *Military Innovation in the Interwar Period*. Cambridge: Cambridge University Press, 1996.

Nagl, John A. *Learning to Eat Soup with a Knife: Counterinsurgency Lessons from Malaya and Vietnam*. Chicago: University of Chicago Press, 2005.

Nerín, Gustau. *La guerra que vino de África*. Barcelona: Crítica, 2005.

Núñez Calvo, Jesús Narciso. "XC Aniversario del patronazgo de la Virgen del Pilar en la Guardia Civil (1913–2003)." *Guardia Civil*, no. 706 (February 2003): 78–81.

Núñez Florencio, Rafael. *El terrorismo anarquista, 1880–1909*. Madrid: Siglo XXI de España, 1983.

Nye, Robert A. *Masculinity and Male Codes of Honor in Modern France*. New York: Oxford University Press, 1993.

"La Oficialidad de la Guardia Civil." *REHGC* 16, no. 30 (1983): 11–21.

O'Neill, Megan, and Anne-Marie Singh. Introduction to *Police Occupational Culture: New Debates and Directions*. Edited by Megan O'Neill, Monique Marks, and Anne-Marie Singh. Oxford: Elsevier, 2007.

Opisso, Alfredo. *La Guardia Civil y su tiempo*. Barcelona: Molinas y Maza, n.d.

Ortiz Villalba, Juan. *Sevilla 1936: del golpe militar a la guerra civil*. Córdoba: Imprenta Vistalegre, 1998.

Palacios Cerezales, Diego. "«En la era del aeroplano». La policía y sus modernidades en el periodo de entreguerras." *Ayer* 135, no. 3 (2024): 23–48.

Parejo Fernández, José Antonio. *La Falange en la Sierra Norte de Sevilla (1934–1936)*. 2nd ed. Seville: Universidad de Sevilla, 2007.

Pastor Martínez, Roberto. "Una página del movimiento obrero riojano. Sucesos de Arnedo, 5 de enero de 1932." *Cuadernos de Investigación Histórica* 10 (1984): 193–207.

Payne, Stanley G. *The Collapse of the Spanish Republic, 1933–1936: Origins of the Civil War*. New Haven, CT: Yale University Press, 2006.

———. *Politics and the Military in Modern Spain*. Stanford: Stanford University Press, 1967.

———. *Spain's First Democracy: The Second Republic, 1931–1936*. Madison: University of Wisconsin Press, 1993.

Pena Rodríguez, Alberto. *El gran aliado de Franco. Portugal y la Guerra Civil española. Prensa, radio, cine y propaganda*. A Coruña: Edicios de Castro, 1998.

Peristiany, J. G., ed. *Honour and Shame: The Values of Mediterranean Society*. Chicago: University of Chicago Press, 1966.

Pitarch, José Luis. *El honor y el honor militar*. Barcelona: Ediciones Grijalbo, 1984.

Pitt-Rivers, Julian. "Honor." In *International Encyclopedia of the Social Sciences*, 6:503–11. Edited by David L. Sills. New York: Macmillan, 1968.

———. *The People of the Sierra*. Chicago: University of Chicago Press, 1961.

Ponce Alberca, Julio, and Diego Lagares García. *Honor de oficiales. Los tribunales de honor en el ejército de la España contemporánea (siglos XIX–XX)*. Barcelona: Ediciones Carena, n.d.

Posen, Barry R. *The Sources of Military Doctrine: France, Britain, and Germany between the World Wars.* Ithaca, NY: Cornell University Press, 1984.

Pozuelo, Vicente. *Los últimos 476 días de Franco.* Barcelona: Editorial Planeta, 1980.

Preston, Paul. *The Coming of the Spanish Civil War: Reform, Reaction and Revolution in the Second Republic, 1931–1936.* 2nd ed. London: Routledge, 1994.

———. *Franco: A Biography.* London: Harper Collins, 1993.

———. "Margarita Nelken: A Full Measure of Pain." In *Doves of War: Four Women of Spain,* 297–408. Harper Collins, 2002.

———. *The Spanish Holocaust: Inquisition and Extermination in Twentieth-Century Spain.* New York: Norton, 2012.

Puell de la Villa, Fernando. *Historia del Ejército en España.* Madrid: Alianza Editorial, 2000.

Pulido Pérez, Agustín M. *La Guardia Civil ante el Bienio Azañista, 1931/33.* Madrid: Almena ediciones, 2008.

Radcliff, Pamela Beth. "The emerging challenge of mass politics." Chap. 9 in *Spain since 1808.* Edited by José Alvarez Junco and Adrian Shubert. New York: Oxford University Press, 2000.

———. *From Mobilization to Civil War: The Politics of Polarization in the Spanish City of Gijon, 1900–1937.* Cambridge: Cambridge University Press, 1996.

Ramírez Barreto, Faustino. *Listado de las vicisitudes de los alumnos del colegio de guardias jóvenes "Duque de Ahumada" (1.853–2.003) (con motivo de la celebración de su 150° aniversario).* Valdemoro, 2002.

———. *Semblanza histórica de la Asociación Pro-Huérfanos de la Guardia Civil.* Madrid: Asociación Pro-Huérfanos de la Guardia Civil, 2008.

Rey, Fernando del, ed. *Palabras como puños: la intransigencia política en la Segunda República española.* Madrid: Editorial Tecnos, 2011.

———. "Reflexiones sobre la violencia política en la II República española." In *Conflicto político, democracia y dictadura: Portugal y España en la década de 1930,* 19–97. Edited by Mercedes Gutiérrez Sánchez and Diego Palacios Cerezales. Madrid: Centro de Estudios Políticos, 2007.

Rivas Gómez, Fernando. "Los documentos de la época fundacional (I–II)." *REHGC* 12, no. 23 (1979).

———. "La enseñanza de la Guardia Civil." *REHGC* 7, no. 13–14 (1974).

———. "El entierro del Alférez de los Reyes y su trascendencia histórica." *REHGC* 20, n. 37 (1987): 141–78.

———. *El Frente Popular: antecedentes de un alzamiento.* Madrid: Librería San Martín, 1976.

———. "Rebeldía y represión en Casas Viejas." *REHGC* 16, no. 29 (1983): 125–58.

———. "La República en marcha." *REHGC* 9–10, no. 17–19 (1976–77).

Rodrigo, Javier. *Los campos de concentración franquista. Entre la historia y la memoria.* Madrid: Siete Mares, 2003.

———. *Hasta la raíz. Violencia durante la Guerra Civil y la dictadura franquista*. Madrid: Alianza Editorial, 2008.

Rosen, Stephen Peter. *Winning the Next War: Innovation and the Modern Military*. Ithaca, NY: Cornell University Press, 1991.

Rosique Navarro, Francisca. *La reforma agraria en Badajoz durante la IIª República (La respuesta patronal)*. Departamento de Publicaciones de la Excma. Diputación Provincial de Badajoz, 1988.

Rubinstein, Jonathan. *City Police*. New York: Farrar, Straus, and Giroux, 1973.

Rubio López, Bernando. *Nuestros soldados*. Bolaños, 2004.

Ruiz, David. *Octubre de 1934. Revolución en la República española*. Madrid: Editorial Síntesis, n.d.

Ruiz Manjón, Octavio. *El Partido Republican Radical, 1908–1936*. Madrid: Tebas, [1976].

Sacanell Ruiz de Apodaca, Enrique. *El general Sanjurjo, héroe y víctima*. Ediciones Altaya, 2008.

Salas Larrazábal, Ramón. *Los datos exactos de la guerra civil*. Madrid: Ediciones Rioduero, 1980.

Sanchez, Sarah. *Fact and Fiction: Representations of the Asturian Revolution (1934–1938)*. Leeds: Maney Publishers, 2003.

Sánchez G.-Saúco, J. A. *La revolución de 1934 en Asturias*. Madrid: Editora Nacional, 1974.

Schein, Edgar H. "How Culture Forms, Develops, and Changes." In *Gaining Control of the Corporate Culture*. Edited by Ralph H. Kilmann, Mary J. Saxton, and Roy Serpa. San Francisco, Jossey-Bass Publishers, 1986.

———. *Organizational Culture and Leadership*. 3rd ed. San Francisco: Jossey-Bass, 2004.

"La Seguridad publica en el periodo constitucional." *REHGC* 15, no. 28 (1982): 11–148.

Shubert, Adrian. *The Road to Revolution Spain: The Coal Miners of Asturias, 1860–1934*. Urbana: University of Illinois Press, 1987.

Silva, Lorenzo. *Sereno en el peligro: la aventura histórica de la Guardia Civil*. Madrid: Editorial EDAF, 2010.

Skolnick, Jerome H. *Justice without Trial: Law Enforcement in Democratic Society*. 4th ed. New Orleans: Quid Pro Books, 2011 [1966].

Smith, Angel. *Anarchism, Revolution and Reaction: Catalan Labour and the Crisis of the Spanish State, 1898–1923*. New York: Berghahn Books, 2007.

———. "Barcelona through the European Mirror: From Red and Black to Claret and Blue." In *Red Barcelona: Social Protest and Labour Mobilization in the Twentieth Century*, 1–16. Edited by Angel Smith. London: Routledge, 2002.

Snider, Don M. "An Uninformed Debate on Military Culture." *Orbis*, no. 1 (1999): 11–26.

Spierenburg, Pieter. "Masculinity, Violence, and Honor: An Introduction." In *Men and Violence: Gender, and Rituals in Modern Europe and America*, 1–29. Edited by Pieter Spierenburg, Columbus: Ohio State University Press, 1998.

Taibo II, Paco Ignacio. *Asturias, Octubre 1934*. Barcelona: Crítica, 2013.

Taylor, Scott K. *Honor and Violence in Golden Age Spain*. New Haven, CT: Yale University Press, 2008.

Trullén Floría, Ramiro. "Castilblanco como sinécdoque. El discurso contrarrevolucionario de la Segunda República." *Historia Social*, no. 83 (2015): 55–71.

Ullman, Joan Connelly. *The Tragic Week: A Study of Anticlericalism in Spain, 1875–1912*. Cambridge, MA: Harvard University Press, 1968.

Valero Capilla, Juan. "Uniformidad de la Guardia Civil (IV)." *REHGC* 19, no. 35 (1986): 143–89.

Vaquero Martínez, Sergio. "La democratización del orden público en la Segunda República española: cultura, política y policía, 1931–1936." PhD diss., Universidad Complutense de Madrid, 2018.

———. "Reformar la policía: Los debates sobre el orden público en las cortes constituyentes de la Segunda República Española, 1931–1933." Chap. 9 in *Construção do Estado, Movimentos Sociais e Economia Política*. Coordinated by Joana Dias Pereira, Ana Sofia Ferreira, and Manuel Loff. Lisbon: Instituto de História Contemporânea, 2020.

Velasco de Castro, Rocío. "La imagen del «moro» en la formulación e instrumentalización del africanismo franquista." *Hispania* 74, no. 246 (January–April 2014): 205–36.

Vincent, Mary. *Spain, 1833–2002: People and State*. Oxford: Oxford University Press, 2007.

Waddington, P. A. J. "Police (Canteen) Sub-Culture: An Appreciation." *British Journal of Criminology* 39, no. 2 (Spring 1999): 287–309.

Westley, William A. *Violence and the Police: A Sociological Study of Law, Custom, and Morality*. Cambridge, MA: MIT Press, 1970.

Whyte, William Foote. *Street Corner Society: The Social Structure of an Italian Slum*. 4th ed. Chicago: University of Chicago Press, 1993 [1943].

Wilson, James Q. *Varieties of Police Behavior: The Management of Law and Order in Eight Communities*. Cambridge, MA: Harvard University Press, 1978 [1968].

Wilson, Peter H. "Defining Military Culture." *Journal of Military History* 72, no. 1 (Jan. 2008): 11–41.

Wyatt-Brown, Bertram. *Southern Honor: Ethics and Behavior in the Old South*. New York: Oxford University Press, 1986.

INDEX

65, 67, 68; equipment of, 86–87, 101–102, 184, 202; and executions, 189, 191, 192–93, 194, 198; expansion of, 24, 87; families of, 9, 27–28, 29, 31, 64, 68, 98, 101, 111, 114, 130, 154, 155, 156, 160, 163; and fear, 100, 109, 110, 129, 168, 173, 174, 180, 181, 202; and festivals, 67; financial support for, 94, 113; formation of, 3, 6, 11, 12, 13, 14–18, 21–23, 41, 199; and formation of republic, 80; and foundational documents, 11, 16–18, 19, 20, 25, 57; Fourth Company (Sama) of, 150, 151, 152–53, 155–56, 157, 159; and fugitives, 37, 172; 38, 156–57, 169; and glory, 81, 144, 150, 154, 157, 159, 162, 165, 166; and "good citizens," 32; and guards' lives, 21, 25, 26, 27, 28, 29, 30, 31, 59, 59–60, 72–73, 129, 180, 200; historians of, 43, 128; homages to, 94–95, 176, 200; and housing, 21, 24, 25–27, 31, 32, 39–40, 45, 94, 96, 148, 186; and humanitarian sentiments, 99, 132, 133, 154, 160, 161, 170; and illegal gambling, 37; and information, 196; and inspections, 16, 28, 29, 34, 60, 75, 76; and inspector general, 176; and interrogations, 38, 54; and investigations, 38, 41, 42, 46, 48, 49, 51, 121, 134–35, 168, 177, 181, 183, 198; and isolation, 7, 24–27, 30, 31, 33, 34, 36, 39–40, 60, 72, 98, 200; and judicial powers, 46, 171; and justice, 106, 112, 113, 168, 169, 174, 183; and killings, 122, 169–70, 171, 174, 181, 188, 189, 192; and legalistic policing style, 109, 202; and legal system, 9, 29, 30–32, 37, 48, 67; and letters from prisoners, 52; and liberalism, 11, 20, 33, 37, 57, 104, 173; and literacy, 22, 34, 35, 37, 60, 61, 65, 66, 67; and local communities, 18, 25–27, 28, 30, 31–34, 40, 60, 89, 93–97, 107–8, 125, 150–51, 156–57, 182–83, 189–90; and loyalty, 60, 62, 63, 66–67, 79, 83, 84, 87, 112, 113, 114, 123, 133, 135, 136, 137, 171, 186, 187, 196, 197; and management of posts, 71, 72, 76; and married guards, 26–28, 31, 91–92; and martial law, 58; and masculinity, 92, 95, 155, 160, 163; and mass in Bilbao, 114; and May 13th decree, 16; media coverage of, 96, 111–14, 180, 181; and militarization, 145, 146, 184; and military courts, 29, 31, 53, 134–35;

145, 162, 195, 198; and military jurisdiction, 134, 150, 172; and military justice, 159, 161; and military rebellion, 161, 172; and military service, 59, 65, 67, 68, 72, 75, 76; military structure of, 199; and mining companies, 149; mission of, 17, 18, 44, 46, 57, 63, 82, 84, 95, 101, 112, 187, 199; and monarchy, 121; and name *cuerpo de guardias civiles*, 14; and national conspiracies, 112; and national right-wing press, 96; in the nineteenth century, 37, 39, 41–44, 76, 199; and 1936 uprising, 183, 186–89; and nobility, 63, 111; and nonviolent approach to policing, 21, 76, 166; number of, 84; and obedience, 29, 62, 63, 71, 98, 99, 100, 119, 128, 129, 133, 136, 191; and officers admissions, 74–76; and oppression of workers, 92; and organization, 16, 18, 24, 88, 135; and organizational culture, 22, 39, 42, 65, 67, 79, 96, 101, 103, 104, 123, 124, 126, 128, 135, 146, 147, 165, 197, 199, 200, 203–4; and Oviedo battle, 169; and pairs (*parejas*), 35, 39, 99; and parades, 24, 72; and patriotism, 96; and patrols, 21, 34–36, 38, 39, 47, 50, 67, 76, 154; and payments, 32, 61, 72, 82, 87; and pensions, 53; and personal possessions, 26; and personnel, 16, 21, 61, 67, 135; and police training, 36–37, 38, 67, 76–77; and policing methods, 6–7, 31, 35–37, 38, 76–77; and political power, 44, 45, 101; and political violence, 122–23, 197–98, 203; poor leadership of, 126, 128, 129, 163; and preparation for war, 60; and the press, 165, 167, 170; and prisoner transport, 37; promotion system of, 74, 75; and prostitutes, 191; and protection of people, 14, 16, 40, 94, 96, 105–6; and public perception, 20, 21, 22, 29, 31, 32, 38, 40, 44, 104, 111; and punishment, 30–31, 53, 62, 98, 134, 135, 139, 150, 161, 172–75, 181, 204; and rebellion of 1936, 186–98; and recruitment process, 66–67; and reform, 123, 129, 131, 133, 135, 139, 140, 183, 201, 202; and regional capitals, 43, 194; and relations with public, 60, 71, 72, 75, 76, 89, 93–98, 107, 108, 110–11, 114, 126; and religion, 62, 63, 66, 91, 93, 111, 113; and republican and leftist targets, 190,

www.ingramcontent.com/pod-product-compliance
Lightning Source LLC
Chambersburg PA
CBHW030300100426

42812CB00002B/510